DISCORDS MINGLED

"Discords mingled with concordes not onelie are tollerable, but make the descant more pleasing if they be well taken. Moreover, there is no coming to a close, speciallie with a Cadence, without a discord."—Thomas Morley
["A Plaine and Easie Introduction to Practicall Musicke."–1597]

DISCORDS
MINGLED

by

CARL ENGEL

Essays On Music

Essay Index Reprint Series

BOOKS FOR LIBRARIES PRESS, INC.
FREEPORT, NEW YORK

First Published 1931
Reprinted 1967

LIBRARY OF CONGRESS CATALOG NUMBER:

67-28752

PRINTED IN THE UNITED STATES OF AMERICA

To the memory of
O. G. SONNECK

APOGGIATURA

THE essays, lectures, and reviews, reprinted here with some changes and many — though probably not enough — corrections, first appeared in the "Musical Quarterly," the "Atlantic Monthly," and the "Boston Evening Transcript." Most of them were written at the suggestion of the late Oscar G. Sonneck, familiarly and affectionately remembered as "Oscar Gloom." He also urged me to gather them between the covers of a book.

By one of those unaccountable orders of providence, which we call accidents, I went to New York on October 22, 1928, unaware that Sonneck had fallen gravely ill. When on the following day the doctors decided that an operation was necessary, another "accident" allowed me to accompany him in the ambulance to the hospital. I stayed with Sonneck for several hours before he was taken to the operating-room. As I was about to leave him, never again to see him alive, he roused himself from the somnolence induced by pain-relieving opiates, and he asked me three or four questions. The last one was whether this book had been accepted for publication. I answered him that it had. He nodded silently and smiled approvingly one of those kindly smiles that would occasionally brighten his wise and stolid face. In spite of his inveterate dislike for dedications, Sonneck had given me permission to inscribe the book to him. In fact, I had made the preparation of the book conditional on that permission. And for once he had yielded. I had three reasons for this dedication: I wanted it to be a token of affection for a true friend, a small tribute of high regard for an eminent predecessor, a just retribution for the guilty one who lured me into writing about music.

If anyone knows that too much music, and certainly far too much about music, is being written nowadays, it should be the grave-digging librarian. In spite of such knowledge, to fling prudence to the winds and deliberately add to the glut by unearthing what already reposed in the burial-ground of newspaper and magazine seems doubly and unpardonably rash.

Yet even a grave-digger, in sanguine moments, is liable to beget offspring. And concerning it he is apt to have the same illusions and maintain the same pretensions that animate a less macabre parent. It rests with the children whether or not the father shall be forgiven.

C. E.

Library of Congress, Washington.
Easter, 1930.

CONTENTS

DISCORDS MINGLED

PARALLEL OCTAVES

SCHUBERT'S FAME

(*1828–1928*)

WHEN Beethoven died, he was a famous man. Famous not only in the city or the country of his adoption, but far beyond. In Paris, by the King's command, a medal of gold had been struck in his honour. From St. Petersburg, Prince Galitzin had sent him a request for string quartettes. The Philharmonic Society of London had played an important part in the composer's life. His name and some of his music had reached the New World, still severed from the old by weeks of sailing and years of immigration.

Beethoven's burial assumed the proportions of a great public show. In the Titan's funeral procession — on March 29, 1827 — the edges of the pall were borne by eight *Kapellmeister*, indistinguishably distinguished pygmies. They were accompanied by thirty-six torch-bearers, dressed and gloved in black, with black crape flowing from their smoky torches and sprays of white flowers fastened to the left sleeve. Among them walked Franz Schubert, torch in hand, carrying on his shoulders, unseen, the dead master's robes.

As he put out his torch and approached the open tomb in the cemetery of Währing, Schubert did not know how near was his own hour of extinction, how soon his own grave would be dug but a few steps from where he then stood.

The business of burying Beethoven done, the immense crowd dispersed. The various funeral ceremonies, at the house, at the church, at the cemetery, had taken several hours. Delays had added to the fatigue. Hunger and thirst called back the living. On the return from Währing — in the company of his friends Schober, Schwind, and Fritz von Hartmann — Schubert went for supper to the alehouse called "Schloss Eisenstadt," in the Nagler-

gasse. There they chatted over their mugs until nearly one
o'clock in the morning, talking of Beethoven, his music, his personality, the tributes paid to his genius.

Silent, at table with the four, sat Death. The blow he had just
dealt to Music was as nothing compared to the blow he was then
preparing. His eyeless stare was holding his next opponent in the
game, his set grin spread agape. The stakes would be royal.

Twenty months later the match of Schubert v. Death came off.
The struggle was brief. Though a hundred years old, the score has
not been settled to everyone's satisfaction. Was it fair play? Death
can be cruel, tricky. No more so than life. His sins of omission out-
number those of commission. He can tarry too long as well as
be precipitate. On the whole, however, his average of timely and
judicious strokes is probably a high one, considering that perhaps
he is entitled to make as many blunders as are made by birth.
Death is fantastic, irresponsible. He loves to take risks, he has
the gambler's instincts. His most spectacular coups are won in
a flash.

When Schubert died, at the age of thirty-one, his friends seemed
justified in putting on his tombstone the inscription: "Music has
buried here a rich possession, but much brighter hopes." They
did not know at the time how large a legacy the dead had left
them. There was the natural expectation that a man of thirty-
one had yet a long and fruitful life before him. But who will
say what the years would have done for Schubert? Fifteen had
sufficed for him to finish an enormous number of compositions;
among them were enough so marvellous in quality that they placed
him for all time among the greatest musicians. Still, his equipment as a composer was incomplete. And he knew it. On June 18,
1812, he had his first lesson in counterpoint. There were but few
to follow. On November 4, 1828 — two weeks before his death —
Schubert called on Simon Sechter, first court-organist, and asked
him for instruction in fugue-writing. It was agreed that the
studies would be based on old Marpurg's "Treatise on the Fugue."
Death interfered with these plans.

It is idle to speculate of what avail Sechter's instruction might
have been to Schubert. The particular charm of Schubert's best

music lies in its spontaneity and youthful exuberance. If there is a "music of the heart," as opposed to "music of the brain," it is Schubert's. And such music is disdainful of contrapuntal crutches. It walks in superb unconcern where fancy leads. The thought of an ageing, fugue-writing Schubert — juggling with *dux* and *comes* in singles, pairs, and triplets — seems depressing and absurd. As well might Constable or Corot, at the height of their skill in landscape-painting, have gone in for a course in anatomy.

Hardly was it because he thought it would make him a better composer that Schubert wanted to perfect himself in counterpoint. With all his native modesty, he had quite a clear idea of his own worth as a musician. But then, there is the story of the position of second court-organist, with a yearly salary of 500 gulden, which became vacant in 1825 when Sechter moved up to be first organist. Count Moritz Dietrichstein, then "music-count" of the imperial court, was anxious that Schubert should have the position. The applicants for it had to submit to an examination, to a test on the organ. The test consisted in improvising fugues and other contrapuntal knick-knacks on given themes. The 500 gulden would have meant salvation. But Schubert refused to compete. He did not submit to the test, and wisely. It is more than likely that he would have failed, or come out with his reputation singed. Although still far from famous, Schubert already was esteemed as a composer of unusual merit. He could ill afford to risk defeat in an official contest in which not God-given talent but man-taught prowess was the essential.

When his incomplete equipment as a manipulator of counterpoint forced him to abandon the hopes of getting this post as organist, Schubert is said to have remarked: "I should be subsidized by the State, so that I might compose without let or care." The same opinion or wish has been voiced by other composers. But, as a rule, they were men incompletely equipped for the struggle of life. And they went under.

If, in 1828, Schubert decided to take belated lessons from Sechter, he may have felt that, after all, some office with a fixed income attached to it was a desirable thing, and that, in order to obtain it, he had to perfect himself in contrapuntal technique.

But Schubert in a position of this kind is no more conceivable than a chamois curbed and harnessed. Nor could another "Forty-eight" or "Kunst der Fuge" have flowed from Schubert's pen. His mission lay in another direction. Now, at the point when he was about to swerve from that direction, Death stepped in and laid down his trump. Perhaps the card was well played. Anyhow, what seemed a victory proved the reverse. For the dead have a way, sometimes, of taking from Death the last trick with the joker of posthumous fame.

*   *

*

Schubert was not a famous personage when he died. For one thing, he died too young to have achieved wide renown in a day which had not begun to develop the modern methods of advertising and rapid contact. Moreover, he did not possess the sort of personality that lent itself to self-propelling or organized publicity. According to one of his intimates, Schubert's salient characteristic was the opposite of salience: a "lovable simplicity" (*liebenswürdige Schlichtheit*), which had earned him the affectionate nickname of *"Schwammerl"* (little toadstool). His precocious musical gifts were early recognized. Lang, the director of the school at the "Convict," remarked again and again in the class reports, from 1809 to 1812, that young Franz was "a musical talent," "a particularly musical talent," and that "he fiddles and plays difficult pieces *prima vista*." Nevertheless, Schubert was not a *Wunderkind* of the Mozart stamp. Nor did he have a Leopold Mozart for father, to act as a martinet and travelling impresario. The fifteen-year-old freak Mozart, under his paternal thumb, had been more of a European celebrity than the thirty-five-year-old master at his death.

Another reason for Schubert's comparative inconspicuousness during his lifetime is the fact that, among the great musicians of his time, he was the first *bourgeois* composer, the first who was not either born within the purlieus of a palace or attached to the person and service of some *grand seigneur*, with the obligatory

doles and patronage and livery. The wind of independence had
burst from the cave of revolt. Though its first fury was spent,
there were the fears and the hopes of another squall. In Schubert
and his music breathed something of that German *Volksseele*—
soul of the people — which, with lyre and sword, was headed for
the stormy spring of 1848.

In March, 1825, Bauernfeld wrote: "Schubert is always the
same, always natural." But in his nature there was a strange
mixture of pride (the knowledge of his musical superiority) and
diffidence (the sense of his social inferiority). He was the life
of the party among his equals, friends, and cronies. He never
tired of playing for their dances. In the right place his geniality
and good nature knew no bounds. Out of his proper element he
was lost. When he accompanied the family of Count Esterhazy
to Zelész, in 1818, as music-teacher of the young *comtesses*, his
status in the household relegated him to the *communes* or servants'
and retainers' quarters. The Count was "fairly raw," the Countess
"haughty." Here poor *"Schwammerl"* had little to look for. He
may already have secretly adored one of his pupils; for company
he was reduced to the "very pretty" chambermaid. In a few
weeks' time his isolation became more and more apparent to him.
"If with every day I did not learn to know better the people who
surround me, I should fare as well as I did in the beginning. But
I see that I am alone among them, except for a couple of really
good girls. My longing for Vienna grows daily." It was the mood
of his homesick "Wanderer," who found that happiness dwelt
where he was not. When he returned to Zelész for a few months
in 1824, it was perhaps chiefly because of the attraction of a
"certain star" who now was six years older and probably six
times more adorable. But she remained a celestial body six hundred light-years distant from the earth-born fungus.

*   *

*

There was a great deal of the Bohemian in Schubert. After
his return from Zelész to Vienna, in the autumn of 1824, the

painter Moritz von Schwind wrote to Franz von Schober: "Schubert is here, well and heavenly light-minded (*himmlisch leichtsinnig*), rejuvenated through bliss and sorrow and gay life (*heiteres Leben*)." Here is the whole man, also his whole music, from his greatest and profoundest songs to the most inconsequential and prettiest of his dance tunes. This constant wavering between happiness and misery, Goethe's "*himmelhoch jauchzend — zu Tode betrübt,*" was a personal trait of Schubert's as well as the mark of the romantic *Zeitgeist*. It was a weakness of character, carrying with it the danger of over-indulgence in complacent morbidness; among the first dozen poems set by Schubert were "Hagar's Lament," "The Maiden's Lament," a plain "Lament," "A Corpse Fantasia," "The Parricide," "Gravedigger's Song" — cheerful subjects to choose for one hardly more than a boy. The Werther-bacillus was deadly; but it was also the cause of a highly poetic sensitiveness. So the scales are probably balanced.

From Zelész on September 21, 1824, Schubert wrote to his friend Schober, who was in Breslau at the time: "I hear that you are not happy! That you must sleep off the rapture of your despair! So Schwind writes me. Although it grieves me greatly, it does not astonish me, for that is the lot of almost every sensitive person in this miserable world. And what should we do with happiness, since unhappiness is the only charm (*Reiz*) left to us?" But *Reiz* also means stimulus. Taken in that sense, Schubert saw clear. It was Heine's "*Aus meinen grossen Schmerzen mach' ich die kleinen Lieder.*" The pains blossomed into songs; but they were real pains, for all that, devilish real, perching on the sill of dawn and spreading their sombre wings before the sunrise.

The natural recourse lay in the "gay life." The tavern was the temple of companionship. Bacchus and Gambrinus were its gods. Schubert never degenerated into a toper; but he sacrificed much, too much, to the indispensable solace of good talk and good beer. Psychical self-preservation brought with it physical self-destruction. His spirits rose, while his power of resistance dropped. Probably it was never very high.

Franz was the twelfth child of his parents. At his birth, his father was thirty-three years old and his mother forty. She bore two more children. In 1812 she died of typhus, at the age of fifty-five. The following year the father, then in his forty-ninth year, remarried; he had four children by his second wife, making eighteen in all. Of the children by his first wife the majority died at birth or in infancy; only five survived. It was by the rarest good luck that Franz lived to see manhood. If caution might have added to his years, a less "heavenly light-minded" person could not have abandoned himself so recklessly to his superlative gift of creation. The Great Mathematician casts up our sum by rules of His own.

It is sharpening the tragedy of Schubert's life to rather a fine point, but unquestionably in his case — as in some others where genius died young or took a "bad turn" — the disparity between the mental and the physical endowments, between creative strength and weakness of character, based on some innate and unremedied shortcoming, must account for the inner conflicts and premature end.

*   *
*

Sir George Grove seemed to think that Schubert's friends did not always take proper care of him, that they did not help him financially, that they failed him in critical moments. The accusation or innuendo is unjust. There is plenty of evidence to the contrary. Obviously, in the last malady medical aid came late and was inadequate. But Schubert had been ailing and had recovered so often that the gravity of the trouble was not suspected — either by him or by others — until it was past curing. Sir George believed that Schubert had premonitions of his death. It would be strange if a mind and temperament like Schubert's had not frequently played with the thought of ultimate dissolution. But the signature "your true friend till death," in Schubert's letter to Anselm Hüttenbrenner of January 18, 1828 — cited by Grove as "singular" proof of his contention — implies the confidence in a long, undying friendship rather than the expression of dark forebodings. And the authenticity of the death-bed remark, "Here, here is my end," supposedly made "in a slow, earnest voice," is at least doubtful, like many another alleged "last words." Three days of delirium and approaching coma may have prevented the actual knowledge that his song had reached its final cadence. What is certain is Schubert's written request, addressed to Schober a week before his death, for books by James Fenimore Cooper to lighten the tedium and misery of his condition. The will to live was still in him. He was then in the hands of a doctor. The picture he paints of himself — incapable of eating or drinking, feebly tottering back and forth between bed and armchair — is pathetic.

In September, 1825, Bauernfeld had written to Schubert, who was with Vogl in Steyr, proposing to take some "decent quarters" in Vienna which Schubert, Schwind, and Bauernfeld would share. Schubert politely but firmly declined the offer. He had had experiences "with such bachelor and student arrangements." He must have thought of Mayrhofer and Schober. Much as he cared for some members of his family, he could not live with them either. He preferred his independence. But that meant a certain loneliness and the want of a ready comforter in times of need. It also meant a more frequent resorting to the nightly gatherings of his chums. Bauernfeld's diary, for October, 1825, contains the entry: "Schubert is back. Tavern and coffee-house life with the friends, often till two, three o'clock in the morning."

The most harmless and most genuine of Schubert's social pleasures were the animated reunions of his friends in the easy freedom of congenial surroundings. Here the reading of Goethe, Tieck, Kleist, Heine, and other "modern" authors furnished these young sages with ample matter for heated debate or sentimental debauch. And seldom did they disband without having some music of their composer in ordinary. The event, in regular solemnization, was known as a *"Schubertiade."* The cult attracted many proselytes. The ministrants varied. It was high-mass when Michael Vogl's voice and the composer's touch on the keys combined — a combination which no one who ever heard it could forget. It was parochial worship during his lifetime. The great Schubert congregation formed slowly after his death.

Unquestionably, the warm admiration he found in the midst of these friends, the many opportunities to perform and judge the effect of his smaller vocal and instrumental works, was an incentive to Schubert's desire and faculty for creation. He was by no means an "unrecognized genius." But he was too much of a genius to find in recognition a remedy for his fits of depression.

Left to himself, Schubert fell into brooding. To his friend Leopold Kupelwieser, whose pencil and brush have immortalized his chubby, spectacled face, he wrote on March 31, 1824: "I am the most unhappy, most miserable being in the world. Imagine a man whose health will never be right again and who in his despair is making matters worse instead of better; imagine, I say, a man whose brightest hopes have come to naught, to whom the happiness of love and friendship offer nothing but bitterest pain, whose enthusiasm (at least inspiration) for the beautiful is threatening to vanish, and ask yourself if such a man is not miserable and unhappy? . . . In this joyless and friendless way I pass my days, save for an occasional visit from Schwind, who brings me a ray of those sweet days of old." The "reading circle" (*Lesegesellschaft*) had died of too much beer-drinking and sausage-eating. Friend Leidesdorf (his impecunious publisher) was a "truly deep and good being"; to be exposed to the infectious melancholia of this worthy mope brought danger to the atrabilious Schubert. They were birds of a feather, with plumage raven-black.

This was before the second visit to Zelész. On the return from it to Vienna the skies looked rosier. There is credible testimony that a re-formed, if not reformed, circle of boon companions did its best to fill Schubert's existence with cheer. The diaries of the brothers Fritz and Franz von Hartmann, especially for the last two years of Schubert's life, give reassuring indications that his "heavenly light-mindedness" was more firmly established. On the night of March 26, 1828 — after Schubert's only "private concert," which earned him "immense success and good receipts" — Franz von Hartmann recorded that all went to "The Snail," where they "jollified until midnight." The home-going, through the quiet and dimly lit streets of Vienna, after such parties, was accompanied by joking and singing of the merry band, much to the annoyance of the neighbourhood. A little life so soon to be rounded with eternal sleep was entitled, by special dispensation, to stay awake until the small hours "in the morn and liquid dew of youth." The Hartmanns were scrupulous timekeepers. There are many entries of late returns with Schubert from one or the other — and sometimes from more than one — of the familiar haunts. When the season invited, they went on excursions to Grinzing and farther into the country, up into the mountains. There was no better tonic for Schubert's mind and soul than the natural beauties of Upper Austria and Steyrmark, of Gmunden and Gastein. Wherever he travelled, he found old friends to welcome him and made new ones. Affection and admiration he had galore, but neither fame nor money.

* *

*

In one of Schubert's earliest letters to Schober and his other friends, written on August 3, 1818, during his first stay at Zelész, he announced that he was living and composing "like a god." He had just set Mayrhofer's "Einsamkeit" and wrote: "I believe it is the best thing I have done, because I was without a care." It is amazing that in later days the constantly recurring cares never really slackened nor impaired his extraordinary rapidity of work or fertility of invention. He wrote on and on, poured out one composition after the other, often three or four songs in one morning, and a long piece of chamber music in less than a week. Yet, once this thread of facile inspiration was cut, the end remained dangling. He was incapable of mending it, or in too great a hurry to bother with it. Hence the number of "unfinished" works, a prey to the mania of "completers." Nobody knows the precious hours he wasted over impossible opera libretti. He had poetic intuition, but lacked literary discrimination. A besetting delusion misled him into vain attempts at writing for the stage. Schubert took these failures much to heart. Yet the delusion is not difficult to explain.

Schubert, the most prolific song-writer in musical history, was primarily a dramatic, not a lyric composer. The dramatic style pierced through in his music before he turned out a true *Lied*. By the first he came naturally, the second he evolved. Schubert's early ballad compositions were still the offshoots of the eighteenth-century solo *"cantatille"* and *"scena."* The subject had changed from the prevailing mythological type to one of fantastic legend. But it was only another form of the old dramatic narrative, set in different sections to follow the story, interspersed with recitatives. His "Hagar's Klage," the settings he made of Schiller's "Der Taucher" and "Die Bürgschaft," are examples of the species that represents Schubert's "origins."

A musical relationship between Schubert and Zumsteeg has been widely proclaimed. There is a patent link. But it is not so much a direct strain inherited by one from the other, as it is a common root from which sprang both the elder and the younger branch. That root must be sought in the lyrico-dramatic hybrid into which the *"Cantata da camera"* had developed, with the German duodrama, monodrama, and melodrama as last derivatives. Zumsteeg died in 1802. It is far less remarkable that Schubert's setting of "Hagar's Klage," written in 1811, should bear a certain resemblance to Zumsteeg's setting of the same poem (published in 1797), than it is that Schubert's setting of Matthisson's "Adelaïde," composed in 1814, should have been so unlike Beethoven's (also published in 1797, after much sketching and revising). Beethoven's setting — the composer still called it a "cantata" — was nothing but an aria according to the classic model, sprawling out in the approved text-repetitions, indulged in to serve a formal demand of the music, not a declamatory or inherent need of the words. "Adelaïde," more than any other of his compositions, had contributed to popularize Beethoven's name. It took courage for a seventeen-year-old boy to try his hand at the same poem. Yet what Schubert achieved with it was, not a step, but a leap beyond Beethoven. The shape of the song is terse and balanced; there is Schubert's characteristic divination of the latent word-melody; his vocal line combines economy with expressiveness; his modulations are free but convincing; at the end of the song the accompaniment, before settling into the tonic major, slips in and out of the minor with an uncanny power of suggestion, so typical of Schubert's magic. The vestiges of the dramatic instinct remain always conspicuous.

Seldom do we get a glimpse — as in Schubert's letter to Bauernfeld and Mayrhofer of May, 1826 — of downright boredom coupled with the admission: "I am not working at all." Ordinarily he produced like a machine; with machine-like speed and regularity he turned out his products, some perfect, others less so. He was not the patient artisan of second and third thoughts. There exist two and more versions of a few songs. Their differences are slight. They do not show anything like Beethoven's long and bitter struggles for perfection. In some instances the changes are not absolute improvements, nor do they seem to reflect the composer's own judgment. His interpreters may have had something to do with them. In the later versions of "The Erlking" the melodic change that stresses the "you" in "don't *you* see the Erlking" savours of the theatrical over-emphasis dear to certain singers. Musically the discarded phrase was better. Of the earlier and almost more remarkable "Gretchen am Spinnrad" — Schubert wrote it in October, 1814 — there exists but one version, apparently the first and only one. The fact that the key, D minor, and the time, six-eight, and the "illustrative" figuration in sixteenth-notes of the accompaniment are the same as in the spinning-song of Haydn's "Seasons" does not diminish the wonder of Schubert's originality.

*   *

*

Schubert had written nearly one hundred and fifty songs between "Gretchen am Spinnrad" and "Der Erlkönig." For six years they remained in manuscript. Thanks to Vogl's initiative,

"Der Erlkönig" appeared at last in March, 1821, as Schubert's Opus 1, and a month later "Gretchen" followed as Opus 2. Robert Schumann, unfortunately, was born too late to do for Schubert what he did for Chopin's Opus 2 and Brahms's Opus 1. There was no one similarly competent and enthusiastic to introduce Schubert to the musical world. And he was the last person to court public attention. Schubert lacked Beethoven's eccentricities, Chopin's mundane graces, Liszt's virtuosity, Wagner's showmanship. He was simple, a trifle uncouth, honest, and rather shy. Some of his friends, at least, saw his drawbacks. Schober, from Breslau, wrote to Schubert on December 2, 1824: "If only you could procure yourself a few alarm-drums in the shape of critics who would constantly without end talk about you in all the papers; it would probably work. I know some quite insignificant people who in such a manner have become famous and popular; why, then, should not you resort to it, who merit it in the highest degree?" But Schober might as well have asked poor Schubert to turn himself inside out.

Grove is, at the least, inconsistent in judging Schubert's cronies. With one hand he pats them approvingly, with the other he raps them severely. They did not, as he says, "virtually live upon Schubert's carelessness and good-nature." If it is an indictment of them, it is an indictment of Schubert, too. Thrift was unknown to him. He lived for the moment, whether golden or sunless. He never earned so much or so steadily that he could have laid up savings had he tried. Apparently it mattered little to him. On July 10, 1826, Schubert wrote to Bauernfeld: "It is impossible for me to go to Gmunden or anywhere else, I have no money at all, and in general things go very badly with me. But I don't care and am cheerful." Nor was he the only one in this predicament. A few weeks later, in August, Bauernfeld confided to his diary the sad but not unusual intelligence that "Schubert is penniless, like the rest of us." Which did not prevent them from having a good time when they got together.

Schubert was a Bohemian, with the qualities and faults of the tribe. His friends — gay, brilliant, irresponsible, stimulating, devoted — were Schubert's richest earthly belongings. He depended on what they gave him as much as they gained by what he gave them. The thing they could not bestow upon him, with their best intentions, was celebrity and a competence. Their circle was rather a humble and hermetic one; in no other could Schubert have moved. When Grove bemoaned the fact that, unlike Beethoven, Schubert did not count among his familiars "crowned heads and nobility," eager to push him into the limelight, he might as well have lamented the inability of a purring puss to snarl like a Royal Bengali.

It is hardly fair to say that "of his important friends few knew, or showed that they knew, what a treasure they had within their reach." Schubert's important friends were Vogl, Ignaz von Sonnleithner and his sons, Count Moritz Dietrichstein (witness Dietrichstein's letter to Vogl written in January, 1821: "Since I have fathomed the genius of this youthful, robust, and uncommonly promising composer, it is one of my most fervent wishes to work for him *sub umbra alarum tuarum*, as much as I can"), Bishop Dankesreither of St. Pölten, the singer Anna Milder, the publisher Matthias Artaria, Kiesewetter, Rochlitz, young Josef von Spaun, and old Salieri; all of them certainly "knew" and showed that they did. The Gesellschaft der Musikfreunde in Vienna knew, and the Steiermärkischer Musikverein knew. Beethoven, whether or not he actually said that in Schubert lived "the divine spark," also knew that here was a musical talent of the first order. That the knowledge was not more general or more loudly trumpeted into the world was probably due to a circumstance alluded to in a remark (August, 1823) by Beethoven's nephew Karl in one of his deaf uncle's writing-tablets: "Schubert is being praised a lot, but people say that he hides himself." The behaviour evidently deserved the reputation. It was not a very helpful reputation.

Still, the expressions of admiration and confidence abounded among those who knew. Josef Hüttenbrenner proved a good prophet, when, as early as 1819, he wrote: "Schubert will truly shine some day, a new Orion in the musical heavens"; and he showed considerable daring as well as acumen when, three years later, he recommended Schubert to the publisher Peters in Leipzig with the words: "To tell you in short and without exaggeration, he is a second Beethoven." That was less than two years after "Der Erlkönig" had for the first time been sung in public.

The novelty of Schubert's music either puzzled the listeners or entirely conquered them. Only those who were steeped in stagnant tradition withheld their approval. What the professional musician and critic objected to most, the freedom and unwonted restlessness of Schubert's modulation, charmed unprejudiced ears. It was not surprising that so many musically untutored but sensitive artists — poets, painters, and the rest — were the first who succumbed to the spell of Schubert's "modernity."

* *

*

The Vienna papers, so far as they took any notice of Schubert during his lifetime, were generous enough in their praises. Berlin and Leipzig took longer to accept the innovator. Clannishness rather than ignorance was the cause. Beethoven had raged against "*die Leipziger Ochsen.*" The attitude of these critics was frigid, to say the least. There is perhaps a reason for it. To-day Schubert's music is the common property of the world. However, when his first songs appeared in print, it can be easily imagined that the cold, intellectual Northerners did not quite know what to do with these warm products of a Southern brain and temperament. To the insular Briton they were even more "foreign." In 1833, at one of the "German soirées" given by the music publisher Wessel in London, William Gardiner tells us that he "heard some songs of Shobert [*sic*], a new author. His 'Erlking' sung by Madame Schroeder [-Devrient] and accompanied on the pianoforte by Madame Dulcken, certainly was a most terrific thing of its kind. The alarming intonation of the vocalist, and the awful thunder which the pianist threw into the bass, had a dramatic effect purely German."

Fétis, in 1830, published in a book of "Curiosités Historiques de la Musique" an article on the "actual state of music in Germany." The greatest curiosity about this article is the fact that Schubert's name is nowhere mentioned and that the only "*jeunes compositeurs*" referred to in passing are Wolfram (1789–1830) and Mendelssohn. Wilhelm Christian Müller's "Einleitungen in die Tonkunst" (1830) contains a brief appreciative notice on Franz Schubert, "*dieser Lieblingsdichter unserer singenden Jugend.*" But his name is set in ordinary type, whereas Onslow's, for instance, was deemed worthy of the capital letters that spelled fame. Schubert's turn was not far off.

When Robert Schumann, ten years after Schubert's death, came to Vienna and wayfared to the holy places of music, he found a wild rosebush planted on Beethoven's grave, but "Franz Schubert's resting-place is unadorned." Schumann called on Schubert's brother Ferdinand. There he discovered the heaps of manuscripts left by Franz. The unearthing of the great C major Symphony and the subsequent performance of it under Mendelssohn in Leipzig were the first results of this visit. The remarkable series of posthumous publications extended over fifty years. So far as "new works" were concerned, Schubert did not die in 1828 at the age of thirty-one, but lived to be well over eighty. No wonder that people began to shake their heads incredulously.

Next to Schumann and Mendelssohn, no one helped more to spread the name and fame of Schubert than did Liszt through his playing of Schubert's piano music and his transcriptions of Schubert songs. On his production of Schubert's opera "Alfonso and Estrella" at Weimar, in 1854, love's labour was lost. In England Sir George Grove became the acknowledged Schubert specialist and apostle of his music. Grove's article on Schubert in the third volume of his "Dictionary of Music and Musicians" was the first biographical and critical account of Schubert's life and works in English. It was the tribute of a rabid enthusiast determined "to throw a perfume on the violet." The resultant odour was not pleasing to all. The "Edinburgh Review," in 1883, thought the article "disproportionate," which it was; it remains so to-day for reasons of piety. The Scottish critic candidly averred that not only did he not share Sir George's enthusiasm to anything like the same extent, but thought it desirable, "in the interest of true musical criticism," that musical readers generally should not share it. "Artistically, Schubert comes before us as almost the typical example of the self-taught genius, with the reservation, however, that he did not teach himself enough. . . . His attitude towards the art was throughout his life that of a very gifted amateur, who wants art just as far as he can get enjoyment out of it, and turns away at the point where hard work begins. . . . Is there no relation traceable between the style of Schubert's life and the style of his art? The possibility of such a relation we heard incidentally suggested once by the remark of a dignified and gentle-mannered old lady, after hearing a sonata of Schubert's, that there was something in his music which always gave her the idea that he was not a refined man."

This little spray of flowers plucked from the venerable "Edinburgh" exhales all the aroma peculiar to the Victorian age. Priggery was making the last stand against the advancing fame of Schubert.

The friends were assembled at Schober's to hail the New Year, 1828, Schubert's last year on earth. There were about a dozen of them. When the clocks of Vienna struck midnight, the friends clinked their glasses of Malaga, and drank to health, happiness, and success. Then Bauernfeld read rather a sentimental poem of ten stanzas which he had written for the occasion. One of them, curiously prophetic, may be translated thus:

> The charm'd flow of words, the fountain of song,
> Divine though they be, will be drained before long.
> No voice, in the throng, can sing without end,
> For even the singer must turn and wend;
> The source is hastening toward the seas,
> And he toward the source of his melodies.

If the grim gambler was present again, he must have appre-

ciated this stanza. The game was lost and won at three o'clock
on the afternoon of Wednesday, November 19, 1828. Death
found that his adversary held the highest trump. And the prize, in
laurels, is incomputable.

Shortly before he died, Schubert read the proofs of the second
part of his "Winterreise." It contains some of his finest and most
touching songs. They are imbued with the serene resignation compounded of a tear and a smile. They disclose the fearless pessimism
of an emancipated spirit.

Schubert's father was wholly conversant with the routine of
dying. He had buried nine children and one wife. The impending
loss of Franz properly filled him with the concern that animates
every good Christian whose faith craves the solace of the last
sacraments. Beyond this, he seems to have been unable to grasp
the significance of the event. The father's letter to Ferdinand,
written on the day Franz died but before his actual death, may
move us to ponder what separates fathers and sons. In a letter to
Franz from his oldest brother, Ignaz, written October 12, 1818,
there occurs this revealing postscript: "If you should write to
Papa and to me jointly, do not touch upon religious matters."

Not all the brothers of Franz were alike. From Steyr, in July,
1825, Franz wrote to his father and stepmother a long letter
which contains the following passage in reference to his brother
Ferdinand: "He surely must have been sick again 77 times, and
must have 9 times thought that he was dying, as if to die were
the worst thing that can befall us. If only he could see these
heavenly mountains and lakes, the sight of which threatens to
crush and annihilate us, he would not set so great a store by this
petty life of ours, but would think it a great happiness to be
returned to the incomprehensible forces of the earth for a new
life."

The spire of St. Stephen's Church is visible far out in the
Austrian plain. What draws the eyes of the world to Vienna is
the hallowed dust of Mozart, Beethoven, Schubert, and Brahms,
returned to the incomprehensible forces of a soil forever sacred.
And not the least precious of its immortal ingredients are the

a martyr and hero, by commemorating the one-hundredth return of the day on which Beethoven's spirit passed from his mortal shell to continue a living presence in his deathless music, the property of all mankind.

*   *

*

When Romain Rolland, on the afternoon of March 28, 1927, appeared in the large assembly hall of the Vienna University, to deliver his "Tribute to Beethoven," the dense crowd greeted him with demonstrative applause. The demonstration was intended not as a greeting to Rolland the musicologist or the novelist, but to the man who had dared to place himself in time of strife and hatred "above the turmoil." His address, delivered in the programme of the international congress of musicologists, only summed up what every other official speaker had voiced, when Rolland closed with the words: "We, the sons of all peoples on this earth, are solemnly united in Beethoven. He is the radiant symbol of Europe's conciliation and of brotherliness among all men."

That might have been called the "keynote" of the Vienna celebration. It was a musical celebration with political significance. It was sponsored by the Austrian Government and the city of Vienna. It was attended by the Apostolic Nuncio to Vienna as the representative of the Pope, by delegations from twelve European nations and the United States of America.

The American delegation was composed of three members — Hon. Albert H. Washburn, American Minister to Austria; the chief of the music division in the Library of Congress; and the secretary of the Beethoven Association in New York, O. G. Sonneck. Among the delegates from European countries were six cabinet ministers, the most conspicuous and the most eagerly watched being the head of the French delegation, Edouard Herriot, quondam Socialist mayor of Lyons, ex-premier of France, then French minister of public instruction. One of his colleagues was M. Henri Rabaud, director of the Paris Conservatory, and well remembered in America as a war-time conductor of the Boston Symphony Orchestra. Mascagni represented Italy.

In the following, the salient impressions of an eventful week are set down as they presented themselves to one member of the American delegation:

Saturday, March 26, at 10:30 A. M. From the residence of the American Minister in the Krügerstrasse (the handsome old *palais* of the Esterhazy and Erdödy families) the Minister's automobile, bearing a small American flag on the windshield, takes the three delegates the few blocks to the grey and massive building of the Musikverein. Delegates and Austrian officials assemble in the "Kleiner Saal," prior to the opening ceremony in the adjoining large hall. The head of the Austrian protocol presents the visitors. A polyglot conversation begins which is to last seven days and nights.

A clock strikes eleven. The "Grosser Musikvereinssaal" is filled to the last row of the top balcony with a surging, straining audience. All eyes are directed toward the first boxes on the left of the stage as the President of the Austrian republic, Dr. Hainisch; the Federal Chancellor, Dr. Seipel; the Cardinal Prince-archbishop of Vienna, Dr. Piffl; and the foreign guests file in. The stage is filled with the chorus of the Society of Friends of Music and the Symphony Orchestra. In the centre a huge white bust of Beethoven, against a background of evergreens, dominates the scene.

Felix Weingartner, with earnest, sober gesture, beckons the musicians to begin the funeral cantata written upon the death of Emperor Joseph II (February 20, 1790). It is early Beethoven, a work of the Bonn period. It was written as a *pièce d'occasion;* it serves in the same capacity to-day. Among the ladies of the chorus youthful faces are in the minority. Long-handled lorgnettes help the eyesight, but not the voice. The soloists, chorus, and orchestra do their parts well enough; criticism is suspended. It is not a concert in the ordinary sense; it is not quite so good, and yet better.

The cantata over, Professor Guido Adler steps to the speaker's

The foreign delegates and Austrian officials, who were the guests of the Austrian President, Mr. Hainisch, at the State luncheon on the occasion of the Beethoven Centenary in Vienna in March 28, 1927.

desk; he is the dean of the musicological faculty at the University of Vienna and chairman of the executive committee in charge of the official celebration. If any man deserves the highest praise for his share in the success of the festivities, it is this little man with the patriarchal white beard, high forehead, world-wise kindly eyes flashing from behind his gold-rimmed spectacles; in mellow voice and precise diction he calls upon the President of Austria formally to open the proceedings. Dr. Hainisch stresses the international character of the celebration; he expects that it will tend to further "intellectual co-operation in every field." The applause is adequate. Much louder and prolonged hand-clapping greets the second speaker, Dr. Ignatz Seipel. The political barometer rises. A red face, bald head equally red, a sharp profile, tight lips, but the look of unbounded courage and determination. The ecclesiastical garb completes the picture of the militant priest. Seipel is the man of the hour. He is the first speaker to refer openly to the late war and its disasters. The world, he exclaims, is athirst again for the sources of idealism. Schiller's "Ode to Joy" furnishes not only him but most of the speakers with apposite quotations. When he dramatically shouts *"Seid umschlungen Millionen,"* the thought involuntarily crosses the listener's mind of the millions that the war has *"verschlungen."* And when the Chancellor thrusts out his arms in a final appeal that "all men become as brothers," one cannot help contrasting this oratory with the news in the Vienna papers that in these very days of fraternal embraces an armed conflict between Italy and Yugoslavia has barely been averted, that the doctors of the Vienna *Krankenkassen* are threatening to go on strike, and that the Socialist leader in parliament has declared the labour unions to stand ready at any moment to paralyse the industrial life of the country. Saint Ludwig van Beethoven, pray for us!

The American Minister speaks for the United States. He praises Beethoven as the "apostle of liberty in the philosophical sense of the word" — a sense Americans have reason to seek consolation in. Be it proudly said that Mr. Washburn is talking in excellent German, to the visible and audible delight of the Viennese. After the ceremony, as the delegates one by one leave their box, Dr. Seipel presses Mr. Washburn's hands and thanks him effusively for the gracious compliment. Echoes of this gratitude reflect from everywhere and for the length of the festivities.

The speeches of the Austrian authorities and the foreign delegates are on record. They are broadcast as far as the current will carry them. But the gesture must join the word, especially in the cases of the Belgian Vandervelde — the best orator of the lot — and Mascagni — the most theatrical. Naturally, some of the speeches are better than others. Felix Weingartner's face occasionally is indication of that difference. He seems relieved when at last he can once more take up his baton and conduct Beethoven's Fantasy for piano, chorus, and orchestra, Opus 80, with which the ceremony comes to an end. Not without the wish, however, that the pianist might have been of a calibre with the occasion.

On the same day at five o'clock — the hour in which Beethoven died — the city of Vienna, in the beautiful city hall, profusely decorated with potted plants and flowers, receives the delegates and a picked crew of city magistrates for a private view of an exhibition of Beethoven relics. But the crowd is too large; a proper appreciation of the wealth of the exhibited treasures is impossible.

There is just time enough to rush to the hotel and dress for the opera. Gluck's ballet "Don Juan" and Beethoven's "Ruins of Athens" (in a version by Richard Strauss and his librettist, Hugo von Hoffmannsthal) make up the programme. The delegates occupy the "*Mittelloge,*" the former royal box, and are given a taste of regal splendour combined with democratic simplicity. Dr. Seipel is the courteous host; the head of the protocol acts as ubiquitous steerer. The performance — intended primarily as a spectacle — is excellent; the colourful stage pictures are charming, some of the dancing and grouping most effectively devised. But the method of doing away with the footlights and of treating almost every scene as a chiaroscuro in which obscurity overbalances clarity, soon wearies the unaccustomed eye. And the trouble becomes acute as other performances take place under the same conditions. The ear, on the contrary, takes unalloyed pleasure in the sounds that come from the orchestra pit that isn't a pit. Here is a lesson in negative and positive experience.

*　　*

*

On Sunday morning, March 27, at 9:30, the foreign delegations and the musical societies of Vienna make their pilgrimage to the Central Cemetery and deposit floral tributes on the sacred tomb. Laurel and gold predominate, with ribbons in a gay assortment of national colours. The American delegation has difficulty in making headway through the crowd and the police cordon. But finally it succeeds in laying down a simple three-ringed bouquet of long-stemmed red roses, white lilacs, and blue hortensias. Meanwhile the male choral organizations of Vienna are gathered and intone (after a fashion) "Die Himmel rühmen." Their leader stands on an improvised platform, with his back to the grave. And with their backs to the grave stand the listeners, with bare heads some of them, despite the certainty of catching a cold in the raw March air. Moving-picture cameras are rattling away. Pietro Mascagni stands before the heap of ribbons and wreaths, with the tragic mask of grief, while from every angle photographers "snap" him and the tombstone. A cemetery is dangerous ground. As a stage it must be reverently used. Here the arrangements are marred by confusion. Wisdom prompts an early departure. Beethoven will smile more approvingly upon the scene when the police cordon is broken, when the singers and delegates have dispersed, and the waiting multitude of anonymous citizens, many of them clothed in poverty, will be allowed to file by the grave and place upon it their humble bunches of spring flowers.

At twelve o'clock "Missa solemnis" in the large hall of the Konzerthaus. Franz Schalk conducts; the chorus is the superb one of the opera; at the first desk of the violins Rosé leads the Viennese Philharmoniker. The soloists rank among the best of Vienna's opera. But it is not the performance of one person or group of persons that raises this mass to the pinnacle of the celebration. It is rather the grandeur of the work, the dramatic life of this religious composition. "From the heart it came" — and to the hearts it goes. Here the spirit of Beethoven truly descends upon musicians and audience. A great soul has suffered, a great mind has wrought, and grandeur has been paired with beauty as never before or since. What if one critic deems the conductor unequal to his gigantic task, what if another shrugs his shoulder at mention of the soloists? There are people with long memories of past performances. Let them remember to their detriment. No slight shortcoming can diminish the effect of this music, can obstruct its way to the heart, as the composer wanted it to go, can detract from the impressiveness of the occasion. The dimensions of the work, the strain on the musicians, unfortunately make an intermission necessary. At the end of the mass, the enthusiasm will no longer be repressed. Deserved applause rewards the performers. Some people stay to recall the conductor and soloists; others want to flee into quiet and solitude, to weep for joy.

Out in the "cottage" quarter of Döbling lives Hofrat Professor Dr. Guido Adler. At four o'clock on Sunday afternoon he is at home for the foreign participants in the international musicological congress that holds its meetings at the university during the week of the festival. The number of guests is too large for even the spacious and yet cosy house. It is a typical Viennese *"Jause"*; coffee, tea, chocolate, sandwiches and cake of every description are passed, while musicologists from far and near renew acquaintances or delight in meeting face to face the men whose writings they have known for long. Their names would fill a column. You hear French, German (in several dialectic varieties), English, Polish, Italian, Danish — a very babel of languages. Everybody seems to speak everybody else's tongue. Romain Rolland and his sister are there. Professor Adler is everywhere. His face beams. His vivacity and freshness belie the tremendous piece of work he has accomplished in planning and preparing this rich programme of music and musicological sessions. And not merely with a kind word does he turn from one to the other; he enters into technical discussions at one moment, and at the next he gives solicitous advice to the stranger in Vienna regarding the smallest detail of personal comfort and convenience. No wonder the man is loved by everyone as much as the savant is admired.

The performance of "Egmont" at the Opera House, on Sunday night, is the occasion for a storm of applause that greets Weingartner when he appears at the conductor's stand. It is a greeting and a leave-taking. Weingartner is forsaking Vienna for Basel. A nervous, brilliant rendition of the overture proves that an ageing king goes prematurely into voluntary exile. Goethe's drama is listened to reverentially; Herriot seems wrapt in thought; no one but he knows upon what his attention is focused. Does he look for historic parallels? The stage is in dimness most of the time. The buxom actress who takes the part of Clärchen turns her back to the audience while behind the scenes Lotte Lehmann, latest idol of the Viennese, sings the Clärchen-Lieder. A rather clumsily managed piece of stage business in an otherwise exceptionally smooth performance. The new scenery of Professor Alfred Roller is distinguished by a refreshing absence of "tradition."

The third day, Monday, March 28, brings the *déjeuner* given by the President, Dr. Hainisch, to the foreign delegates at the foreign office, the famous *palais* on the Ballhausplatz. The President, in the large salon, moves slowly from group to group with a gracious word for everyone. His English is as fluent as his French; but his cordiality rings truest in the broad accents of his native Viennese. With his high stature, full white beard, slightly closed eyes, and benevolent smile, he is eminently dignified and at the same time engagingly "republican." From the walls of the reception room pictures of Habsburg emperors and archdukes seem to gaze wonderingly upon the assembly.

The table is laid in the beautiful long hall — exquisite in its plainness of white and gold — wherein a little over one hundred years ago the Vienna Congress held its momentous debates. To the four doors then giving access to the room, a fifth one had to be added at the time in order to solve the knotty problem of precedence, by having the ambassadors of the five contracting nations enter simultaneously, each one through a door of his own. To-day the questions of etiquette are no less perplexing. The seating has been arranged according to the sacrosanct precepts of state etiquette. To have found entertaining neighbours — Swiss on one side and French on the other — is a matter of personal luck.

In the middle of the long table sits the President; he has at his right the Papal Nuncio, at his left the envoy from Berlin, the "nationalistic" Reichsinnminister von Keudell. Opposite the President sits the Chancellor, Dr. Seipel; from his right and left evolves a similar order of dignitaries and delegates, foreign and domestic. There is a welcome absence of speeches and music. The table is adorned with heavy gilt ornaments and tasteful floral decorations. The menu is a choice one. The list of beverages is worth recording; it comprises Sherry, Schwechat beer, Vöslauer Goldeck 1924 (white), Ruster Perle 1925 (red), Schlumberger Privatkeller 1917 (champagne), and a variety of liqueurs with the coffee and cigars. *Tout comme chez nous!* The conversation is as animated as it is polyglot. His Eminence Monsignor Sibilia, in his carmine-hued robes, stands out in the company of black cutaways. However, in his case, it is not only the clothes that make the man, but the head, a fine Roman head, keen dark eyes, mobile features, expressive movements of well-shaped hands — the perfect type of the prince of the Church. And while he is intently talking to his neighbour on the right, one has the impression that he does not miss a word that is spoken on both sides of the long table, the longest, it is said, that has been laid under the republican régime. The occasion is indeed a memorable one. But already the heaping measure of music and official entertainments begins to weigh a little upon the traveller from afar.

The weight becomes almost unbearable when on Monday evening he attempts to hear two concerts going on at the same time: that is, the beginning of one and the end of the other. The first brings rarely performed works by masters, great and small, of the eighteenth century, forerunners of Beethoven. A chamber orchestra under Professor Heger (who directs his men deftly, discreetly, and without baton) plays a suite by J. J. Fux (1660-1741), the chapel-master of Emperor Charles VI. Minuet and Passepied betray their kinship with the *Ländler;* it is Austrian music. After a few harpsichord pieces, competently played by Alice Ehlers, there follows the composition of a trail-blazer, the little-known G. M. Monn (1717-1750), the first organist of the beautiful Karls-kirche in Vienna. It is a concerto for 'cello and orchestra, the solo part played by the incomparable Pablo Casals. The rest of the programme must be sacrificed in order to find the way in a drenching rain to the small hall in the near-by Konzerthaus, where the Rosé Quartet play Beethoven's Opus 130 in its original form, with the great Fugue (Opus 133) for a finale. The players are in excellent form, they officiate with authority and conviction. But they cannot alter the impression that the composer wisely substituted later another finale for the fugue. Those who have strength and courage left repair after the concert to the former royal castle, the imposing Hofburg, where the Austrian minister of public instruction, Dr. Schmitz, receives the visitors and guests in the hall of ceremonies.

* *
*

The fourth day of the celebration offers another quandary: the choice between a concert of chamber music played by a trio of masters — Casals, Hubermann, and Friedmann — or an evening of historic opera in the lovely Redoutensaal of the Hofburg. The latter is too unusual and attractive to pass by. The programme comprises Henry Purcell's "Dido and Æneas," Pergolesi's "Serva Padrona," and a short ballet by Rameau. The hall is in white and gold, hung with priceless tapestries, and illuminated by huge crystal chandeliers. The stage has no proscenium arch; it is simply a raised prolongation of the room, with curved double stairs in the centre leading to an upper door, while from the sides the stage is reached from improvised low wings. A red silk curtain reaching halfway up is pulled back, and the scene discloses a picture of rare charm and colour. The costumes belong, perhaps, to a period

which is a little later than the time in which Purcell's opera was
written (ca. 1688), but it is authentic rococo, the women in wide
hoopskirts, the Trojan soldiers in pseudo-Greek armour, and
plumed helmets over long, curly wigs. Hans Gál is responsible for
the musical "revision" of the score. Eye and ear are too en-
grossed for the moment to permit musico-historical scruples to
spoil the æsthetic pleasure; there are times when learning is a
hindrance. The orchestra, under Schalk, sounds now and then a
little thick, but it never covers the voices. Mme. Gutheil-
Schoder's stage management provides such quaint and delightful
pictures that to quarrel with their historic accuracy would be
pedantic. Frau Born as Dido looks queenly and makes it difficult
to understand that even the Olympians could have bullied Æneas
into leaving her and the hospitable shores of Carthage. The other
parts are well distributed, though none of the singers stands out
by virtue of tonal quality or vocal bravura.

"La Serva Padrona" enlists two capital singers who are also
excellent actors, the basso Mayr and the soprano Mme. Schumann,
favourably known in America, where she appeared in concerts with
Richard Strauss. Although Strauss is absent from Vienna for the
moment, to the apparent satisfaction of a large section of the musical world, he manages to share the front page of the papers with
Beethoven when the wild rumour is spread that he has suffered a
stroke of paralysis in Dresden. Wife and son leave by airplane for
the Saxon capital, to learn to the relief not only of themselves but
of everybody that their illustrious husband and father is conducting
concerts in Königsberg, at the eastern confines of the Reich, and is
enjoying the best of health. The excitement is admirably sustained
by the later news that Strauss intends to sue the source whence
came the false alarm.

Wisely indeed the programmes are so arranged as to afford
variety and to prevent a surfeit of the music of one man, be it
Beethoven himself. Thus on Wednesday, March 30, at noon, a
specially invited public is privileged to listen in the chapel of the
Hofburg to a choir of men's and boys' voices, singing sacred and
secular compositions of the thirteenth, fourteenth, and fifteenth

centuries, under the direction of Dr. Rudolph Ficker. The very first number, a motet by Perotinus, reveals the strange beauty of this music. Whoever may have thought of these "Gothic" composers as groping tiros in a "new art" has a surprise in store. Limpid counterpoint, floating rhythms, and bold melodic patterns hardly savour of crude antiquity. Our ear has been re-educated to listen to progressions of fourths and fifths without being in the least disturbed by them. To-day, perhaps more readily than fifty years ago, this music is again able to move us. An Italian secular song of the fourteenth century evokes all the arts and graces of the Renaissance. A remarkable motet by Dunstable reminds us of the leading rôle played by England in these years of early musical development. The programme has the great merit of brevity. Too much of this music would, after all, fatigue our ear. Not all of it is equally good. Not all of it seems to have escaped the arranger's retouching. But in its simple contours it outlines a whole world of song, the passing of which we have cause to regret. And the concert will undoubtedly remain one of the most memorable in a week too closely packed with unforgettable experiences.

Although the orchestra concert, on the evening of the same day, may not differ much from innumerable similar programmes in and out of centenary years, the conducting of the Eroica by Weingartner has something vital and Nordic; the conducting of the Eighth by Casals — in sheer contrast — is electrifyingly Latin, without quite demonstrating that this great artist is as marvellous a conductor as he is a violoncellist. While Weingartner leads like an infallible and unconquerable commander, Casals incites, conjures, and rushes headlong forward, often carrying after him orchestra and audience. Rosé, again at the first desk of the violins, gives the tone to this admirable body of string players with his vibrant, incisive articulation of every phrase and his instantaneous response to the slightest indications of the conductor.

A gala performance of "Fidelio" at the opera, on the evening of Thursday, March 31, marks the end of the official celebration. The large auditorium is bright with gay frocks and dazzling jewellery worn by Vienna's proverbially fair sex. The men wear their decorations, and some of them, like Mascagni, wear several pounds of stars, crosses, and medals on their chests. The red, white, and red band of the new order of the Republic crosses the breast of the President, who sits with his wife and aged mother in one of the proscenium boxes. The centre box is given over once more to the foreign delegates, Dr. Seipel doing the honours. The old nobility is represented, but sparsely. The absence of all military uniforms robs the scene of its former brilliancy. Nevertheless, Vienna is trying hard to look its old self.

Lotte Lehmann is singing the part of Leonore for the first time; and, strange to relate, Piccaver too is new as Florestan. Both are astonishingly competent; yet there are moments when this or that name belonging to the past rises from oblivion and outshines in retrospect the stars of the evening. The chorus and orchestra, however, are still superb. The new scenery and lighting follow the school of the obscurantists. There never was a darker dungeon in Spain, or even in the Schlüsselburg, than the dismal hole wherein languishes Florestan on the Vienna stage.

All the more bright and glittering is the scene in the Imperial salons of the opera, which are thrown open after the performance to a throng of invited guests. Before supper is served, Professor Adler claps his hands for attention, and in a few touching words, betraying his emotion, he bids farewell and *au revoir* to the foreign visitors. Herriot replies. As the celebration began with a quasi-political gesture, so it ends. Herriot's voice rings through the rooms with the inflections of the experienced tribune. In the name of Beethoven, let there be peace, unity, co-operation. These are words sweet to the ears of Vienna and the listening world. What greater fame could mortal man achieve than to serve the cause of peace, to see his life-work made the means of joining again what hatred and ignorance, greed and jealousy had sundered? Music has reaped new honours, accepted new responsibilities. By the tomb of Beethoven, under the spell of his harmonies, we have consecrated ourselves anew to the cause of brotherly love. Beethoven should be satisfied. No honour would have pleased him better.

"HOME, SWEET HOME"
(1 8 2 3 – 1 9 2 3)

CELEBRATION the world over marked in 1923 the one-hundredth anniversary of "Home, Sweet Home." Not very old, after all, when you consider that the emotions of homesickness, *Heimweh, mal du pays,* date probably back to Adam and Eve's pained glances at the shut gates of Eden. But old enough to have been coæval with (if not the inspiration of) so many splendid "developments" in real estate, so many building loan companies nobly helping you to "own-your-own," so many ingenious plans for making sweeter and sweeter that little two-room flat with bath and kitchenette. If home has lost nothing of its pristine humbleness, the benefits of modern improvements and the solicitude of a jovial janitor have imparted to it a sweetness exceeding anything imagined by the poet and his generation.

Comparatively few are the people nowadays who inhabit the house of their fathers. All the wider is the appeal of the song in praise of it. Every tongue with a term to express the sense of nostalgia has appropriated tune and words, bodily or in a slightly altered form. That originally it should have been an English ballad, best beloved among the songs of English-speaking races, is not surprising.

The Anglo-Saxon, although pre-eminently a colonizer, a roamer abroad, a trader searching foreign lands and seas, nevertheless holds to his native ways, clings to the thought of his castellated hearth. No matter how far from his shire or spire, he retains a longing for "that happy abode" of his childhood and the vicinity of his baptismal register. Nor is the longing always suppressed, but it seeks utterance in the simple and tender strains of a melody that has become a universal symbol for the aspirations of the human family. And these aspirations will find a voice, even though — viewing the matter dispassionately — there is no gainsaying that frequently it is best to dwell at a reasonable distance from one's own relations, and that true comfort is oftenest met farthest away from that "village half hid by the woods."

At a public sale in the Anderson Galleries, New York, on the evening of March 6, 1923, was sold to the highest bidder the autograph score of Bishop's opera "Clari; or, The Maid of Milan," containing the song "Home, Sweet Home." It brought $1,590.

The lucky winner in the contest, or the man who wanted it worst, was Mr. Hiram W. Sibley, that munificent founder and maintainer of the Sibley Music Library, which is attached to the University of Rochester, N. Y. Thanks to Mr. Sibley's generosity and public spirit, the score, which came to America in 1884, will now securely remain in this country.

"Clari; or, The Maid of Milan," was performed for the first time on May 8, 1823, at Covent Garden, London. Speaking of this première in his annals of the venerable playhouse, H. S. Wyndham indulges in the following foot-note: "It is sad to relate that the original MS. of the opera, formerly in the possession of the late Mr. Julian Marshall, is now in the United States." How much sadder the author should be when he reflects upon the now assured permanency of so cruel a loss.

But why this note of national grief? Has not America a valid claim to the autograph? The poem of this immortal song was written, not by an Englishman, but by an American, John Howard Payne — although for the sake of truth and fairness be it remembered that the appealing words are but a paraphrase of Thomas Bayly's text which he wrote for the "Sicilian Air" that formed part of the song collection entitled "Melodies of Various Nations," published by Messrs. Goulding in 1821. Like many other melodies in this collection, the "Sicilian Air" was arranged, and largely invented, by Sir Henry Rowley Bishop. It was corner-stone, lintel, and roof-tree of "Home, Sweet Home."

Anyway, America had its share in "Clari," even if the whole story was "borrowed" from a ballet by the same name which Rodolphe Kreutzer set to music in 1820. Kreutzer is remembered to-day, not by any of his thirty-odd operas, but only by exercises, caprices, and a few concerti for the violin; by a sonata for violin and piano which Beethoven dedicated to him; and by the novel which the late Count Leo Tolstoi based on the strange and rather dubious assumption that this sonata is not a piece to be played in a drawing-room before a company of ladies in low-neck dresses. Kreutzer's music for the ballet of "Clari" was deemed "excellent" by Bishop himself when he attended a performance of it in Paris during his third continental visit, in August, 1822. He wrote in his diary: "This ballet is one of the most interesting I ever saw." Herein he agreed with Payne, who, too, had seen it in Paris and turned it first into a play.

Evidently Payne's operatic transformation of the story did not greatly impress the critic who after the London première wrote: "Mr. Howard Payne has taken the trouble to convert a very fine Pantomime into a very indifferent Opera." But the British public wept over it, even as the Parisians had been moved to tears by Mlle. Bigotini's acting. The plot is of the simplest.

Clari, an innocent and trusting country maiden, has been persuaded by a dashing and wily duke to elope from her paternal home and follow him to his château, where the marriage ceremony is to crown their happiness. The lover showers gifts on his beloved — the opening chorus is the entrée of the *valetaille* in Clari's boudoir, delivering costly tokens of the duke's affection — but the plain band of gold is not among them. Clari, overcome with remorse, breaks forth in what is supposed to be a folk-song, in which she laments her folly by extolling the unique advantages of home. At this point the audience is likely to lose control over its lachrymal glands, not to regain it until the final curtain. In fact, the salty flow will pour ever more freely as in the third scene of the first act strolling players, invited to cheer the dejected Clari on her birthday, unwittingly and injudiciously enact a playlet the situations of which are duplicating exactly her own unfortunate plight. When the strains of her very lamentations come from the lips of her counterpart, she can barely hide her anguish. The play becomes reality to her. She rushes forward to stop it at the moment when the father violently denounces his errant daughter. She collapses. At this point stage directions have it: "The duke and tenantry stand astonished," which seems natural enough.

In the second act the duke's astonishment has turned to annoyance. He tells Clari bluntly that they can never wed. The action drags along artificially until it receives new impetus by Clari's nocturnal escape. Returned, in the third act, to her paternal roof, paternal curses greet her. But the repentant duke overtakes the bird flown from the gilded cage. He promptly offers his hand and half of all he surveys, which change of mind does not fail presently and pleasantly to affect the irate parent's attitude. "His eyes turned upward, and streaming with tears, and with a choked voice," the father exclaims: "Heaven bless ye!" Thus with embraces and a background of merry villagers all wreathed in approving smiles, the last tableau is one profoundly moving and thoroughly satisfying.

To apprehend how far a critic's callousness may go, let us ponder what the London "Times" had to say after the first performance: "We do not very well understand the morality or the pathos of this scene, but it concluded the piece and was greatly applauded."

The device of the play within the play, precipitating the catastrophe, is the same in "Hamlet," in "Pagliacci," and in "Clari." Anyone wishing to form a precise idea of just how long a space of time is covered by one hundred terrestrial years should read the dialogue and songs in "Clari."

There is interest in examining some of the contemporary judgments pronounced on Bishop's music. One critic wrote: "We have no belief that Mr. Bishop ever intended that any part of his fame should rest upon this work; it is composed of temporary materials, gathered together with theatrical haste." Stern judge and gentle prophet, could you to-day name any one among the many, many compositions of Sir Henry that is apt to call for centennial commemoration — save that "Sicilian Air" in "Clari"? Even though we may not express ourselves with certainty on just what were the composer's intentions when he wrote this music, it would seem that he was determined on "putting across" Clari's song of "Home, Sweet Home." He succeeded.

The air appears first, in augmentation, as part of the overture. Next it is sung in its conventional form by Clari. Then it must serve, of course, as climax for the interpolated playlet. The third act brings it as a chorus intoned by the peasants to welcome the penitent daughter (in gingerly six-eight time); and at the very end it reappears (in three-four time) for a last and graceful bow.

Mr. Frederick Corder, in the "Musical Quarterly," January, 1918, gives poor Bishop a rather severe scolding for having written what amounts to one of the very earliest examples of an opera based on at least one "Leitmotiv." Nor do the rhythmic and harmonic variations to which Bishop subjected the tune in the course of the play seem quite so atrocious as the indignant Mr. Corder would have us believe. It is plain that Bishop, or someone else, must have thought well enough of the tune to write, or suggest the writing of, the whole opera round this one melody.

That the music of the opera is mediocre no one will deny. At the time of its first performance it was thought to possess "nothing that is distinguished by originality of conception, ingenuity of adaptation, or elegance of effect." But the verdict was by no means unanimous. One reviewer said: "The overture is a spirited composition à la Beethoven [!]. . . . In the few bars of adagio, we find an extreme minor third employed in a manner that is new and somewhat foreign to our present feelings." Musical theorists will please take note.

And who wrote this melody of "Home, Sweet Home"? Certainly not Payne; nor did he hear it trilled "by the sweet voice of a peasant girl" in Italy, as a romantic fable would have us believe, for the weaving of which the poet himself is partly to blame. In the "Clari" score, made up of the single numbers, the caption title of the song informs us that it was "composed and partly founded on a 'Sicilian Air' by Henry R. Bishop, composer and director of the Music of the Theatre Royal, Covent Garden." Mr. Corder, as well as Mr. Richard Northcott in his "Life of Sir Henry R. Bishop,"

seems satisfied that the "Sicilian Air" and its subsequent evolution
were wholly the work of Bishop. Mr. Henry Davey, historian of
Britain's music, is naturally more guarded and is content with
saying that the melody "is almost certainly Bishop's own." When
it had achieved instant and phenomenal success, the composer
blushingly "confessed" that he alone was guilty. As a matter of
fact, the tune was in the air. There is a vague resemblance between
it and one of the (equally problematical) "Maltese Melodies" and
"Norwegian Tunes" published (ca. 1805) by Edward Jones, "Harp
Master and Bard to H. R. H. the Prince of Wales." This resemblance is of no more significance than that with half a dozen genuine folk-songs. Take, for example, the beginning of the refrain in
"Home, Sweet Home," with its characteristic upward sweep to the
tonic followed by a stepwise descent to the dominant and the drop
into the mediant, which is note for note the same as a phrase in
"The Last Rose of Summer." The stuff such tunes are made of
floats about us everywhere.

The second decade of the nineteenth century witnessed one of
those passionate revivals of the folk-song and the belief in the
plenary inspiration of "the People." The demand for these vocal
gems was larger than the known supply. Publishers (even then)
formed alliances with poets and composers, and set up in wholesale manufacture of folk-songs. Mr. Power had Thomas Moore;
Messrs. Goulding, d'Almaine, Potter & Co. had Thomas Bayly,
the author of "Rough Sketches of Bath." Mr. Corder concludes
"from its extreme rarity at the present day" that the Goulding
collection "cannot have sold well." The copy in the Library of
Congress (containing all three volumes) came to Washington via
Calcutta, India, where it was "imported and sold by James Ja-
cobs." Books are good travellers.

Both publishers, Power and Goulding, had recourse to Bishop
for the "Symphonies and Arrangements," though the second one
of the Goulding volumes was arranged by Sir John Stevenson.
These symphonies, or rather introductions and postludes, were
Bishop's forte. In them he gave the reins to his fancy. Nothing
more peculiar and inappropriate could well be imagined than, for

instance, the sophisticated introduction and postlude of the original "Sicilian Air."

When Moore and Bishop collaborated on the "National Melodies" for Power, the poet wrote to the publisher on May 1, 1821: "Keep Mr. Bishop's learning down as much as you can!" The poet speaks familiar speech. When it came to producing newly "discovered" pearls of folkish melody, Moore and Bishop indulged in a harmless game of mutual deception. Moore, at Power's instigation, submitted his tunes to Bishop for revision; he passed off one of his own as a "Swedish" song, and Bishop thought it "delicious." But the poet had misgivings about the imposture and wanted to call it a "Moorish" air! When Bishop's turn came to own himself fashioner of one of these jewels, Moore — a trifle incredulous and disdainful — wrote to Power on July 8, 1822: "That air (which I had not the slightest idea was Bishop's) has been floating in my memory for many, many years." Precisely; there is a similarity of cast, a propinquity of inflection, in so many of these genuine and spurious folk-songs, that the tune is practically shaped and on the point of birth long before it is put to paper. The embryology of folk-music is a fascinating study.

None of which should detract from the merit of Bishop's setting of Payne's words, or of Payne's adaptation of Bayly's words to Bishop's revised tune. Words and music are here inseparable. It is due to the American, John Howard Payne, as much as to the first knighted musician of Great Britain if the world celebrated the one-hundredth anniversary of "Home, Sweet Home" as of something still fresh and alive in millions of hearts.

"Home, Sweet Home" was sung on the night when it first saw the footlights at Covent Garden by the performer of Clari, Miss Maria Tree. This young singer whose merits had "already raised her to a high degree of favour with the public" — as a contemporary reviewer said — made her auspicious début in 1820. She had three gifted sisters, the oldest of whom was Mrs. Quin, a famous English dancer. Anne, according to Joseph N. Ireland, "had a line of singing parts and chambermaids peculiarly her own, while Miss Ellen (later Mrs. Charles Kean) in her earlier days was recognized as the most finished walking lady and the most promising high comedienne of the times."

Maria's voice compared favourably with "that of her coadjutor, Miss Stephens" — incomparable Kitty! — but it still lacked volume and sweetness. By 1822 Miss Tree's singing had much improved and she was "every night confirming the favourable impression she made upon the public as a dramatic singer." Leaving aside the question of the real authorship in the tune of "Home, Sweet Home," one gallant first-nighter wrote: "Come whence it may, we know not any land, however favoured by Phœbus, that can produce a chauntress to sing it with the same feeling and taste that so highly distinguished its performance by our charming countrywoman, Miss M. Tree."

Maria owed her chance thus to immortalize herself to the fact that in 1823, the year of "Clari," extraordinary Kitty Stephens was no longer a member of the Covent Garden company. Kitty, aged nineteen, had appeared on that stage for the first time in September, 1813, as Mandane in "Artaxerxes." Her salary was twelve pounds a week, half of which went into the pockets of her singing-teacher, Mr. Welch, although her earlier training under Signor Lanza, from her twelfth to her seventeenth year, had laid the real foundation for her art. Her weekly salary had gradually been increased to twenty pounds. In 1822 she asked for a raise of five pounds. Since one of the agreements between actors and management of the theatre was that if the salary of one member should be raised, those of all the others were to be correspondingly augmented, the increase was diplomatically offered to her in the form of a "bonus"! Kitty would have none of it. Emboldened, she retorted with a demand of ten pounds for each performance, or the unprecedented salary of sixty pounds a week. The management's reply was brief and in the negative. Whereupon Miss Stephens left Covent Garden. Breaking a long-established tacit pact, she offended all professional ethics by going straight into the enemy's camp: Mr. Ellison, the manager of Drury Lane, was only too glad to welcome Miss Stephens on any terms.

The spoiled prima donna acted rather ungratefully. Her colleague Mrs. Salmon told William Gardiner that Mr. Thomas Harris, the patentee and chief proprietor of Covent Garden, had stipulated with the musical director that Miss Stephens should have the choice of all the songs in Handel's oratorios, whether for soprano or bass, as being "the first singer" in England. "Of course," Mrs. Salmon added, "I am obliged to take up what Miss Stephens pleases to reject."

Old Thomas Harris was very much concerned about the music for his theatre. In February, 1818, when Bishop was writing music to Thomas Dibdin's "Zuma; or, The Tree of Health," Harris asked for advance samples from the score "for my daughter Fanny to play to me." He had decided views in the matter of songs and who should sing them. Annexation and interpolation of musical numbers would be unhesitatingly suggested by him to author and composer if he thought it in the interest of the box office. On one occasion he wrote: "I remember a most beautiful air of Mazzinghi's in Cobb's 'Ramah Droog,' beginning 'Happy were my days'; it never failed to electrify the audience and was a great support to the piece. If Braham or rather Kitty had it, with appropriate words, its success would be certain." Note the "rather Kitty." Moreover, why not learn from these older and wiser ways? It might prove of great help to a budding school of operatic composers if in their works were included such ancient favourites as the "Evening Star" and the "Anvil Chorus," "with appropriate words."

Thomas Harris died in 1820. After the retirement of his son and successor, in 1822, the managing committee, under the direction of Charles Kemble, evidently failed to instruct the musical director with regard to Kitty's privileges. No wonder that, when on top of this she was refused the increase in salary, she bolted. At Drury Lane her employment was not so congenial as it had originally been at Covent Garden. Opportunities to shine were fewer. The provinces, with their spectacular and Gargantuan festivals, however, were a never failing field of new successes. Kitty was quick in discerning the value of "Home, Sweet Home" for these occasions. She took it up at once and made it, after all, her song.

At the first opportunity Miss Stephens had, the York festival
of 1823 — and no musical festival of the times was possible without her — she sang Bishop's and Payne's new ballad. The musical
debauch at York lasted from Tuesday, September 23, to Friday,
the 26th, with performances in the morning and evening. Nineteen
thousand five hundred tickets were sold. "Home, Sweet Home"
appeared on the programme of the Thursday night concert. It
was sandwiched between a violin concerto of Viotti's, played by
the second concertmaster, Mori, and "Robin Adair" with variations, sung by Mme. Catalani.

Measure the fortitude of your ancestors when you consider that,
besides these three numbers, at the same concert were performed:
Beethoven's C Minor Symphony, immediately followed by
"Charlie is my darling," sung by Miss Travis; also the "Egmont"
Overture; also five excerpts from operas by Rossini, among which
the "Cenerentola" Overture, and the "Largo al factotum," sung
by Signor Placci; also the whole finale from Mozart's "Figaro,"
plus the "Non più andrai," sung by Catalani; also two glees for
men's voices; also a Venetian air arranged by Bochsa and sung by
Mrs. Salmon; also a Fantasia for French horn played by Signor
Puzzi; also an aria by Muzio Clementi; also a song by Dr.
Pepusch; the whole topped off with "God save our gracious
King," vociferated by Mme. Catalani, who achieved the distinction of making herself heard above the entire "supporting" soloists,
chorus, organ, and orchestra. And this, consider, was a short concert! The affair on Friday morning, with all the encores, lasted
nearly seven hours.

Catalani had the strongest voice. Mrs. Salmon's was the finer
quality of tone and higher polish of execution. Now meditate this
appraisal of Miss Stephens: "She has a voice at once so rich and
smooth that it seizes upon the ear, whilst the purity and propriety
of her style is in perfect accordance with the national estimate
of what the English alone can appreciate, because it forms the
basis of their natural character, and with a trait which is emphatically their own, namely with chaste singing."

Reduced to simpler language, Miss Stephens, the Briton's favourite of a hundred years ago, like Miss Mary Pickford, the world's favourite of to-day, was probably the apotheosis of sweet dullness. Indeed, one traitor to his country is said to have remarked of our chaste idol — Miss Stephens, not Miss Pickford — "there she stands, as insipid as a boiled pig!"

A few days after the York festival, in 1823, Kitty sang "Home, Sweet Home" at Birmingham. That feast lasted from the 7th to the 10th of October. Artists and programmes were much the same as at York. "The portions best received were principally English, and above all Bishop's most touching ballad of Home. It was loudly encored." Song and singer became almost inseverable. When Mme. Catalani at the Newcastle festival, October, 1824 (despite the presence of Catherine), in some unaccountable way managed to sing "Home, Sweet Home," the papers boldly announced that it "was a failure." How Kitty must have chuckled! She was too firmly enthroned to fear a usurper.

Kitty was an institution. Her voice still was lovely; it still reached easily to D above the staff. Besides, she was comely. When George Harlow painted her portrait she can have been little more than twenty. A reproduction of it adorned the "European Magazine and London Review" for January, 1818, as illustration to an article on the fair sitter. She had a singer's throat, full, squarely set; dark eyes and curls; a slightly tilted-up nose; and prettily pouting lips. The artist put animation into her face, a mischievous little smile. As a singer she is said to have been rather frigid, but "in private society she threw off every tinge of coldness." John Jackson, R. A., painted her when she was a little more mature. His portrait of her hangs in the National Gallery, London. Apparently she had the secret of preserving voice and looks alike. Both exercised their spell.

One gentleman was for a long time constantly seen at her performances, seated in a front row. He followed her from festival to festival through the provinces to Ireland and back to London. He could not find the courage to speak to her, much less propose. His days ended in a lunatic asylum. At first Lord Milton, then His Grace the Duke of Devonshire, were for a while in assiduous attendance upon Kitty. But her heart was undecided. Still, she got into Burke's Peerage.

Apollo's crown was not all that a kind fate had destined for this daughter of a carver and gilder in Park Street, Grosvenor Square. Born in 1794, "lucky Kitty Stephens" was forty-four years old when in 1838 the fifth Earl of Essex — a widower variously reported as being then anywhere between sixty-eight and eighty-two years old — married her and placed a coronet on her curls. He had long been her ardent admirer, but his joy in the possession of the nation's darling was to be short; he died the next year. Although it had been said of her that on the stage "for great ladies she was not well suited, either in person, voice or style," she spent half of her life as the Dowager Countess of Essex, reaching the more than biblical age of eighty-eight. She died, February 22, 1882, at her town house in Belgrave Square.

"Home, Sweet Home" brought luck to everyone except its authors. Payne's checkered career came to an end in 1852, far from his home land, in Tunis, where he was American consul. Payne was sent twice to Tunis, the second time never to return alive. He was buried in Africa; but in 1883 his body was brought to America for burial in Washington.

On the morning of the day on which Bishop died, the London "Times" published an appeal for the subscription of funds to aid the composer, who was "labouring under pecuniary embarrassment." That was April 30, 1855; Bishop died of "cancer of bladder and atrophy of kidney," his unhappy home wanting the wife and mother to bring solace to his last hours.

Bochsa — harpist, composer, forger, bigamist, and adulterer — who had been the first to make an instrumental arrangement of "Home, Sweet Home," in the year of its publication, somewhat acidulated the air in the Bishop household when in 1839 he eloped with Bishop's second wife, the singer Anna Rivière. Mme. Bishop was twenty-nine, Bochsa was fifty, or only three years younger than Bishop. The lady's conquest by "the old harpist Bochsa" leaves Mr. Corder nonplussed; says he seriously: "And when one thinks of the many brilliant songs Bishop wrote for his wife, while

Bochsa's attempts at composition were — but there! There is never any sense or reason in these things." As if connubial felicity depended on the brilliance of the partner's musical contributions!

The "Musical Quarterly Review," in 1824, spoke in an article on Bishop's music as follows: "Twenty of his pieces we know to have worn out three sets of plate, and of 'Home, Sweet Home' written only last year no less than thirty thousand copies have been sold." Mr. Northcott says: "No fewer than one hundred thousand copies of the music were sold during the first year, but Bishop was paid only £20 for his share of the immortal work." Do these figures refer to Great Britain or are they supposed to include America?

Seven months after the London première "Clari" was given for the first time in New York, at the Park Theatre (November 12, 1823). Mr. Pearman, who at Covent Garden had "created" the part of "Jocoso, Valet to the Duke," was touring the States and probably brought the music of "Clari" with him. The libretto was advertised "among new dramatic pieces just published" in the New York "Statesman" as early as October 28. This American edition of the libretto contained the London cast. In announcing the play for Mr. Pearman's fourth performance, his vocal soli were temptingly enumerated; so were those of Mrs. Holman in the part of the maid Vespina (not, as Mr. Northcott erroneously states, in the title-part). Clari was sung by a Miss Johnson, probably the later Mrs. Hilson, long the ornament of the Park Theatre. Miss Johnson, "then in the full pride of her youthful beauty," was "very affecting." But of Clari's ballad not a word. The play was repeated on Monday, November 17, "having been received with the most decided approbation," as the advertisement in the "Statesman" said. The visitor from London had promised, for his benefit night on the 20th, "The Siege of Belgrade," but instead a third performance of "Clari" became necessary "by particular desire." In this announcement Clari and her performer were altogether omitted!

From New York, Pearman went to Philadelphia, where he introduced the novelty. William B. Wood, Philadelphia manager, wrote, in his "Personal Recollections of the Stage," that "by one of those amusing blunders which still are common, the bill announced all the music except 'Home, Sweet Home,' one of the sweetest things in it." Perhaps it was intention rather than a blunder. For it was distinctly Mr. Pearman's party; and he was one of the first actors to travel the land as a "star."

In spite of the fact that the performances of "Clari" in America, that season, were far from numerous — "Undine; or, The Spirit of the Waters," for instance, was much oftener on the billboards — and notwithstanding the studious ignoring of "Home, Sweet Home" in all the advertisements, the song must have immediately found favour with the public in New York and Philadelphia and Boston, as it had done in London and the provinces. Witness the American reprints of "Home, Sweet Home," which began to appear early, and rapidly multiplied. Counting in these pirated editions, Mr. Northcott's figures for the sales of the first year would not seem improbable.

Can anyone estimate the number of times the song has been printed since?

SUSPENSIONS

THE MOZART COUPLE

NOT long ago, a youthful Mozart — impersonated by two charming actresses — tripped the boards in Paris and New York. Legend will not leave hands off him. Once more poetic fantasy had dressed him up as Cherubino, touched him with the light of unreality, and put "clever" lines in his mouth. Yet what playwright could invent a story more dramatic than the life of Wolfgang Amédée? No contrivance of fiction can outrun plain truth: those thirty-six brief years of earthly existence burdened with a measure of glory and wretchedness never attained before or after and crowded with labours that yielded a beauty unmatched, incomparable.

The truth about Mozart has had a singular way of slipping between the lines of rhapsodic or prudish biographers. Not that there was cause for hiding the true likeness of the man. The musician would stand undiminished were he suddenly revealed a forger, bigamist, or murderer. Mozart was nothing of the kind; only, besides being superhumanly endowed in one direction, he was eminently human, or humanly weak, in other directions. There are several reasons why these weaknesses, these lesser traits — although not less important for the accurate and complete picture — have been passed over or deliberately effaced.

The chief reason, obviously enough, lies in Mozart's own music. With its sparkle and grace, its warmth and purity, it was largely responsible for the determined efforts to represent the man who wrote it as an idealized dream-figure: music so divinely perfect must be the creation of a perfect divinity. Nature is not so simple. She delights in contrasts rather than in parallels. That fact is not always appreciated. Thus the retouched and prettified portrait could gain the wide acceptance it enjoyed so long.

If the portrait was a fraud, it was a pious fraud, an excusable one. In perpetrating it, the original blame rests mainly upon Mozart's first extensive biography, written by Georg Nikolaus von Nissen, the Danish diplomat who in 1809 married Mozart's widow, thereby legalizing his relations with her, which had probably begun some ten years earlier. It is a common thing that people who do not rigorously uphold the conventions behind closed shutters, hang decorum out of the open window. Some are hypocrites, others are not; they simply lack the energy or the desire to go through the fuss of defying Mrs. Grundy. If they are "different," they prefer to be so quietly rather than ostentatiously.

Among critical biographers, too, there is the decorous, if not the hypocritical, school; and there are the fussy, defiant "revelationists." Neither is apt to get at the truth and nothing but the truth. One paints too rosy, the other too black. A gallery of waxworks and a rogues' gallery are about equidistant from a gallery of master-portraits.

If a single biographical master-portrait of Mozart is still lacking, there are scattered all the elements of one throughout the monumental revision of Jahn's work by Hermann Abert, the painstaking research of Wyzewa and Saint-Foix, and lastly the courageous treatment by Arthur Schurig. But that is comparatively recent history. Nor has all the documentary evidence been produced, more than a century after the case came into court. When Schurig brought out a separate volume on Constance Mozart, he placed the principal blame for this delay upon Johann Evangelist Engl (1835-1921), for many years the secretary and archivist of the Mozarteum in Salzburg, "the narrowest head" — wrote Schurig — "that I have encountered in my eventful life. He closely kept from every student of Mozart the documents that he was guarding; and every page that this man has written in his miserable provincial German is full of mistakes or misleading remarks."

On the whole, Constance has fared badly at the hands of Mozart's biographers. She has been painted too persistently in som-

bre hues, while on her husband were lavished all the bright tints
in the rainbow. Schurig's is the first contribution toward a fair
estimate of Constance Weber. But how fair? Is it a final judgment? Does she deserve all the blame that still clings to her?
And if not, is there perchance a modicum of credit due her? In
plumage man and wife differed probably less than is generally
accepted. To all intents and purposes of the blessed state called
matrimony, they were birds of an identical feather. Light-
hearted, both young and somewhat frivolous, of the same caste
in a severely caste-divided world, they "fitted," inwardly and out-
wardly. What girl of nineteen, what woman of any age, was to
have "understood" the composer Mozart? The man Mozart
wanted a wife, he wanted to get away from the Archbishop's
thraldom and from the father's surveillance. He wanted a home
of his own, and he had twelve different ones in Vienna during the
nine years of his married life. Poor Cherubino!

Yet where was Mozart's choice? Who were the eligible girls
in Salzburg or Vienna pining to marry a jobless and penniless
genius? No one so far has come forward and suggested to whom
Mozart should have offered his heart and hand. Did he fail to
inspire confidence among the "better families"? As a matter of
fact, those families still regarded a composer, no matter how much
they admired his music, as several degrees lower in the social
scale. It was not the rule then for a musician to pick a rich bride
and sit back in comfort. Gluck married money, but he was the
exception; and his was a love-match consummated only after the
bride's objecting father had died. With Wolfgang and Constance
it was the bridegroom's father who objected, violently, blind
with rage, demanding that the bride's mother, whom he accused
of intrigue and connivance, be put in irons and branded as "se-
ducer of youth"!

That there was seduction is more than probable, and seduction
meeting with little resistance; but allow Wolfgang the modest
merit of a facile victory, won without the aid of an indulgent
rather than a pandering mother-in-law-to-be. Fate threw Mozart
into the arms of the Webers. There was no escape.

Mozart met Fridolin Weber, *Hofmusikus* and father of four daughters, at Mannheim in January, 1778, while on his way to Paris, accompanied by his mother. It was Aloysia, she of the warm, opulent voice, who first turned Wolfgang's head. But he would have surrendered to any pair of languid eyes and tempting lips. He was twenty-two; father and mother had kept him too long on the leash. At Augsburg he had found in his little cousin, the "Bäsle," first a willing victim to be coaxed into dark corners; and then he made her the recipient of letters into which drained dark currents of his mind. That was green fruit, and the taste of it unhealthy. But Aloysia, seventeen and a singer of parts — "I vouch for her singing with my life," he wrote to his father — here was sugared ripeness too sweet to resist. And the poor, worried mother knew it. On February 4 she secretly appended a post-script to one of Wolfgang's letters to his father, in which she gave vent to her annoyance and her fears. The effect of this news on the father in Salzburg was to be foreseen; on February 12 he gave his son peremptory orders: "Away with you to Paris — and soon!" In Paris, on July 3, Mozart's mother died.

Wolfgang met Aloysia again about Christmas-time in Munich, where she had been engaged for the opera. But the few intervening months, the change of place and conditions, had made a great difference. Aloysia was blown, flippant, cruel. When she saw Mozart in a red frock-coat and golden buttons, covered with black crape as a sign of his mourning, she ridiculed his "livery." Mozart retaliated at the piano with an improvised air sung to the classic invitation of Götz von Berlichingen. Cherubino's was the retort unknightly. In 1781 he qualified Aloysia as "a false, evil-minded coquette."

The Webers went to Vienna in September, 1779, because Aloysia, through the influence of her "protector," Count Hadik, Minister of War, had received a call as prima donna to the court theatre. Fridolin Weber died the following month. Cecilia Weber, the widow, gathered round her the four daughters and — with an eye to the main chance — let rooms to "paying guests." In October, 1780, Aloysia found a husband in Joseph Lange, an estimable man and capable actor. He became one of Mozart's intimate friends. But not until Mozart had written of him almost as disparagingly as he continued to speak of the now definitely lost Aloysia.

This was the situation when Mozart arrived in Vienna on March 16, 1781. His relations with the Archbishop in Salzburg were near the breaking-point. Cherubino, as afraid of the parental fetters as he was disgusted with the archiepiscopal ones, swam in the soft, caressing air of a Viennese spring, immersed in freedom, drowning in a flood of sensuousness. Events moved swiftly. On May 2 Mozart took up lodgings with the Weber family. On May 9 be handed his resignation to the Archbishop. On June 8 the break was accomplished.

Here enters Constance, though for a little while longer she remains in the background. The fulminating epistles which old Leopold Mozart must have sent to his son when he learned of the latter's new address we can only imagine — for the letters themselves, all of Leopold's letters to Wolfgang from January 12, 1781 to his death, in May, 1787, have been destroyed — probably by the one who had the most reason to resent them, who felt least flattered by their damnatory candour. We may be sure that father Leopold fairly bombarded his son with commands to change his quarters. Wolfgang demurred; on July 13 he still insisted that he could never find a pleasanter, cheaper, or more convenient domicile. What a distant father failed to achieve, the sparrows on the housetop did. First softly, then with increasing brazenness, they were twittering "things" about the ardent young boarder and one of his landlady's pretty daughters. The twitter filled the neighbourhood; somehow it reached Salzburg. In less than two weeks the wind had veered completely, with storm-clouds on the horizon: *"Mon très cher Père!* I say it again, that I have long [?!] intended to take other lodgings, and only because of the gossip of the people; I am sorry that I am forced to do it because of silly talk, not a word of which is true. Just because I live with them [the Webers], I am supposed to marry the daughter! Nothing is said about being enamoured, they skipped that;

instead, I take lodgings in the house, hence I marry! I never was farther from marrying than I am now." And more in the same vein. No mention of Constance; what references he makes to Madame Weber's daughters and his conduct with them cunningly suggest the remnant of a tepid and playful interest in "the married Mademoiselle." Aloysia as lightning-rod! But the bolt is not ready to strike. Instead, a fog descends upon the scene; for a while we can only dimly follow the action and identify the actors.

Is Arthur Schurig right when he maintains that at this point Mozart really had no idea of marrying? Possibly. Is he right also, when he pretends to distinguish "already" the intriguing hand of Madame Weber? Did it require intrigue to throw Wolfgang and Constance together? Cecilia Weber may have "simulated motherly objections," but it is not necessary to assume that they were calculated to hasten rather than frustrate the union. Wolfgang wrote to his father in the letter of July 25: "If I were to marry all those with whom I have joked, I might easily have two hundred wives!" Patently, he was bragging. He was trying to soften the father's anger and dissipate his suspicions by exaggerating the truth. Still, the "joking" with Constance had probably gone beyond his fooling with the "Bäsle." The "joke" was not irreparable in its consequences, except that Wolfgang, far from anticipating Don Giovanni with his *mille e tre*, or even with a modest two hundred, was captivated and was racked with his desire for the one girl whose intimacy he had been able to enjoy sufficiently to give him a foretaste of what secure, legitimate, and full possession of a wife would be like.

Meanwhile the birds continued their annoying twitter. Wolfgang fled them at last; about September 1 he took a room "Auf dem Graben." But he could not flee the birdlime which his own nature had spread for him. On December 15 he sits down and writes to his father, makes a clean breast: "Nature speaks in me as loud as it does in everyone else, and perhaps louder than in some big, strapping fellow." He pleads his domestic bent, he claims the need of a solicitous housewife. He prepares the father as gently as he can, leading gradually to the dreaded disclosure that the chosen one is *"eine Weberische"* — dear Constance, "the martyr among them, and therefore perhaps the best-hearted, the most competent."

Leopold Mozart's desperate protests were of no avail. The marriage contract was signed August 3, 1782, and on the following day the wedding was celebrated in St. Stephen's. The irksome period of betrothal had lasted nine months. It did not pass without lovers' quarrels. Constance was nineteen, seven years younger than Wolfgang. She was a child of her day, almost as light and giddy a day as our own. She committed the modish sin of having permitted a *"chapeau"* — a dude — to measure the calf of her leg with a coloured ribbon, in the sight of other people. Knee-long skirts now make unnecessary such investigation. One hundred and fifty years ago it formed a sort of parlour-game. But poor Cherubino was highly offended at the behaviour of his affianced. He wrote her an indignant letter, upbraided her, and lulled himself in hopes that Constance was what her name implied. We have no proof that she was other.

The married life of Wolfgang and Constance lasted 112 months; during 54 of them Constance was with child. The first-born arrived on June 17, 1783, and lived two months; the last was five months old when Mozart died. Of the six children only two survived their father and mother: Karl (1784-1858) and Franz Xaver Wolfgang (1791-1844).

Whatever reflected glory Constance derived in later life from the growing fame of her first husband, while she was his wife her existence was humble, precarious, and none too happy. She gained the reputation of having been a poor housekeeper, extravagant and improvident. That may have been largely reflected odium. During her widowhood and after her second marriage she proved herself the reverse; she exhibited shrewdness, she reckoned with every kreuzer. In 1808 she wrote to Karl in Milan: "Your last letter did not give me much pleasure, because it contained nothing hearty, and for such a cold, empty letter it is a pity to pay the high postage." She avoided using envelopes whenever she could, folding the letter sheet after the fashion of the time in order to save on the postal charge.

Beginning with 1783, Mozart seems to have fallen into debts of which he never ridded himself. The letters to his friend and brother-mason Puchberg for small or large loans are pathetic. They were seldom in vain. Yet posterity erects no monuments to mere Puchbergs. Emperors are protected against oblivion, even when they can do no better than appoint a Mozart, after composing a "Don Giovanni," *Hofkompositeur* with eight hundred florins a year. Mozart was then thirty-one; he had five more years to live. His son Wolfgang at seventeen earned more; in 1808 he was engaged as private music-teacher to the children of Count Bavorowski at Podkamien near Lemberg, with a thousand florins a year, lodging, food, firewood, and candles free. And he wrote no "Don Giovanni."

Mozart left his family penniless, burdened with debts, most of which Constance paid off in a comparatively short time. But it was no easy matter. Her first grief stunned her. When Wolfgang succumbed to a *"hitziges Frieselfieber,"* on December 5, 1791, Constance — inexperienced, impractical, mistaught even — felt dazed and lost. She is said to have slipped into the bed from which the corpse had been taken to catch the malady that killed her husband. That is probably another one of the many legends. At any rate, she was too ill to follow the bier on December 6. The story of the funeral, the unmarked grave, remains painful reading. Painful also is the thought of Baron van Swieten, a friend of some means, missing his chance and arranging — to "protect the widow" — for the cheapest burial that could be had. It cost eleven florins, twenty-six kreuzer. Constance paid for it.

We do not know with whom originated the idea of having Constance submit a petition to Emperor Leopold II five days after the coffin of her husband had been lowered into the poor-pit. The petition resulted in the imperial sanction of a benefit concert which took place December 28; it netted the widow enough money to satisfy pressing creditors. The inventory of December 19 is a curious document. Among the debts were 282 florins due one tailor, 13 florins due another; 208 florins due the upholsterer; 179 florins due for medicines. In all, Constance paid 918 florins in debts after Wolfgang's death; this did not include any loans, the exact figure of which is not known. Among the assets, estimated at 592 florins, were 60 florins in cash; a personal wardrobe, including coats of white, bluish, red, brown, black, and mouse-grey cloth, held to be worth 55 florins; the silverware consisted of three spoons valued at 7 florins the lot; the two most precious objects among the household goods were a billiard with five balls and twelve cues, put down at 60 florins, and a fortepiano at 80 florins. What would Mozart's viola, estimated at 4 florins, bring to-day? Then there were manuscripts, whole piles of them. No one could tell their value. Do we know it now?

Whatever influence Constance had on Mozart, she did not interfere with his work. She may have created a condition to push it. Generally Mozart is credited with having worked harder after his marriage than before. Arthur Schurig, too, speaks of the "enormous" amount of music written by Mozart during those nine years. That becomes easily evident if one consults the Köchel catalogue or the "Nouveau Classement" of Wyzewa and Saint-Foix. According to the latter, 381 works fall into the twenty years of composition before the marriage, and 201 works into the last nine years of Mozart's life. To be sure, many of them are fugitive songs, brief canons, occasional arias, duets, and the like, hastily written for interpolation in other people's operas, to satisfy importunate singers.

There is a perceptible swing in the direction of Mozart's work, coinciding approximately with the time of his marriage; and that arc of deflection has never been properly traced or measured. Even a casual survey brings out a few facts to which attaches more than a superficial significance. Despite the figures, the "enormous" takes on a qualitative rather than a quantitative meaning, and statistics again would seem to be a dubious guide. After his marriage Mozart composed only 5 of his 46 symphonies, but they were the greatest; he added no more serenades and divertimenti to the 33 he had written before his marriage. After

August 4, 1782, the date of the wedding, came only 8 of his 23
stage works, but among those were his master-operas; and "The
Abduction from the Seraglio," of course, was the sweat of the
bridegroom-fever that burned his marrow. During his married life
Mozart wrote: 11 of his 27 string quartets (on the last day of
1782 he finished the first of the six quartets dedicated to Haydn);
all but one of the piano trios, quartets, and quintets; only 7 of
his 42 piano and violin sonatas; 25 of his 54 concerti (mostly the
piano concerti written for himself); only 4 of his 17 piano sonatas, but all 5 of the piano fantasies; none of the 17 organ
sonatas; of his more than 40 shorter vocal compositions for the
church only the single "Ave verum"; of his 18 masses only 1,
besides the final "Requiem." And that mass was the great unfinished one in C which he had "vowed in his heart" to write for the
occasion of his wife's first visit to his father and sister in Salzburg. The young couple arrived there in July, 1783. On August
25 the music was performed in the Church of St. Peter, the missing sections being taken from another of the composer's masses.
His vow was kept, his conscience quiet. And to give the event its
fullest import, the soprano part was sung by Constance. As a
"muse," or inspiration, Constance would not seem to have been
very lucky. For not only this mass, but all the other compositions
that Mozart dedicated to her, were destined to remain unfinished.

Not until 1808, seventeen years after Mozart's death, did his
widow make any effort to visit his grave — only to learn then
that there was no grave. This has always been considered as conclusive evidence of the indifference with which Constance regarded Mozart. Yet her letters to her sons show that she held
Mozart's memory sacred. On March 5, 1806, she wrote to Karl:
"Remember always my earnest admonition, that no son of
Mozart's must be allowed to turn out a mediocrity." Constance
had a musical salon. We know that, in 1807, Monday was her
jour fixe. Musicians from far and near met at her home. Of
Seidler, the violinist, she wrote to Karl enthusiastically: "You
should hear him play your father's quartets!"

After Mozart's death, Constance not only developed orderliness and economy — virtues which were probably latent in her — but showed musical judgment. Of Asioli, with whom Karl was living and studying in Milan, she wrote: "The cantatas of his that I know are certainly very empty." She wanted Karl to study in Vienna with Albrechtsberger, "that dear, skilful man, whom your father so greatly esteemed." When her son Wolfgang obtained his position as music-teacher in the family of the Polish count, she ascribed it wholly to the fact that he had been a pupil of Albrechtsberger. Her solicitude for her children was as great as her veneration for their father. She displayed sincere emotion when in 1810 she sent to Karl in Milan, with the *vetturino* Christoforttei, carefully and lovingly packed, "the pianoforte of your father. It is as good as it was, I should say even better than it was; first, because I have taken great care of it, and second, because Walter, who made it, has been kind enough to overhaul and refelt it for me. Since then I could have sold it many times; but I hold it as dear as I do my children, and therefore I shall let no one have it but you, if you promise me to take as good care of it as I did and never to part with it." The instrument is now in the Mozart Museum in Salzburg.

When Karl paid no attention to his mother's wish that he come to Vienna and study with Albrechtsberger, she bluntly put to him the question: "Have you other prospects or are you in love?" At the thought of marriage she gave him this excellent bit of advice: "Only I beg of you, in case you marry a rich girl, that you will never depend on your wife. You must always try to earn your livelihood and never live on the bounty of a woman."

Family history repeats itself. How like the postscript of Mozart's mother in Mannheim, with the first "warning" about Aloysia, reads this postscript at the end of a letter from Constance to Karl, dated September 14, 1808: "From Signor Piastrini I learned to-day that you have taken lodgings in the house of a singer. Karl, Karl, beware!" A mother's heart forever beating anxiously lest danger overtake her brood; but a wife's heart calming down at last in the peace, security, and ease she had not known before. From Copenhagen, on November 13, 1810, Madame von Nissen wrote to her son Karl Mozart: "As far as I am concerned, pray believe that I never was so well off. . . . I have my competence, have a brave, dear husband, who is respected, carries me on his hands, and loves me above all things." And, loyal to both, she always signed herself after the death of her second husband, in 1826, "Constance, widow of state-councillor von Nissen, formerly the widow of Mozart."

The Mozart legend is securely closeted within the chambers of countless hearts. Here it rests unassailable, and in each of these tabernacles worship is offered to an idol, smiling under the halo of unquestioned sanctity. How could it be otherwise? Did ever man breathe greater purity, heavenly grace, and solace divine into immortal sound? Yet he stood "at the very junction-lines of the visible and invisible." Strains of unearthly loftiness mingled with "such a Bacchic reel and rout and revelry of beauty as leaves one staggered and giddy." There dwelt in his body a double soul, saint and satyr, indissolubly made one.

The biographers of Mozart, until the beginning of this century, have blindly followed Otto Jahn in overdrawing the halo and covering up the hornlets. As if the latter could disfigure what can never be anything else but the fairest face in music. Even the lines of anguish, the betraying droop of heavy lids, cannot dim the ray of smiling loveliness. Still, on the smile alone were fastened the eyes of all those who have worked upon the legend.

In one of her essays, Alice Meynell says that "rather affected objection" is taken every now and then to the publication of certain facts in the lives of poets, although these are all, in the strictest sense, biography. The chief source for Mozart's biography is the letters, those of the master himself and those of his prolix father. In some of the letters penned by the young satyr, we catch an unexpected sight of the cherub's troubled twin: Mozart, composer of the Jupiter Symphony, the familiar of stable-boys. Bare of all romantic tinsel, the naked truth only increases the stature of this superchild, until we know not what to marvel at more: the godlike spirit or the human heart torn by passion and woe.

Let Francis Thompson, better qualified, now have the final word: "The difference between the true poet in his poetry and in his letters or personal intercourse, is just the difference between two states of the one man; between the metal live from the forge and the metal chill. But, chill or glowing, the metal is equally itself. If difference there be, it is the metal in glow that is the truer to itself. For, cold, it may be overlaid with dirt, obscured with dust; but afire, all these are scorched away."

DIE WAGNERDÄMMERUNG

A T a notorious murder trial in Cincinnati, some years ago, a man who had killed his wife entered the usual plea of "not guilty by reason of insanity." A lunacy commission examined the defendant and found him to be "technically sane." However, the alienists pronounced him a "dangerous psychopath," because in their opinion the man was "amoral, lacking a sense of ethics, emotionally unstable, being subject to unrestrained outbreaks of temper and rage, and egocentric to a pathological degree." The characterization of this murderer fits, word for word, the technically sane musician Richard Wagner.

It was eminently sane, and at the same time distinctly amoral, that Wagner appropriated the wife of his friend Hans von Bülow, when he found her not only more to his liking than his own, but essential to the completion of his great work. The sense of ethics remained curiously undeveloped in the man who was a master in the art of using and abusing his acquaintances. In order to convince ourselves of his emotional instability, we need but look through Wagner's letters, exultant or hyperbolical at one moment and whimpering or in despair at the next. All his life he suffered from an uncontrollable temper; his last fit of rage was apparently responsible for the attack of angina pectoris that caused his death. By testimony of friends and foes alike, his colossal egoism knew no bounds. Such was the man Wagner; a person whom a lunacy commission might have declared a "dangerous psychopath" — a musician whom the world acclaims as one of the greatest of all times.

Destiny, that uncertain agent, is generally held answerable if of two men, afflicted with the same psychopathic shortcomings, one turns out a murderer and the other a genius. The difference be-

tween the two lies in the different direction and application of
the identical proclivities. The criminal is a born law-breaker; so
is genius. The criminal breaks the laws of God and man; genius
breaks the canons of social convention and artistic tradition. The
criminal defies the law, until he is brought to justice. Genius
assumes a position apart from and above the rest of humanity;
he is a law unto himself. Haled before the tribunal of human
prejudice, he is broken on the wheel of ignorance.

Whereas the criminal, as a rule, is bent upon destruction for
low personal ends, genius is constructive as well as destructive in
the high pursuit of an ideal. The essential attribute of genius is
the faculty to create. There is no musical genius that has more
lustily demolished and more gloriously built up than Wagner.

Although Wagner had the makings of a first-class murderer,
destiny — or inheritance — gave him constructive faculties wherewith to overbalance his destructive tendencies. By the very
nature of his character and his endowments, the man and the
artist in Wagner were two separate beings. He himself, undoubtedly, was aware of it. He knew that if his art commanded admiration, his character was not above reproach. He had too much
intelligence not to see the conflict. But he wanted others to be
blind to it. In his famous "Communication to my friends" (of
1851) he announced that he could not consider those his devotees
who loved him as an artist only, and withheld their sympathies
from the man. And he was right. He could not change; he had
to be taken as he was, even though it meant to put up with the
impossible. The one friend willing to take him so was Liszt. In
October, 1852, from Weimar, Liszt wrote to Wagner: "You cannot and shall not be other than you are, and so I revere, comprehend, and love you with all my soul." Liszt, the most loyal and
generous of friends, spared no effort in his show of devotion. But
eventually he, too, was placed before the grave and hopeless
problem of reconciling his feelings for the artist Wagner with
those for the man.

The problematical in Wagner's nature, ideas, and work is the
reason that more has been written about him than about any

other musician. And we still go on writing, reading, talking, about this extraordinary man, although we have not begun to gain free access to his entire biographical or musical papers. Wagner's biography, like his autobiography, is incomplete. A prodigious lot of letters is available. But important sections — those that would help most in rounding out the picture of the man — are lacking. Perhaps they are lost; or they may have been destroyed. There is reason to suspect a secret censorship at work in certain quarters. The bulk of the letters which his first wife, Minna, wrote to Wagner have never been published. They may still be at Wahnfried; and, again, they may not. The rest of the Burrell material, lately come to light, adds much to our knowledge. Wagner's letters to one of his passing flames, Mathilde Maier, left at her death with the instruction that they should "not be published during Cosima Wagner's lifetime," were mildly disappointing. And Cosima, dying at ninety-two, outlived her husband by forty-seven years.

Wagner's life, Wagner's music, are seemingly inexhaustible subjects; partly because a good deal of each has yet to be told or put in the proper light; partly because the romantic element that so strongly pervades both, his life and his music, is a constant temptation to commentators and rhapsodists. The quarrels, long and bitter, that Wagner's person and music stirred up in such quantities, are now happily ended. "*Der Fall Wagner*" — the case of Wagner, as Nietzsche sarcastically called it — has lost actuality. What anti-Wagnerians we now have in our midst complain, not about the licence, but about the tameness of his music. Such is the speed with which our ears form new allegiances. And yet Wagner's fantastic story has lost nothing of its romance, and his music is likely always to represent the highest crest of the romantic wave in art.

Mozart was fourteen years old when Beethoven was born, in 1770. Wagner was fourteen years old when Beethoven died, in 1827. Mozart is the musical consummation of the eighteenth century, as Wagner is that of the nineteenth century. Beethoven is the towering bridge that connects two epochs, the classic and the romantic — or the predominantly formal and the predominantly emotional.

There have always been highly emotional individuals who temperamentally correspond to the type that we call the romantic. It is a psychopathic type. St. John, the writer of the Apocalypse, is an early literary example. Dante is a later one. But after occasional appearances throughout the ages, the conditions that had produced certain "romantic" individuals became general and shaped the mentality of entire generations. The romantic spirit became contagious. Probably the most infectious case was that of Jean-Jacques Rousseau. With him began in earnest the epidemic of morbid introspection, of exaggerated emotionalism, of passionate curiosity about the so-called secrets of nature. Romanticism, in art, was a new order of artistic conceptions due to a psychic disorder in the artist. He lived in a world of dreams. But he found the centre of the universe in himself. Abnormal sensibilities gave the artist a sort of clairvoyance. Poetry and music began to work with black magic. Theoretically, art still dwelt in the empyrean of pure thought. In effect, art caught man where he is weakest, by his sensibility. Wagner described his earliest aim in composition as "a bold glorification of unfettered sensualism." That was more or less the aim of all romantic art. In its attainment Wagner went farthest. He thought that he was opening a new era. In reality he was the closing apotheosis of a magnificent pathological interlude.

Wagner's supreme position among his romantic predecessors and contemporaries is due not only to his remarkable talents, but to his exceptional chances of unfolding these talents. His mental and physical constitution permitted him to overcome more hardships, and to live a longer physical and artistic life, than was given to any other great musician of his time. Consider what the lives of these romantic composers were: Weber, the first of them, died at the age of 40; Schubert died at the age of 31; Mendelssohn lived to be 38; Chopin succumbed to consumption at 39; Schumann fell into hopeless insanity at the age of 44 and died two years later, but as a composer he had practically ceased to exist at 40. It was a soft and hapless lot.

If Wagner overshadows these men — some more, some less — it is principally because he possessed rude health, had tough powers of resistance, and lived out the biblical three-score years and ten. Had he died as young as Schubert, "Tannhäuser" would have remained an unfinished opera. Had he lived a creative life only as long as the longest enjoyed by these other composers — that is, had he died in 1853, at the age of forty — we should have been without a single note of "Tristan und Isolde," of the "Meistersinger," of the "Nibelungen," and of "Parsifal." In other words, we should have had not one page of the "greater Wagner." That Wagner produced those greater works is due to three factors: his phenomenal gifts, his phenomenal capacity for work, and his phenomenal luck.

It has become the fashion of late to attack on their human side persons of superhuman achievement. There is no hero who, like Achilles and Siegfried, does not have a vulnerable spot. Saint and sinner may be opposites, though not a few saints reached their blessed state only after they had conquered sin. Genius and sinner are not necessarily opposites; on the contrary, more often are they identical. We have seen a Wagner afflicted with the psychopathic taints found in a murderer. To spread these taints before the world in an effort to diminish the stature of a giant is contemptible. To dwell on them as a complement often needed in greatness — mental, not moral greatness — is legitimate. Only by thus seeing the whole man, down to his lowest depth, can we measure the height to which his mind soared. And were it not for that depth, perhaps the height would never be reached.

The complex character of Wagner resolves into a fairly simple and consistent pattern, if we reduce it to the traits that make up the "theatrical" type. It is a very common type. There are many excellent actors in this world who never step before the footlights. There are not a few actors to whom the earth offers barely a large enough stage. In a powerful personality, the traits of the "theatrical" type may exert a maleficent or beneficent

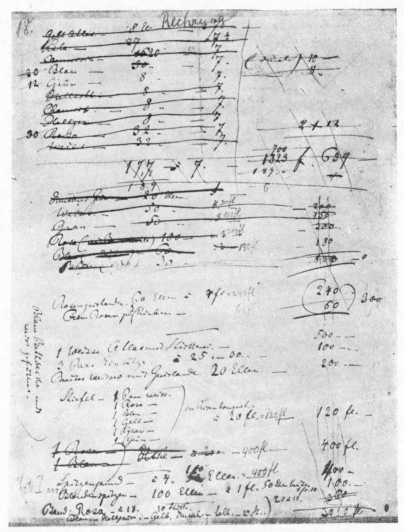

One of the statements in Wagner's handwriting for material furnished him by the milliner, Bertha Goldwag, in Vienna, totalling 3010 gulden.

—(*By courtesy of the Library of Congress.*)

influence, or both. We need think only of Nero, Pope Leo X, or Napoleon I.

The chief traits of the "theatrical" type might be summed up as follows: an innate dual or multiple personality (resulting in duplicity or multiplicity of behaviour), an imaginative exuberance, an absorption in unreality, a craving for public show and applause, and a lively dramatic instinct.

Wagner possessed all of these qualities. He came by them naturally. He inherited them. They were developed by his early surroundings. His father, Friedrich Wagner, was born in the same year as Beethoven, and died when Richard, the youngest of seven children, was six months old. Friedrich Wagner, a police clerk, was exceedingly fond of the stage and, according to his son Richard, was inclined to take a gallant interest in actresses. When Friedrich's widow, ten months after her husband's death, married his friend the actor Ludwig Geyer, the home in which Richard grew up was completely permeated with the theatrical atmosphere.

When a boy is seized with the theatrical fever, there is, as a rule, no cure for him. The world of the stage holds irresistible allurements. They emanate not alone from the excitement, the glitter, the crowd, of the evening. In the grey light of the morning after, the wings and the empty pit, shrouded in darkness, have unique and mysterious attractions. Young Wagner surrendered to them completely. While still in school, he wrote dramas. They were of the romantic kind, full of adventures and valorous knighthood. Romanticism had rekindled a lively passion for ancient sagas and tales of mediæval chivalry. Wagner never outgrew these tales. In Eisleben, where he spent some time with a brother of his step-father, the boy ingratiated himself with a soap-boiler's family on account of the stories he told. His talent for spinning a yarn was precocious. Later in life he was forever reading his dramatic texts to those who would listen to him. With his strong Saxon dialect he declaimed, and with a profusion of gestures he acted, the involved and interminable narratives of his remodelled Germanic myths. And evidently he carried off the illusion so successfully that his hearers forgot that the gods and Valkyries were talking in Leipzig brogue.

If we accept Wagner as flesh and spirit of the theatre, the contradictions of his character resolve into harmony. His apparent inconsistencies only accentuate his trueness to type. We understand the ease with which the professed revolutionary and socialist of 1849, who for thirteen years lived in exile as a "political refugee," changed to the familiar of kings and princes. We are inclined to forgive the very duplicities of the man to whom life was but a succession of different scenes in which he played different parts. His mask was his armour. And he had need constantly to defend and save himself for the only business that counted with him — the act of composing.

Creating was a sublime ritual, with the accomplishment of which nothing earthy or profane was allowed to interfere. As a composer, Wagner lived in a state of hallucination and in a world apart. Lack of money, from which he suffered so much, was unbearable to him. Yet it never really hampered his inspiration; it merely spoiled his joy in life. To escape want, he would curb his pride; but he never sacrificed an ideal. As Wagner grew older, he became more dependent on external things He demanded not only comfort but luxury; and his ideas of luxury often showed strange aberrations of taste. To gratify his love for richly decorated rooms and sumptuous garments, he was ready to squander his last penny and run up debts. In the Library of Congress are the garish samples of silk and satin for house-robes, bed-covers, and pillow slips that he ordered from a milliner in Vienna, together with fourteen letters that he wrote to her full of minute directions. The setting and costume for his own person acquired increasing importance. Most often place and action in Wagner's life suited each other; be it Paris and poverty, the lake of Lucerne and love, or Bayreuth and beatification. Fortune indulged him by selecting his beloved Venice and a stately palace on the Grand Canal for the final curtain.

Wagner's theatrical instinct led him to dramatize and poetize his entire life. Nor were intrigue and melodramatic complications foreign or distasteful to his nature. He could play any part that the circumstances called for. But he was cut out for the spectacular and glamorous leading rôle. He excelled as a talker, less in dialogue than in monologue. Still, he headed the most brilliant company of players ever assembled. He took pains to surround himself with a cast of friends and admirers who ably supported him in the most marvellous tragicomedy of life.

Many of his contemporaries, quite naturally, saw in the protagonist of the tragicomedy only a clever mountebank. Yet, obviously, for a jester he was too deadly in earnest, for a trickster he was too superb an artist. This impractical hotspur, this rampageous blusterer, was the most methodical and patient craftsman. If a composer's manuscripts give any indication of his creative methods, compare Beethoven's feverish scrawls with the cool, collected, neat handwriting of Wagner. Here is evidence of a control which has an almost fatalistic assurance. It is strange to see the musician lay down his pen for a stretch of years, busy himself in the meantime with literary work, and then take up composing again with a fresh vigour and a richer gift of expression. Periods of real idleness Wagner never knew. When he lamented that he needed "rest," what he meant was leisure to work. His supply of energy was inexhaustible. Tchaikovsky, in a letter from Paris to his brother Modeste, once wrote that he had spent the morning furiously at work in order to earn "the right to do nothing." Wagner was always clamouring for some right or other: the right to live, the right to possess the woman he craved, the right to realize his dreams; but never did he ask for the right to do nothing. He lived passionately, he loved passionately, he worked passionately; and he wrote music drenched with all the passion he was capable of.

The only frenzy that Wagner never knew was the religious fervour born of implicit religious faith. He was full of passion, but void of compassion. He never experienced the rapture and contrition of Bach or Franck. He believed in himself. His wisdom was the fruit of selfish struggle, not of a man *"durch Mitleid wissend."* For a long time he had been an avowed atheist. Christ interested him as a dramatic personage. In 1848 Wagner sketched a play with the title "Jesus of Nazareth." He dropped the plan. Later in life the mysticism of the Christian legends appealed to him. But it was only a superficial and perhaps a superstitious concern. His mystico-symbolical "Parsifal" is first and last a musical spectacle, not a spiritual revelation. It is theatrical religion; or the Christian heaven done over by the man who undertook to renovate Valhalla. Nietzsche roundly condemned the text of "Parsifal." He saw in it, not a profession of faith, but an apostasy. In one of his notes Nietzsche wrote: "Wagner's 'Parsifal' was primarily a concession to the Catholic instincts of his wife, the daughter of Liszt." Here Nietzsche erred. Cosima's Catholicism was not very deep-rooted. In the Library of Congress are some unpublished letters of Wagner to the lawyer who handled the divorce of Cosima. In one of these letters Wagner inquired whether Cosima's conversion to Protestantism should take place at once or later, according to whether such a conversion was needed to facilitate the divorce or her re-marriage.

No, "Parsifal" was hardly a concession to the daughter of Liszt. More likely was it dimly and darkly felt or intended as a last challenge to father Liszt himself. Poor, grand old Liszt had been pushed into the background by his son-in-law. When the composer Liszt realized that Wagner was threatening to monopolize for years to come the opera stage and the concert platform, he took refuge in the music for the church. Then began the period of Liszt's religious compositions. Here he hoped, perhaps, to find at last a niche for himself that he could keep unmolested. But again Wagner tried to smoke him out with his own fumes of myrrh and frankincense.

What Nietzsche objected to, chiefly, in "Parsifal" was the introduction of "the tiresome theme of love" — as he called it — into what purported to be the poetic treatment of a spiritual subject. All of Wagner's stage works are built on Nietzsche's "tiresome theme of love," but with variations; in the minor key of renunciation, and in the major of salvation and redemption. There are tiresome stretches in all of Wagner's operas, but they are not those that deal with love. To him love was the ruling motive in life. It was the core of his being, the well-spring of his inspiration. When the full measure of love came to the man who had written "Tristan und Isolde," he, too, rose to the stature of his own heroes. From Lucerne, where Cosima von Bülow had joined him, he wrote on November 18, 1867, to Baron von Düfflipp, the private secretary of King Ludwig, that unless the conditions for the shielding of Cosima's honour which he, Richard Wagner, laid down in this letter were promptly accepted, he would be compelled to renounce forever the favour and protection of his exalted friend and royal master. This was not a vain threat. Here we have a glimpse of the man at his best and noblest. If he were in the wrong, he would take the consequences. But give up Cosima, never. For above Munich, above the King of Bavaria, above everything, came his need of the one person who had made him feel that under her affectionate and devoted care he would finish his "Nibelungen." The future proved him right.

Wagner's self-confidence sprang largely from his belief that he had been born a *Universalgenie* — as the Germans call it — a universal genius. In the years of Wagner's adolescence the world had been treated to the sight of two such geniuses with whose fame the earth reverberated: Napoleon and Goethe. The Emperor, at Bautzen, had carried off one of his last spectacular victories on May 21, 1813, one day before Richard Wagner was born in near-by Leipzig. In 1832, the year of Goethe's death, Wagner—then nineteen years old—had tried his hand at some music for Goethe's "Faust." When he was twenty-six, he wrote in Paris the orchestral piece known as "A Faust Overture." Three years before, about the time he had married the actress Minna Planer, at Königsberg (so he tells us in his autobiography), he was projecting an overture entitled "Napoleon." He gave up the idea because (as Wagner writes) he was unable to decide whether he "should express the annihilating stroke of fate that befell the French Emperor in Russia by a beat of the tam-tam or not." Tchaikovsky overcame these scruples and in his "1812" Overture introduced heavy artillery.

Napoleon and Goethe appealed to the imagination of young
Wagner because they represented the sort of "universal genius"
that he was beginning to consider himself. Napoleon was not
only the brilliant strategist and irresistible leader of men, the
juggler with crowns and thrones, but the daring engineer who
provided France with a network of unsurpassed roads, and the
wise legislator who gave to his country an exemplary code of laws.
Above all, he was the most consummate and resourceful stage
director, who never miscalculated an effect, not even in the hour
of his bitterest reverses. The dispatch-bearer who brought to
Paris the news of the burning of Moscow and the impending
retreat from Russia, also brought in his pouch a new constitution
for the actors and actresses of the Comédie Française which the
Emperor had personally drawn up in the smouldering ruins of the
Kremlin. France could feel reassured.

Goethe, on the other hand, was the foremost lyric, epic, and
dramatic poet of his time, was novelist, historian, traveller, geolo-
gist, botanist, inventor of a new science of colours, architect, nu-
mismatist, collector of antiques and engravings, theatrical manager, and minister of state. In 1825 Goethe told Eckermann that
at one time he had hoped to build a German national theatre for
the production of his plays — a hope which Wagner, fifty years
later, realized for his musical dramas in the "Festspielhaus" at
Bayreuth.

Less of a clear thinker than Napoleon, much less of a poet
than Goethe, Wagner shared with them a prodigious versatility.
At least he did some things extremely well and could not resist
dabbling in others that he did not do so well. His mania for
writing is a case in point.

Wagner was forever scribbling. And to everything that he
wrote he attached an importance which he was forever trying to
impress upon others. When Wagner, in 1871, decided to publish a
complete edition of his prose and verse, he gave as a reason his
belief that whoever is master of an art is best qualified to expound
that art. This is perfectly true. The trouble is that Wagner was
not content to write about the one thing he understood supremely

well — music — but that he pronounced dogmatically on politics, on religion, on philosophy and æsthetics, on criticism, on the peculiarities of the Jewish race, on the drama, on everything that came into his buzzing head and aroused his interest or his ire.

The bulk of Wagner's prose writing is polemic or argumentative. Because he differed from the rest of men, he had need of explaining and of defending himself. He thought that he was setting down eternal axioms, when in reality he played prosecutor or made speeches for the defence, according to which side he was on. In one of his articles he wrote that he was proud, not of his achievements as a musician, but of the convictions he had gained from these achievements, which he was now able to hand down — evidently for the improvement of posterity. But his convictions were simply those of a man who considers himself always to be in the right, who is driven by motives all of which he deems just, and who resorts to means that he allows no one to question. Wagner was not an original thinker or a true philosopher. He picked up ideas wherever he found suitable ones — namely, those which lent added strength to his conviction that his behaviour, his actions, his character, his art work, were unimpeachable and unsurpassed. Therefore his artistic theories and his views on life were nothing more than the reflections of his personal development as artist and as man.

Artistic theories become unpleasantly loud every time someone shouts from the housetops his artistic contrariness. With theories the artist challenges the world; he conquers it with master works. When the fight is won, when the truth of a new artistic doctrine has been proved, when the new idea has emerged fully hatched from the egg of theories, then the shell of its early and necessary prison should drop like a cumbersome and confining protection no longer needed. We must give Wagner credit for having seen this much sooner than his followers did. He knew he had won the battle, long before he had spread his richest banners to the wind of public opinion. In July, 1853, he wrote from St. Moritz to Liszt: "I don't care to, I can't, and I won't *theorize* any more;

and he is not my friend who lures me into this damn business." Perhaps because Wagner the man had enemies all his life — hosts of them — the artist Wagner felt obliged to keep on theorizing to the very end.

That Wagner the librettist did not know how to write poetry is now generally conceded. But to say that he was not a poet, that he was insensible to "the poetic atmosphere and aroma of words," is missing the mark. There are unforgettable lines in Wagner's plays, there are strains of music which in our memory remain inseparable from the words. There are instances where the dramatic pregnancy of the words outweighs the music. Take the returning Tannhäuser's outburst in the last act: "*Schweig mir von Rom!* (Speak not of Rome!)" Here is the real climax of the whole opera — and it is the words, not the music, that make us conscious of it. In spite of the wonderful symphonic web, there are few passages in Wagner's operas more tedious than Wotan's harangue to Brünnhilde in the third act of "The Valkyrie" and Brünnhilde's defence. Yet Wagner never wrote anything nobler and tenderer than the last words of the sorrowing father when, as a punishment for her disobedience, he takes from his child her divine nature: "*Denn so kehrt der Gott sich dir ab, so küsst er die Gottheit von dir* (For thus turneth from thee the god, thus doth he kiss the godhead from thee)." With this cry of the blood ringing in our ears, the marvellous chords of transition (known as the "sleep-motive") well up from the orchestra; and then begin the orchestral fireworks with the dancing flames in the wood-winds and the glockenspiel. There is certainly a "poetic aroma" about the words of that simple question which young Siegfried — who had never known his parents — asks himself: "*Aber wie sah meine Mutter wohl aus?* (But how was my mother's face?)" Take the soliloquy of Hans Sachs on the morning after the riotous night and his world-wise explanation of the rumpus:

> *Ein Glühwurm fand sein Weibchen nicht;*
> *Der hat den Schaden angericht.*
> *Der Flieder war's: — Johannisnacht.*

A glowworm could not find his mate,
He did the damage perpetrate.
'Twas lilac time — eve of St. John's.

There are many such instances which show that Wagner could
hit on the appropriate verbal phrase, on the felicitous turn of
words, or what the French call *"le mot juste."* And in such instances the words are appropriate, not only because they fit the
dramatic situation, but because they have that poetic quality
which unfetters our fancy and makes us read deep beneath the
words those things that no words can express. They certainly
always unfettered Wagner's fancy and enabled him to write music
which helps to make this deeper meaning unmistakable.

And yet of any sustained poetic writing Wagner was incapable.
All that he needed was now and then — in the salient moments —
the salient phrase. That sent him headlong into the music and
acted like the twist that sets the music-top spinning. Once only
did he reverse the process. That was when the emotional climax
of his life had inspired him to write the lovely "Siegfried Idyll"
for Cosima's birthday on Christmas-day, 1870. He had put into
this music what was best and most lovable in him, his gratitude
for the joy over the birth of a son, for the happiness in the shelter
of a peaceful home. When he tried to couch these same sentiments
in words, he contrived to write two fine lines for the opening, but
the rest of the poem is plain doggerel. And in no line did he match
the lofty and serene beauty of the music.

Wagner's theatrical mind, his early affiliations with the stage,
predestined him to become a composer of dramatic music. He did
not write suites and fugues like Bach's and Handel's, or symphonies like Haydn's and Mozart's, nor chamber music like Beethoven's. These were the masters of a preponderantly formal
music. The nearest musical relative of Wagner was, not Weber
or Marschner, but Gluck. Wagner wrote dramatic music because
he was an absolute slave to emotion. He could not think musically without being stirred emotionally. The most formal piece of
music that Wagner ever wrote is that contrapuntal masterpiece,

the prelude to the "Meistersinger." Yet it owed its inception to one of those emotional flare-ups in which Wagner's musical fecundation produced the finest results. The incident took place on a wild-goose-chase to Venice, in December, 1861, to revisit his "Tristan" muse, Mathilde Wesendonck, and borrow money from her husband. The story is worth telling in Wagner's own words:

"Wesendonck, who always went about armed with huge field-glasses, and was ever ready for sight-seeing, only once took me with him to see the Academy of Arts, a building which on my former visits to Venice I had only known from the outside. In spite of all my indifference, I must confess that the 'Assumption of the Virgin,' by Titian, exercised a most sublime influence on me, so that, as soon as I realized its conception, my old powers revived within me, as though by a sudden flash of inspiration. I determined at once on the composition of the 'Meistersinger.' . . . I had spent four dreary days in Venice, and now started by train on my dull journey to Vienna, following the roundabout overland route. It was during this journey that the music of the 'Meistersinger' first dawned on me . . . with the utmost distinctness I at once composed the principal part of the overture in C major."

This story, no doubt, reveals a thoroughly characteristic and common occurrence in Wagner's life. An emotional crisis had to start his creative activity. And in these moments of highest tension Wagner was in the truest sense a seer endowed with second sight, who translated into music what he saw and felt.

Wagner possessed to a phenomenal degree the gifts of clairvoyance and clairaudience. There is no other way of explaining what he did. If a poetic vision sprang up in his mind, it was accompanied by its musical counterpart. Wagner always heard what he saw, what he felt, what he thought — and he saw farther, felt deeper, and thought more passionately than any musician had done before him. His faculties of clairvoyance and clairaudience became more and more acute as he grew older — or the progress continued at least until the completion of the "Nibelungen." In the music of "Parsifal" there is no really new note. It is a musical summing up of the man who had developed his powers to their limit. Yet "Parsifal" furnished the indispensable coping stone to the monument of Wagner's music.

As the monument rose to ever greater height, the builder never ceased to be mindful that it should increase in architectonic richness of design. Wagner had no patience with those who were content indefinitely to repeat themselves. In a famous letter that he wrote to Liszt in 1852 he expressed his disappointment in Berlioz because the Frenchman had not developed, had not succeeded in composing something that was different from what he had written before. It sounds as if he were pointing to himself as a model when he writes: "Children, do something new, something new, and again something new! If you cling to the old, the devil of unproductiveness will get you and you are the sorriest lot of artists."

It is useless to speculate what Wagner's music would have been like, in the end, had not his first sojourn in Paris, from September, 1839, until April, 1842, been a hopeless failure. Had he succeeded in giving "Rienzi" in Paris, and had the production brought him fame and fortune, possibly the world might have lost the revolutionary Wagner for one content to turn out more "grand operas" of the lucrative Meyerbeerian formula. However, probability is against it. Wagner, in Paris, did the lowliest hackwork to keep the wolf from the door; but he never sold his art. To nearly everyone he ever corresponded with, he complained about his lack of funds or openly hinted that a loan or gift would be welcome; but unlike the letters of Tchaikovsky or those of other prominent musicians, his correspondence is singularly free from complaints that his inspiration was forsaking him. Even while starving in Paris — starving for food and for recognition — he went to work on "The Flying Dutchman," which set the curve for the stupendous arc that his later operas described. Great as the distance between the beginning and the end of this arc may seem, there is no mistaking the connection of the two. The first fruit of Wagner's and the last do not differ enough in savour to suggest that they grew upon different trees. Nor did the soil that nourished them ever cease to drink in the fertilizing influences of predecessors and contemporaries alike.

At sixty-seven, when Wagner wrote the music for "Parsifal," he did not compose better tunes, or melodies of a different cast, than he had at twenty-seven, when he finished "Rienzi." He never lost his fondness for a certain Weberian sweep of melody and orchestral rush, at times not altogether free from a blustering swagger. In spite of the improved wind instruments that he found pliant to his advancing chromaticism, he never got away from the grandiloquent Beethovenian themes built on the open notes of the valveless brasses. Although in his autobiography — which swarms with the names of contemporary musicians — Chopin's name does not occur a single time, the purling cascades and flowering garlands of sound that Chopin bequeathed to music were a legacy on which Wagner drew heavily until the end. The harmonic opulence and rhythmic nervousness of the Hungarian Liszt passed into Wagner's music to stay there; and, admittedly, they gained by the transfer.

To certain mannerisms Wagner clung throughout his evolution. The ultra-romantic *gruppetto,* as an emotional tremor, runs through his first opera, "The Fairies"; it still turns up in the most significant place of Kundry's narrative in the second act of "Parsifal." In forty-five years Wagner had discovered nothing better. The *gruppetto* followed by an upward leap of a sixth might almost be called an obsession of Wagner's. It stands out prominently on the first page of the "Rienzi" overture; it plays an important part in "Tannhäuser"; Brünnhilde resorts to it in rousing Siegfried to new deeds; and it contributes notably to Isolde's final apostrophe. But apart from these tell-tale birthmarks, the music of Wagner in time changed its face so completely as to amount to a transfiguration.

On the technical side, the development and originality of Wagner's music are centred in three points: modulation, variation, and orchestration. Wagner's increasing mastery of modulatory devices, of thematic changes, of orchestral colouring, constitutes his greatest contribution to music. In these three points he

showed himself the daring innovator and inventor on whose discoveries all of our subsequent music rests. Without his growing
command over these three means he could never have originated
what he called his "endless melody." For — far from being longer
than ordinary melodies of four, eight, or sixteen measures — this
"endless melody" is in reality the composite of a limited number
of pregnant but short motives, joined one to the other in endless
repetition. The marvel, that this repetition escapes being tiresome, is due solely to the infinite art with which Wagner learned
to handle the three chief tools of his musical craft.

In itself his technical mastery of modulation, variation, and
orchestration would have availed him little, had not Wagner
learned to produce with these tools results of unparalleled musical
characterization, of unfailing psychological effect. Whether it be
fire or water he tries to depict, whether it be the dark and clammy
caves of Nibelheim or the bright cerulean abode of Lohengrin,
his elements are unmistakable, his colours are true. The storm in
"The Flying Dutchman," the "murmurs of the woods" in "Siegfried," those ravishing last eighteen measures of the second act
of the "Meistersinger," with the empty, moonlit street of mediæval Nuremberg returning to its nightly peace — these are but a
few samples of Wagner's musical brush-work and the vividness
of his amazing tonal pictures. He was not only a painter of large
canvases, but he excelled as a miniaturist. In a detail, such as the
single chord which occurs on the word "*blau*" (blue) when Tristan, in the beginning of the opera, points to the distant shore of
Cornwall, we can measure the subtlety with which Wagner's
imagination worked. We may truly say that Wagner had only
one sense, his hearing, and that the sharpness of this sense
amounted to clairaudience.

In a letter to Mathilde Wesendonck that has been often quoted,
Wagner confessed that his technique was gradually resolving
into a more and more skilful devising of modulatory transitions.
No doubt, Wagner was right. And he knew that here he was
breaking ground and unearthing virgin gold. But it would be
erroneous to assume that his skill consisted solely in the ease with

which he contrived the passage from one unresolved harmony to the next, or from one key to another. The extraordinary part of such mobile scores as "Tristan" and the "Nibelungen" is the remarkable balance and relationship of tonalities that lie at the bottom of these perpetually fluctuating modulations and deceptive cadences. Only within the last three or four years, Alfred Lorenz analysed for the first time in a deeply revealing study the consistent structure of tonalities that forms the hidden framework of these unwieldy scores. Whether Wagner followed herein a consciously developed plan or was guided merely by his unerring intuition, we cannot tell — at least not without knowing more about the sketches of these operas that are being guarded at Wahnfried more jealously than Fafner watched over his treasure.

A stout volume might be filled with examples showing the adroitness with which Wagner learned to apply the time-worn device of variation to his melodic material and its harmonic metamorphoses. And it is not "variation" in the older acceptance of the word. It is not mere elaboration and figuration of a theme in a display of ingenuity, as we find it in Haydn or Mozart. Nor is it the variation that delights in rhythmic and harmonic modifications of a theme, dear to Beethoven and Brahms. With Wagner a specific motive, to which a specific thought or emotion attaches, is varied or modified according to the slightest change of the thought or emotion. It is psychological variation of a musical theme. A telling example may be seen in the "fire" motive of the "Nibelungen." From its first appearance in "Rheingold" as the symbol of the fire-god, Loge, until it accompanies the lighting of the funeral pyre in the last act of "The Twilight of the Gods," it undergoes transformations that are comparable only to the ever-changing flame itself.

It is astounding with what psychological understanding Wagner went to work by the time he wrote the score of "Tristan." There is nothing in all music like the agonizing tension he creates with a motive of four notes the moment that Tristan, in the first act, heeds at last Isolde's summons and appears before her. Each faces the other without uttering a word, while in the orchestra those four notes, swelling convulsively, are as the spasm that chokes the throat and binds the tongue. And when Isolde and Tristan have regained their voices, that same spasmodic motive rises and falls like the mercury in a barometer, registering the curves of conflicting passions, until the four notes round out, with an ominous storm-warning, the very phrase with which Isolde hails the magic potion that is to seal their doom.

Or take what is perhaps the most pathetic moment in the whole tragedy: when faithful Kurwenal, fatally struck, sinks at the feet of Tristan and, clutching his dead master's hand, apologizes for following him into death. "Tristan! Master! Chide him not if thy man would go with thee!" And as Kurwenal dies, his motive — and the motive that signifies home, Kareol Castle, peaceful and sunny life — returns in the orchestra for the last time, but so subtly transformed as to make it seem the mere shadow, the spectre of the original theme. It is one measure only in a score inexhaustible in riches. Yet that one measure may well serve as a shining example of what meaning the term "variation" had assumed in music when the sorcerer Wagner put his touch to it.

In a broader sense, of course, Wagner's art of "variation," in order to achieve its ends, relied on help from the orchestra. In the one measure just mentioned it is the use of the oboes and bassoons pianissimo and of the muted violoncello that gives its unearthly pallor to a musical phrase which had previously appeared clad in the richest orchestral hues. And the colourfulness, the gorgeousness of Wagner's orchestra was something unknown before him; he trained our ears to a new volume and a new quality of sound. The horn of Siegfried is no longer that of Oberon. King Marke's bass-clarinet has nothing in common with the bass-clarinet in the fifth act of Meyerbeer's "Huguenots." The violins of the "Lohengrin" prelude and the violins in Louis Spohr's "Jessonda" are not the same. The mere visual difference between Wagner's later scores and those of his contemporaries is that which strikes the eye on comparing cotton cloth of a single shade shot through with one or two silken strands of different col-

ours in a conspicuous pattern, and cloth woven out of a multitude
of coloured threads, so harmoniously blended and so deftly arranged that the changing patterns merge one into the other con-
tinuously and overspread the entire fabric of brocaded silk and
velvet. Wagner's methods of orchestration are no longer a secret.
They have been imitated; they have never been surpassed.
Wagner was the first to raise instrumental polyphony to the
pinnacle which vocal polyphony had attained in the age of Palestrina, Lasso, Vittoria, and William Byrd. But whereas these old
masters represent the neighbouring peaks in a high range of contemporary talent schooled in the principles of a slowly developed
style of composition that originated in the Netherlands, Wagner's orchestral polyphony mounts abruptly like a lone volcano
in the plain. And sound flowed from its cone in fiery streams of
molten lava. Even now it has not cooled entirely; the glow of it
still empurples the sky. If it brought devastation, it also brought
unparalleled fertility. Out of Wagner's volcanic ashes grew harvest after harvest of new music.

Since the advent of the newest music — that is, within the last
twenty years or so — the younger musicians incline to be oblivious
of their debt to Wagner. We who have stepped into our fifth
decade are the last "perfect Wagnerites." No person who to-day
is less than forty years of age can possibly feel toward Wagner's
music as those of us do who first encountered it not later than at
the end of the nineteenth century. Then it was at the height of
its glory. It had conquered all opposition. It still retained something of its formidable novelty. The performances of Wagner's
later operas had reached a splendour unknown to Wagner himself.
Bayreuth, the Prinzregenten Theater in Munich, were shrines to
which worshippers from the farthest ends of the globe made an-
nual pilgrimage. And for the faithful not even the beer and
sausages in the intermissions of the four- and five-hour orgies could
break the spell. Those of us who between 1890 and 1900 heard for
the first time "Tristan," "Die Meistersinger," and the "Ring," are
the last beings on this earth who will have experienced the impact
with the full force of Wagner's genius.

If Wagner's music emanated from a person technically sane but actually neurotic and psychopathic, what are we to think of Debussy, Schönberg, and Stravinsky? They have taught our ears to hear things which make Wagner seem like a pompous and garrulous but innocent old man. A new age is talking a new musical language. Nothing can stop the course of progress. The seduction that a fresh aspect of beauty exercises upon susceptible natures is very powerful. But while our conceptions of beauty may change according to the eternal law of satiety and variety, the permanency of the master work remains secure. And Wagner, though receding into the background of time, still looms above his successors as a full-sized master. Wagner's personality, under the scalpel of the biographer, has suffered the disfigurement of a thorough-going autopsy. The post-mortem of the man's character reads like the report of a psychiatrist on a criminal or a degenerate. But there are pages — many pages — of this man's music which prove that human frailty was paired in him with superhuman strength of will and boundless creative energy. The combination produced a phenomenon the like of which we have yet to see.

SCHÖNBERG LUNAIRE

(Read before the International Composers' Guild in New York, January, 1923)

WHEN Dr. Burney — historian of music and father of Fanny — journeyed to Italy, in July, 1770, he did so not, like most travellers before him, to see the sights, but to hear the sounds, all the musical sounds of what was musically still the most resounding country in the world. He went about his errand systematically, manfully. Endowed with British thoroughness and fortitude, he set a record in five months for listening to operas, oratorios, concerts, masses, private *"accademias,"* learned lectures — a record unbroken even by a New York critic in a winter's season. No piece of music was so humble, no performance so indifferent, that it did not seem to merit a mention in his journal or provide him with food for deep and grave reflection.

Thus we are told that at Venice, in August, he heard one night "on the Great Canal" a company of musicians in a barge. The band consisted of violins, flutes, horns, basses, and a kettle-drum, added to which was a singer "with a pretty good tenor voice." That manifestly was music of the people — Italian jazz, if you will — of one hundred and fifty years ago. And when these hired serenaders, duly impassioned, burst into "noise and fury," as he puts it, our placid Briton made the observation that these, too — the noise and fury — "had their effect." The specific effect on himself was that they moved him to ponder "the necessity of discord in the composition of music in parts." He came to the conclusion "that provided the ear be at length made amends, there are few dissonances too strong for it."

Perhaps it is not inopportune once more to recall this century-

and-a-half-old opinion, in a day when the art of music, as on earlier and not infrequent occasions, is being accused anew of showing an offensive prodigality in so-called dissonances. Of ancient standing though the charge may be, only recent developments have definitely placed Burney among the major prophets. Unfortunately, we are not in a position to say whether or not the doctor's ears would have accepted as sufficient the amends that some of our present music makes. It is not unlikely that Burney's ears, in spite of their owner's admirable theories, would have completely failed him in a practical test, could he have submitted to it along the Great White Way that represents our "Great Canal" (inviting comparison by sheer dissemblance), or in the chilling hall that is the home of our *"accademias."* He might have learned, to his confusion, that novel music demands new ears to hear it with. The countless yester-years which sink into the pit of time drag with them innumerable yester-ears.

In Europe, Arnold Schönberg's "Pierrot Lunaire," when first performed, was vehemently denounced and extravagantly praised. This dissension is typical, not exceptional, where Schönberg's music is concerned. Repeated ten years later, "Pierrot Lunaire" startled Berlin anew, cleft it into two hostile camps. Far from soothing the savage breast, these strains incited the meek to riot. The lapse of the decade had not softened the current or veered the wind. In the auditorium of the Berlin Hochschule, "Pierrot" brought on a tempest. Not content with hissing, ill-mannered and boisterous members in the audience resorted to antique latch-keys on which to blow more briskly their whistling gale of disapproval. One of the younger critics jumped up on the stage, in gallant defence of the composer and his work, called the noisy objectors a pack of *"Lausbuben"* — thus discreetly absolving the gentler and less demonstrative sex — and told these people that they had no business to come to such a musical event "without the proper spiritual preparation."

Ladies and gentlemen, I should feel an overwhelming sense of responsibility were I to believe for a moment that your good behaviour on the occasion of the first performance of "Pierrot

Lunaire" in America, depended solely on my persuasive and illuminating talents, or on the success of that "spiritual preparation" which it might seem my privilege to give you. It is fortunate, indeed, that in these climes displeasure at musical performances does not break out in turbulence. So long as in our country it is not made a political issue, we may rest safe that music, be it the worst or the weirdest, will be listened to politely and resignedly. Therefore, your bringing up, your wider acquaintance with ultra-modern music, as well as the happy prevalence of Yale locks and flat keys, render superfluous an initiation such as the public of Berlin doubtless needed.

Nevertheless, it is not impossible that even among you there may be some who — hearing "Pierrot Lunaire" for the first time — will come upon this music with wonder and uneasiness, if not with a painful start. Now, there is a virtue in being told by the doctor that he is going to hurt us. Prepared for it, we generally find his treatment less brutal than the cautioning made us fear. And sometimes we develop a real passion for our doctor. Therefore some of you might be served by a few words of warning, even though I cannot offer you much actual enlightenment. For I may as well confess that, with all my admiration for Schönberg's originality and mastership, there is in his latest music not a little that I still find somewhat difficult to grasp. This deficiency of understanding implies, for the time being, an occasional absence of profit or enjoyment. And in the things of art, I am ashamed to say, I follow the base instincts of a usurer and hedonist.

As you all know, music, the language of tones, has a peculiar way of assuming, now and then, a new speech. And when it does, the result is more complex than that presented in linguistic evolution. I mean not mere diversity in style such as exists between the Germanism of Brahms or Thomas Carlyle and the Latinism of Debussy or Walter Pater. The music of both composers remains music; the English of both writers remains English. To be sure there were many who at first could not understand Debussy. Some people are deaf to the magic of Pater's prose. In Schönberg's latest manner we are facing something different. It is not only a change in style and diction, but an upheaval in syntax and grammar, the bursting flood of a new vocabulary. No wonder that this new language should be a trifle more difficult to make out. What some esteem crude and ugly is evidently the most genuine, the most fitting, expression that Schönberg has found so far for what is in his mind and heart. Unintelligible though it may still be in spots, the dynamic intensity of it, the eloquence of its inflections, unmistakably prove that this language is fraught with meaning and the sincere desire to convey something deeply felt. We can do no less than pause attentively and wait for fuller comprehension of what unquestionably is masterfully wrought.

One of Germany's keenest critics and most ardent champions of modern music, in speaking of "Pierrot Lunaire," called it the only problematical music of our day, because it is "the only one of which the laws are still unrecognizable." The laws of harmony are a shaky structure. Someone is always at it with reinforcements, improvements, and extensions. In the streets of New York, so long as they cannot be altered or widened, new traffic regulations must meet the demands of the swelling vehicular commerce. In the network of harmony, so long as it was founded on inalterable mathematical proportions, the rules of counterpoint and modulation were much like the "go" and "stop," the "turn to the right" and "turn to the left" of the police department. And now that the royal road of music has been made dangerous with the congestion of polytonality and the recklessness of atonality, the theorist, or musical police commissioner, will promptly come along with a new set of traffic rules. The number of musical accidents will then decrease, for a time, and a period of relative safety will prevail — until New York shall have to anchor traffic towers to the clouds, and music adopt measures to prevent the wrecking of skyscrapers by an excess of sympathetic vibrations.

If there be æstheticians who have as yet failed to formulate the "laws" that underly Schönberg's latest music, other composers, either let into the secret by Schönberg himself or through their own ingenuity, have apparently detected his methods. For Schönberg has imitators. Those who are not trying to write music in the Schönbergian manner, but strive to listen to it appreciatively, might at a pinch get along without a knowledge of these laws. That does not relieve us of the duty to find, if we can, the right approach to Schönberg's later style, to find the right ears with which to listen to it.

The fact that different ears hear different things, or that different beings are variously affected by the same sounds, is at the bottom of all musical progress. It forms part and parcel of what we fondly call "the cultural evolution of the race." All goes well until we are suddenly confronted with the depressing discovery that evolution has evolved beyond ourselves, that we have reached the point where we can no longer tell music from musical noise. But remember Burney's prophecy.

Dr. Theodore Lessing, a German scientist, has studied the effects of noise in an interesting monograph entitled "Der Lärm." The author claims that the constantly increasing noise which surrounds us has a tendency to sharpen our ear. The louder and merrier the noise, the finer or more complicated the sounds that we are able to absorb with any sort of relish. According to Dr. Lessing, "we have grown terribly noisy, and at the same time terribly musical." Thomas Hood said to Schopenhauer: "For a musical people, the Germans are the most noisy people I ever met with." Of course, the connection escaped him. You will now, I trust, cherish the blessings of greater noise in the happy certainty that America is the musical nation of the future.

Whatever we may think of Dr. Lessing's theories, this much we know: the ear must accustom itself to a sound, or be in a state of preparedness for it, in order to derive pleasure from it. Almost as soon as this has taken place, the novelty, and with it a great deal of the sensuous charm, begins to wane. Because every discord has a tendency to become a concord, when our ear has heard it too often, rarer and subtler sounds, bolder and richer tone-combinations, must be invented. Music must assume a new speech. Where are the days when a diminished seventh chord could usher in Samiel, the ambassador from hell? In its arpeggiated form this chord survives only in the brilliant improvisations of piano salesmen. Where are the augmented triads of Wotan's Amazons that galloped through so much of post-Wagnerian music? Even a conservative composer of "blues" discards them now as "too slow." And for the use of the naughty whole-tone scale every self-respecting musician, to-day, must apologize.

The ear that can thrill to such antiquated stuff suffers from "arrested hearing." While it may be the lot of any or all of us to find ourselves, some day or other, thus afflicted, there are people born in that state. An ear less fixed and settled, yet not quite ready for the clarinet pieces of Mr. Stravinsky or the violin and piano bits by Mr. Anton von Webern, might be described as possessing "retarded hearing." The ear that reaches forward, insatiable of new sonorities, is gifted with "advanced hearing." Every composer of genius has such an "advanced hearing." Not every person with "advanced hearing" is a genius. In some instances, as that of Scriabin, death comes before the advance has stopped. In others, as that of Debussy, the advance, at first moderate, then strongly pronounced, slackens and comes to a standstill, to be overtaken by other and younger ears. This steeplechase between arrested, retarded, and advanced hearing is known as musical history.

In this race, advanced hearing always wins the stakes, backed by the less musical and often totally unmusical amateurs. A musically trained ear, because it probes deeper into the flesh and sinew of sound, because it penetrates farther into the mechanism of the art, has more to feed on. Hence it is less in need of change. That is why so many excellent musicians are Brahmsites or Franckists, and little else. They get all they want in the music of one or two masters, because they get that music whole. Again, the person whose ear listens only skin-deep, or the less musical person, especially the all-round cultured dilettant, grows sooner sated with one type of music and is ready to fall into the arms of any other that will bring innovation and relief. Therefore we find a papal chamberlain encouraging the first experiments in opera, at the end of the sixteenth century. Therefore did *der Esel* Lobkowitz" get his money's worth, and more. Therefore, "the Wag-

nerites," depicted by Aubrey Beardsley, have become the audience
par excellence that has given the greatest aid to all modern music
since Wagner.

Outside the orchestra of nature, from the roaring thunder to
the chirping of a bird, I believe there are only three sounds which
from time immemorial, in the Orient and Occident, have retained
their unaltered potency; they are: a mother's croon, the bell in
divine worship, and the bugle that calls to battle. All other man-
made sounds have undergone, and are undergoing, constant
changes. Noise is becoming louder, more insidious; our ears are
growing used to music freer and more sublimated. In both these
qualities, freedom and sublimation, Schönberg's "Pierrot Lunaire"
leaves nothing to be desired. It represents a tremendous jump
away — I do not say forward or backward — I say, a tremendous jump away from music as we have heretofore understood it.

Schönberg calls these "three times seven songs" a melodrama.
It is the Guild's most excellent resolve to give only this one work
on that occasion, but to play it twice; once, to enable an attun-
ing, as it were, of our receiving apparatus to Schönberg's æsthetic
wave-length; and a second time, so that we may get Schönberg's
message, or as much of it as — well, as the atmospheric conditions
will permit. Some day, perhaps in our own lifetime, we shall have
returned to the custom of a little *Hausmusik* after supper, and
young friends dropping in on a Sunday evening may take our
copy of "Pierrot Lunaire" from the shelf and read it off at first
sight with ease and comprehension. For the time being, a performance of this work presents many and great difficulties. We
have M. Darius Milhaud's word for it that before these songs
could be given in Paris under his direction, in January, 1922,
the singer, or rather "speaker," of the words, Mme. Marya
Freund, a highly intelligent artist, required two rehearsals daily
for six weeks, while the instrumentalists met for twenty rehearsals of three hours each, until the ensemble was tolerably
perfect. No doubt the knowledge of such colossal difficulties overcome will inspire many a hearer with solemn awe. Again, it is
reasonably certain that there will be others ready to feel with

Dr. Johnson, who upon being reminded by a friend that the feat accomplished by a celebrated violinist to whom they were listening was extremely difficult, replied: "Sir, I wish it were impossible." But Johnson was deaf to the charms of music.

The texts of these twenty-one songs are by Albert Giraud, and were written in French, or more precisely in the French of a Belgian. There is a difference, as M. Milhaud justly remarks. Schönberg used a German translation by Otto Erich Hartleben. When Giraud's "Pierrot Lunaire" was published by Alphonse Lemerre, in 1884, its author was twenty-four years old. Schönberg was ten. Schönberg wrote his settings in Berlin when he was thirty-eight. The first, "Mondestrunken," was written on March 30, 1912; the last to be completed was "Kreuze," on September 9. The forty rehearsals which were needed before this work could be given its first public hearing, that same autumn, started before the music of all the numbers was finished. The score was published in 1914.

Giraud was a native of Louvain. His real name was Kaeyenberg. He was for a time one of the editors of "La Jeune Belgique." That was a good many years ago. The men who then unfolded the banner of youth in Brussels caught in it much of the wind that came down from the Parnassian heights of France. Verlaine's "Fêtes galantes" started a run in moonlight revels, with pale Pierrot as master of ceremonies and Colombine as queen of the night.

Giraud's book entitled "Pierrot Lunaire" (later included in his "Héros et Pierrots") contains fifty rondeaux; each has the prescribed number of thirteen lines, with but two rhymes; the first couplet of the first quatrain is repeated as second couplet of the second quatrain; the last line of each poem is a repetition of the first. The pattern soon palls; the contrivance becomes monotonous and all effect of spontaneity is lost. Hartleben's translation does not attempt to rhyme, which is one advantage; it also varies the metre, which is another. But it retains Giraud's order of lines, without which, obviously, there would be no rondeaux; it succeeds in doing so only with the aid of copious dots, dashes, and ellipses. Now, if anything could be more wearisome than fifty

French rondeaux, chiefly mauve and pearl-grey, it is difficult to imagine — unless it be fifty German translations of French rondeaux, chiefly pearl-grey and mauve. One need but compare the text of Schönberg's third song, "Der Dandy," with Giraud's "Pierrot Dandy," in order to see how a very little word omitted here and another added there alter the particular nuance in a colour scheme in which demi-tints predominate and often take the place of high-lights. When we look in the present direction of poetry, we must confess that, had not the composer Schönberg been attracted by these lunary fancies, there would be little temptation to turn back for a discussion of either Giraud's poems or Hartleben's adaptations.

Schönberg chose twenty-one from among fifty. There was wisdom in his moderation. The selection and arrangement were evidently made with a distinct plan in mind. We can only guess at the intention. The result awakened in Mr. Paul Bekker (a fervid convert of Schönberg's) impressions of a *"Romantik im Zerrspiegel"* — romanticism in a distorting mirror — while a French critic in the "Revue musicale" spoke of a *"psychologie romantique tourmentée"*; and lastly Mr. Edwin Evans found in the music "Teutonic *Herzlichkeit."* Here are men of three different national tastes affected in pretty much the same manner. No doubt this is due primarily to the choice of texts, to the poetic *"Vorwurf,"* as they would say in German. And perhaps it is not without significance that one of the few phrases in the score which are to be actually sung by the reciter is one of three notes in "Rote Messe," over the words *"sein Herz."*

With your permission, I shall now quote a paragraph from one of Schönberg's essays:

"I have written many of my songs to their very end, intoxicated with the initial sound of the first text-words, without bothering in the least about the further course of the poetic happenings — indeed, without realizing them in the least during the trance of composing; and only after days did it occur to me to see what really were the poetic contents of my song. It then proved, to my great astonishment, that never did I do fuller justice to the

poet than when, led off by the first spontaneous contact with the
initial sound, I divined everything which evidently and necessarily
had to follow this initial sound."

This very interesting method apparently applies to translations
as well as to poems in their original language. The first of the
"Pierrot Lunaire" rondeaux which Schönberg set to music was the
one which is No. 1 in the finished work. In the German translation it begins:

> *Den Wein den man mit Augen trinkt,*
> *Giesst Nachts der Mond in Wogen nieder.*

Which is:

> The Wine we drink in with our eyes,
> At night the moon pours down in ripples.

Such is the initial sound that inspired Schönberg to compose
"Pierrot Lunaire." Such is the keynote; and everything else
"evidently and necessarily" had to follow this initial sound.
Which might lead a facetious person to remark that of all in-
ebriating liquors the most dangerous is moonshine.

Once we give up the attempt to fathom why Schönberg thought
this symbolic, moony salmagundi, this show of sentimental
puppets, a fitting carrier for so co-ordinated, so ruthlessly consequential, so vital and pregnant a music as that which he has written for it, we have but to take that music for what it is, detached
and different from any other music we have known before. Then
it becomes our duty to acknowledge the particular mastery that is
Schönberg's, the cleverness with which he has subtilized and
diversified the sonorities of each song. Instead of a dull mono-
chrome, we have the most amazing expressiveness and the most
refreshing variety of tonal colour that could be obtained from a
modest group of eight instruments, in the hands of five players.
When the poet as in No. 8, "Nacht," and No. 10, "Rote Messe,"
has given the musician an opportunity to use stronger pigments,
Schönberg takes advantage of it and achieves a surprising richness
of tone. It is these marvels of sheer sound, unheard till now, as

yet uncatalogued, bewildering and tantalizing, and they alone, that disarm criticism and defy analysis.

"L'alphabet m'appartient," said Casanova. You all know in what this ownership resulted. If the result disquiet timid hearts, it certainly did no great violence to the alphabet. The case is a different one when Schönberg seems to say: "The scale is mine," and proceeds to prove it. Here are the same twelve tones of old, but in horizontal and vertical combinations and permutations of such novelty that the effect is baffling to ear and eye alike. Yet, the first surprise over, one begins to recognize familiar faces in the picture of the score. Rhythmically, above all, things appear much as they have been for some time. Indeed, there is often a rhythmic soberness which, if disappointing to some, must be reassuring to others. While there is infinite elasticity within the musical phrase, and utter freedom in the reciting voice as well as in the accompanying instruments, no unusual or intricate measures are indulged in. We meet even with the rhythmic interdependence born of a canonic pairing or a fugato. In fact, these venerable contrapuntal devices bob up continually. Not only simple canon but imitation in contrary motion, augmentation, and diminution are drawn upon to lend, here and there, organic firmness to the texture.

In the eighteenth number, "Der Mondfleck," we come upon a veritable piece of mediæval cunning. The piccolo runs like a shadow on the heels of the clarinet, or, to be exact, at a distance of two beats, while the violin leads the violoncello, canonically, by a whole measure. Arrived at the middle of the tenth measure, these four instruments retrace their steps, in a merry crab canon, and not without politely reversing the precedence. Meanwhile the piano goes its own unperturbed way in a busy fughetta. Dr. Egon Wellesz, commenting on this tour de force, admits that not in the whole of musical literature, not even in Bach's "Kunst der Fuge," is there anything to compare with it; and he stresses the point that this artifice is not an end in itself, but is justified by the text, which reads: "A white spot of bright moonlight on the back of his coat, thus Pierrot promenades in the soft evening."

This, it must be conceded, is very ingenious. It leads to the question how far, in other instances, the music of Schönberg succeeds in interpreting literally, or by association of ideas, the meaning of the spoken word. Even to broach this question is enough to convict me. For has not Schönberg himself told us that it is nothing but a convenient shift, if the musical critic, unable to grasp the music, solemnly babbles about a composer's not doing justice to the poet's words? But to say that he did, in this instance, would be convicting the composer. Alas, no, the music is better than the words. The composer, prefatorily, warns his players not to create the mood and character of the music out of the sense of the text, but to take their cue merely from the music itself. Where musical illustration was intended, it will be found anyway and does not have to be read into the notes. That simplifies matters.

Now, as to the harmonic fibre of this music, only the very rash or the superlunar will venture, or be able, to say what it is all about. Fearless Dr. Eaglefield Hull, who is at home in every kind of modern harmony, says that "we are much too close to Schönberg's music to be able to assess it at all properly." Is that meant to be inclusive of himself? Does that pledge us to silent acceptance, and leave all the pleasant fuss to our grandchildren? We must remember Schönberg's own words: that the artist does not create anything because others may deem it beautiful, but because he, the artist, deems it necessary. When Schönberg's settings of poems by Stefan George were sung for the first time in Vienna (January, 1910), the composer wrote a sort of manifesto for the programme, declaring that he followed only the dictates of an inner voice, not the traditions of an absorbed and superseded training. Nowhere does this become clearer than in "Pierrot Lunaire." It is disconcerting music: disconcerting because of its inexplicable force; disconcerting by the very lack of amends that Dr. Burney demanded; disconcerting as a piece of impeccable workmanship; disconcerting especially because, all reservations and exceptions noted, there remains the impression of one possessed, tragically possessed, if you will, by the demoniacal powers of imagination, one who is mingling in his delirious speech the accents of a fiery tongue on which descended the spirit of a new revelation.

There are passages in this score that are as a pencil on a child's slate, as gall in the mouth. There are others that grip and enthrall. Oblivious to æsthetic doctrines refuted, to scholastic rules disproved, we are willingly mastered by the intensity or sublimation of the sonorous phenomenon — unstable and elusive — which we still call music. M. Charles Koechlin, after the performance in Paris, could do no less than write: *"C'était de la musique."* It is the music of one gifted with the mystic powers of second sight and second hearing. Listen to the falling petals of moonlight in "Colombine"; to the sombre spectre of night, stalking round to the tune of a passacaglia, while giant moths strangle the sun with their black wings. Mark the flute's anxious fluttering in "Der kranke Mond" which is heard again as a postlude to "Enthauptung." Look carefully at the instrumentation of that page in "Die Kreuze" which tells of the poets who are slain, and bleed to death upon the holy crosses of their verses. Your sense of irony will help you to catch this or that musical aside. The whimsicality of the "Serenade" cannot escape you. And if you are at all sentimentally inclined, the closing number of the work, "O alter Duft," is sure of its appeal. Here again the German translation fails to identify the scent, to suggest the particular *"vieux parfum vaporisé"* that is evocative of

les bleus Elysées
Où Watteau s'est éternisé.

Schönberg's setting is desperately nostalgic. We feel the distance of time and space that separates us from something of which our nostrils barely catch a memory. But who will say that it is the land breeze from Cythera we smell, or a drop of Pompeo Vandini's Bergamot on a piece of old lace, or what?

The musical means with which all this is attempted, and not a little of it accomplished, are at times very complex, and again most simple. The technical skill exhibited in the instrumentation is the outstanding achievement. The flageolet chords of the piano we have encountered before, in Schönberg's "Drei Klavierstücke." There are undoubtedly mannerisms in his music, and some of them may prove irritating. Schönberg's "melodic line" has often a restless way of jumping back and forth from one register to another, in intervals larger than that of an octave. The effect is almost that produced by the changing voice of a pubescent boy. Overdone, the trick becomes exasperating. The atonal nature of this music need not frighten us. What seems unbearable to-day may be mellifluous to-morrow. The amount of pleasure that a receptive and unbiased hearer will derive from this music will be determined, after all, not by the arbitrary count of unamended dissonances, but by the degree to which the triad Watteau-Pierrot-Schönberg enters his conception of a concordant trinity.

Anyone curious to explain the paradox presented in this music, the mixture of aggressive modernity and evident lapse into a blissfully somnolent past, may find a hint for a solution of the problem in that last number, "O alter Duft." There Teutonic, world-wide sentimentality stands revealed in all its blushing nakedness. *"O alter Duft aus Märchenzeit . . ."* a longing for the past that lies destroyed, destroyed by us; homesickness for the land of fairies, by us deserted. Here is the tragedy, but it is not Pierrot's. He does not age, he knows not past or future. It is ours, we who are struggling ever onward, ever backward looking. And when we leave the concert hall, astir under the impact with this new *"Zukunftsmusik,"* might it not so happen that of a sudden we seem to see a glistening of moonbeams on water, to hear a band of violins, flutes, horns, basses, a kettle-drum, and "a pretty good tenor voice," while the bells of San Giorgio Maggiore and those of the Salute are exchanging midnight greetings across the Giudecca? And there, those figures in long capes, slipping under the *felze* of their gondolas, are they not returning from an *"accademia"* at the Grimani's and delightedly discussing the new sonata with which Maestro Galuppi favoured the company? . . . *"O alter Duft!"*

CROSS-RELATIONS

MUSIC WE SHALL NEVER HEAR

*L'orgue de Barbarie, dans le crépuscule du souvenir, m'a fait
désespérément rêver.*

STÉPHANE MALLARMÉ

SOME of us who have not yet been privileged to enter into
direct communication with the spectral world still find in
dreams the strangest of our terrestrial experiences. And of all
dreams, those that we are consciously spinning in moments of an
intensified wakefulness — which has of sleep the peculiar quality of rendering us insensible to our immediate surroundings, while
it begets a swifter pace of thought than does the stimulating
drug — those dreams, indeed, are the most wonderful and most
inexplicable.

It was not, as in the case of Mallarmé, a hand-organ, with its
joyously vulgar tunes, with its old-fashioned and banal song of the
faubourgs, which made me dream so desperately. Nor did it happen in Mallarmé's favourite season, the dying days of summer. It
was on an afternoon in spring, at the side of a crackling fire, for
which a wet and chilly relapse into winter formed a more than
plausible excuse. And it was a story by Maurice Renard, "La
Mort et le Coquillage," which started all the trouble and sent me
on the melancholy and meandering road to music we shall never
hear. But the story, of course, is far more musical than any hand-
organ can ever expect to be; and I feel that I should here reveal
a little about this extraordinary tale, which is the fourth in a
book of seven, one weirder than the other, and all by the same
author. Nerval, a composer, died of what his friends regard as a
stroke of apoplexy. He had been at work, for years, on his masterpiece, "Amphitrite." The prelude, representing Neptune's

train, is a gorgeous riot of tones, of strange, unheard-of harmonies, leading to the brutal chords with which the Tritons announce the approach of the Sirens. But at this point the composer's invention stopped short — he is incapable, is utterly unable to write the haunting song of the Nereids. It is a large sea-shell which came from the beach of Salerno, picked up one evening from the mantelpiece in Nerval's room, that suddenly exerts its unsuspected spell over the despairing musician. He casually holds it to his ear, and what he hears is indescribable. He is hypnotized. Like a prehistoric phonograph, the shell has preserved the sound of miraculous voices, and there can be no doubt to whom they belonged. He rushes to the piano and tries to write down *"la divine clameur sexuelle"* of these women that followed the God of the Ocean. The floor is soon littered with sheets of paper, covered with vain attempts at a transcription of this incredible chant. At two o'clock in the morning Nerval, exhausted, gives up the quest; at four he begins to tremble with fever; at half past five he falls against the marble mantel — dead. The shell drops to the floor and breaks into a thousand splinters. The narrator ends with the question: *"Pourquoi riez-vous?"* and I almost believe that you are smiling, too. But that is my fault, due to my imperfect sketch of an astonishing tale. Read it and you will not laugh. More than that, you will understand the reason for this long preamble.

Supremely futile as it may appear to speculate on the sweetness of the Sirens' song, there is no denying that futile occupations have a charm peculiarly their own. I am inalienably attached to them, and I have long since learned that what my sterner friends brand as a "waste of time" are the happiest hours of my life. The story finished, I began to look into the ever-shifting flame, until my pupils seemed to burst my head, until my ears began to catch long-forgotten sounds, which the relentless tide of time and fleeting fashion had swept into the background of oblivion.

I realize that if I want to tell you something of my shadowy escapade, I must be very careful not merely to offer a long list of names and titles, plucked at random from the past. For the

graveyard of music is a spacious acre, and labyrinthian paths
wind through myriad rows of unremembered tombs. Many stones
have crumbled; they bear no longer the slightest trace of deed
or date. Too many, alas, of these graves are the tragic, though
well-deserved, repositories of still-born effort. Much music lies
buried there that never should have seen the light of day, that
never held a spark of life. Countless fresh mounts testify to an
ever-increasing mortality. On the other hand, there remains not
a little music that is enjoying an unnatural longevity. Ill-advised
performers and conductors drag it from the sick-room with the
fondness that some people have for exhibiting their decrepit relatives of remote birth. It should have been put by long ago. We
may be justly grateful if we never hear it.

But that the Sirens' song should have perished, unrecorded, is
certainly regrettable, in spite of its reputed dangerous effects.
Malicious tongues have it that the fatal consequences were due
to the extreme impurity of intonation indulged in by the ladies
— listeners preferring to commit self-murder rather than stand
the torture. This theory presupposes such an unreasonably superior sensitiveness on the part of ancient tars that I am wholly
disinclined to give it serious consideration. I deplore the loss of
all the music to which Greek mythology makes such frequent and
glowing reference. — And yet was not perhaps Arion overrated?
Would Orpheus in our day still work his magic? The widowed
bard charmed beast and tree; he dared descend to Hades. Would
he have the courage to step before that modern monster, a concert audience composed of critics and connoisseurs? — Hellas was
not the only place of musical prodigies. The ancient history of
the Hebrews tells of remarkable feats. What did the trumpets
blow that felled the walls of Jericho? Some learned Rosicru-
cian might possibly tell you that these destructive buglers carefully ascertained the "vibrations" of the city's mural defences,
and then lustily blew a chord which corresponded to their number.
Did King David, on his harp, use the little finger as well as the
others? What was it the Children of Israel refused to sing, by the
rivers of Babylon, when their captors required of them one of

the songs of Zion, and a song of mirth above all? — The answer
is difficult, perhaps impossible. Still, we are here no longer upon
entirely uncertain ground. Many of the traditional tunes preserved in the Jewish worship date from a dim and distant day.
Some of them are melodies of surpassing beauty and true Oriental line, though hardly the expression of great mirth. They
would suffice to make one feel, in looking backward over many
centuries of musical development, that there must have been
things for the disappearance of which we have good cause to be
sorry. We have not missed so much, perhaps, in not having heard
Nero sing his own odes with a wine-worn voice. He had spared
no effort to cultivate the art of singing and had placed himself in
the hands of Rome's ablest vocal instructors. Did he not, upon
the advice of one of these worthies, lie flat on his back for hours,
supporting the weight of heavy stones on his chest, to strengthen
the muscles of his diaphragm? It appears that the methods of
singing teachers have not materially changed throughout the ages.
It is difficult to conceive how Italy, how the whole of Europe,
could have offered these *maestri* a large enough field of operation,
if their countryman Columbus had not opportunely discovered
America for them. — I will confess that I would give much to
have heard Saint Cecilia extemporize upon the organ, if for no
other reason than to be able to disprove the contention of those
hypercritical historians who argue that the titulary saint of
music did not know one note from another, and that no Cavaillé-
Coll or Skinner existed in her day. Be that as it may, she was
fortunate in having the most famous artists idealize her in painting and sculpture, which gave her as much posthumous advertising as some of our living and constantly photographed organists
attain only by the ruthless dissemination of their innumerable
poses.

But let us take a short cut to yonder corner of the cemetery,
with its long tiers of urns, of table-tombs, of weeping angels,
shaded by willow trees and yews. It was not very long ago that
these names which now you can hardly distinguish were on
everybody's lips, were praised and worshipped. What are two

hundred years? They are enough to wipe out everything except a short, cold, matter-of-fact note in the biographical dictionary. The transitoriness of mundane glory is nowhere demonstrated with more cruel certainty than in the realm of arts and letters. Nature's law is unalterable. The stately sunflower that proudly raised its head must sooner or later fade and wither, like the violet, of proverbial modesty, that bloomed in a secluded nook and was content in pouring out its little soul of nectar. In fact, I am inclined to believe that, of the two, the violet's fate is, if anything, the less bitter. For though its perfume be but a memory, we are apt to keep it pressed between the leaves of a beloved book. The sunflower knows no such sentimental aftermath. Sparrows come and pick the seeds.

Charles VI, of the House of Habsburg, had succeeded his brother Joseph as Roman Emperor of the German Nations. He inherited not only a throne, but wars to wage and arts to cultivate. He neglected neither. The affairs of the Netherlands and of Spain having been settled, the Emperor, nine years after coming into power, decided to take formal possession of one of his most valuable crown-lands, and in 1723 he went to Prague for his coronation as King of Bohemia. To flatter the crowd and to impress the kings, his brothers, he planned to have the ceremonies attended by unusual pomp and brilliance. No function of this sort was complete without music, and it had to be music in its most regal form, the opera. Born at the court of Florence, the opera has always remained a princely offspring, notwithstanding all efforts to breed a species that would more nearly approximate popular taste, and that could be maintained by popular support alone. Charles was very fond of operas and had his private composer supply him with a new one whenever wanted. Johann Joseph Fux was undoubtedly an excellent musician, and Vienna had no other to compare with him. — In 1714 Fux wrote an opera, "Elisa," for the birthday of Charles's aunt, Archduchess Elizabeth Christina, which made a sensation. The Emperor was so pleased with the work that at the third performance — being himself a dilettante of no mean ability — he played the clavecin

in the orchestra, while the composer turned the pages. Fux, to
compliment his imperial master, remarked what a pity it was
that His Majesty had not become a *Kapellmeister*. But Charles is
said to have replied that he was perfectly satisfied with his position. — For the festivities in Prague, Fux, who was then sixty-
three years old, had written "Costanza e Fortezza." The Emperor had spared no costs in engaging the best singers of the day.
An orchestra of more than a hundred men had been assembled
from all over Europe, under the leadership of Caldara. Among
the violinists was Tartini. Quantz had come from Berlin to play
the flute. With him journeyed Weiss and Graun. Prague was
a beehive of musicians.[1] The excitement was great, for rumour had
it that Fux was too ill with the gout to leave Vienna. But the
Emperor would let no gout interfere with his plans to honour his
dear composer, and by his orders Fux was carried in a sedan-
chair all the way from the Donau to the Moldau capital. At the
gala performance, which took place in the open air, it was not the
Cardinal-Primate of Prague nor the Elector of Bavaria who sat
next to the newly-crowned King of Bohemia, but Johann Joseph
Fux, musician, with his feet bandaged in cotton. Quantz, to whom
we owe many sagacious observations on the music and musicians
of his time, wrote about this opera: "The composition is more
churchly than theatrical, but very splendid." Quantz did not care
very much for Tartini's playing. He admired the beautiful tone
and finished execution, but thought his style dry and lacking in
charm. Another violinist in the orchestra was Nicola Matteis,
who had written the ballet music interpolated in "Costanza e
Fortezza." Matteis was born in London, of an Italian father. In
1737, at Shrewsbury, he gave young Burney lessons in French
and in music. Burney tells us that he excelled in playing Corelli's sonatas. We still occasionally hear Corelli's "Follia." But of
Matteis's music there remains as little as of the many operas by

---

[1] "History does not furnish a more glorious event for music, than this
solemnity, nor a similar instance of so great a number of eminent professors
of any one art being collected together."—Dr. Charles Burney: "The Present
State of Music in Germany," etc., London, 1773, Vol. II.

the great Fux, in spite of the fact that Fux was probably one of the most celebrated men of his age, the author of a remarkable treatise on composition, printed at the Emperor's expense, a monumental work for any theorist to have written, long used as a text-book. Mozart and Haydn studied it.

I have mentioned Quantz. His long association with Frederick the Great is known. Frederick's passion for the flute was pathologic, as was his attachment to dogs. His greyhounds accompanied him on campaigns, following the King's travelling coach in a landau of their own, with two footmen in the back who were strictly enjoined not to address the royal favourites with the too familiar "thou." His flute was Frederick's inseparable companion, until he began to lose his teeth.

It is half past five in the afternoon. A rich sunset glow is painting fireworks upon the tall French windows of Sans-Souci, which rises serenely above the crest of its little hill. Quantz and Charles Philip Emmanuel Bach — more famous in his lifetime than his father — are slowly ascending the vine-covered terraces that lead to the castle. They are lost in conversation. On each new level they stand awhile and talk. Quantz is telling Bach of his trip to Italy, in 1725, and of his great admiration for old Alessandro Scarlatti, whom he visited in Naples and to whom he was introduced by Hasse. That name irritates Bach. He will have none of Hasse, even though the people go wild over his music, and though Philip V, at the Escurial, suffering from manic depression, can be induced to go to sleep, every night, only after hearing the glorious *castrato* Farinelli sing an aria from one of Hasse's operas. These tunes are superficial, too sugary and Italian. They will not live. *Musique à la mode* is ephemeral stuff. And as to the fabulous sum that Hasse and his wife, Faustina, are drawing at Dresden, it is preposterous. Quantz promptly changes the subject and tells of his love affair at Naples: how his life was threatened by a jealous rival, how he had to flee to Rome. They laugh — but the proximity of the august presence quickly stifles their merriment. Sentinels are posted on the highest terrace, lackeys flank the portals. Quantz and Bach enter the ante-

chamber and exchange greetings with the courtiers. It is only
petit cercle this evening. A member of the Academy of Berlin,
Dutchman by birth; an English officer, just arrived, the bearer of
a diamond-studded snuff-box with the miniature of George II
and a letter from His Britannic Majesty; a general of the
Guards, who fears the Austrian fire less than these musicales;
two chamberlains — and the illustrious Monsieur Voltaire. These
form the audience. No women. The subdued chatter in the antechamber continues while the King is heard preluding and prac-
tising scales, preparatory to the concert. At the stroke of six the
doors of the music-room open. Frederick, flute in hand, graciously
receives his bowing guests. The candles in the large glass chan-
delier sparkle in the hundreds of crystals. A silver candelabra is
placed on a little mahogany table next to Frederick's music-stand
of rosewood, inlaid with ivory, a present from his sister, the
Margravine of Bayreuth. The walls are decorated with lovely
boiseries, copied from the rooms of Louis at Versailles, on a side-
board stands a beautiful vase, the work of the young china-
manufactory of Berlin, in imitation of the Bourbons' older
Sèvres. And the French philosopher completes the setting for this
imported *Kultur.* Only the music is German, though that bears
strong transalpine traces. The programme consists of three concerti for flute and clavecin. The first and third are by Quantz.
The second is by the King; that is, he has sketched out the flute
part, and Agricola, pupil of Johann Sebastian Bach, has provided
the accompaniment. This is entrusted to Charles Philip Emmanuel Bach, playing one of the new "fortepianos" made by
Gottfried Silbermann. He has a hard task, since the King is somewhat absolutistic in his *tempi.* Quantz, unperturbedly, beats time.
But that is not his sole charge. The piece ended, he is the only
one who is permitted to say "bravo" or express any praise for
the royal flutist, it being taken for granted that all the other people present know less about flute-playing than he does. — Friedrich Christian Fasch, who after 1756 alternated with Bach every
month in accompanying the King, at his first appearance, un-
warned, burst into loud applause, which nearly cost him his posi-

tion. — After the third concerto has been finished, a few words are exchanged. The King has a jest for Voltaire, to which the Frenchman answers with an epigram. The English officer is the recipient of a kind word of thanks. Then the doors open again, and in the antechamber wait three couriers with dispatches from Silesia, Poland, and St. Petersburg. They turn with a click of their heels and spurs, and follow the King, who is humming the andante from the last concerto on the programme. And Quantz wrote something like three hundred for him!

Frederick had one great admirer — not as a flute-player, but as an engineer of battles — and that was Bonaparte. Napoleon visited the dead King's Sans-Souci, and the rock crystals on the lustre in the music-room gently trembled when the footstep that made Europe quake resounded in Frederick's sacrosanctum. That night Napoleon had his field-bed placed in the late King's chamber. Did he dream of flutes or flintlocks?

There are other questions relating to Napoleon and music that are still unanswered. Frédéric Masson, who investigated everything concerning the great Corsican, his person, family, household, and reign, including the price paid for his socks and razors, has left here a lacuna. It seems fairly well established, though, that Napoleon did not have real understanding or taste for music, but that he admitted its value, and even its necessity, in certain circumstances. He did not care for Cherubini; in fact, he harboured an unexplained animosity against him. But he affected the keenest admiration for Paër. After a performance of Paër's "Achilles" at Dresden, in 1806, Napoleon, with the right of the conqueror, claimed the composer from the King of Saxony and gave him a brilliant position. Paër had to follow the Emperor to Posen and organize musical entertainments between battles and diplomatic conferences, probably more because it looked well in the eyes of the awe-struck nations than on account of an unquenchable desire on Napoleon's part to be soothed by dulcet strains. He very seldom stayed for the whole of any concert given at the Tuileries. But at St. Cloud, among his family, he demanded, if he did not enjoy, "a little music." He liked to hear his stepdaughter and sister-in-law, Hortense, sing him Italian romances, which she accompanied herself. Hortense Beauharnais, wife of Louis Bonaparte, Queen of Holland, is said to have had a very pleasing voice, which she inherited from her mother, whose bad teeth and beautifully modulated speech were the occasion of much contemporary comment. Hortense even composed; at least, she is reputed to have written the well-known air *"Partant pour la Syrie"* in collaboration with Louis Drouet, a mere boy when he was made solo flutist to the King of Holland and "musical secretary to the Queen," later entering the services of Napoleon, and finally being transferred to Napoleon's sister, Pauline Borghese. His life was full of adventure; in 1854 he visited New York. Another sister of Napoleon, Elisa Bacciochi, had at her miniature court in Lucca no less a musical entertainer than Niccolo Paganini. He played three evenings a week. But he had to avoid harmonics. For Paganini's flageolets made poor, hysterical Elisa swoon.

There is one instance, however, where Napoleon showed serious preoccupation with music. It was the eve of his expedition to Egypt, shrouded in impenetrable mystery. With the thoroughness that marked everything he undertook, he wanted historians, scientists, artists, poets, and musicians to accompany him to the Pyramids. Arnault, in his "Souvenirs d'un Sexagénaire," tells of these elaborate preparations. Bonaparte had declared: *"Il nous faut un barde qui chante à la tête des colonnes."* Besides the poet and composer he wanted a singer. All three were to be attached to the First Consul's own person and were to receive six thousand francs each, in addition to their regular salary. Ducis pleaded old age, Méhul too much work, and Lays, with the star tenor's characteristic regard for the interests of the public, claimed that a sea voyage might cost him his voice. Méhul recommended Henri-Jean Rigel, *"habile professeur de piano,"* who conducted the opera installed at Cairo and gave there his own "Les Deux Meuniers" in 1799. The singer chosen was Guillaume André Villoteau, who had been choir boy, dragoon, student of medicine, and who achieved fame with his studies of the music and musical instruments of Egypt. What an enterprise, and what a stage-manager was Napoleon! Picture him on board the *Orient*, a night of Mediterranean splendour, his generals grouped around him, eager expectation in the mind of everybody, and Villoteau calmly singing an air from "Bélisaire," by Philidor, prolific opera-composer and champion chess-player of the world.

Méhul, whose setting of André Chénier's "Chant du Départ" was one of the grand songs of the Revolution, had obtained his release only by promising Napoleon that he would write march tunes for the French armies. Did he write any? What has become of them? Did Napoleon, on his white horse and in his green *chasseur* uniform, enter Berlin to the tune of one of them? When the circumspect Prussians returned the visit, they had provided a "Pariser Einzugsmarsch."

The whims of Bellona are strange. Napoleon, after three days of carnage at Leipzig, in October, 1813, saw his luck turn. He was beaten by his father-in-law, Emperor Franz of Austria, musical amateur and quartet fiend. Franz entered the city, which the fleeing French were leaving, with the remark that at last he would find leisure to play a little chamber music again. The imperial quartet was always behind the firing line. At the head of it — if there could be another head than the Emperor himself — was Franz Krommer. Born in 1759, he was only three years younger than Mozart and he survived Beethoven by four years. Showing in his early youth great talent for the violin, he was brought up and kept by the munificence of rich noblemen, until he obtained a sinecure at the Viennese court, in 1812, as "doorkeeper of the royal bedchamber." In 1814 he was named *Hofkapellmeister*, a title which has covered a multitude of mediocrities. But Krommer was by no means considered such in his lifetime. On the contrary, he enjoyed the greatest popular favour. He was the composer of chamber music *par excellence*. He is responsible for no less than twenty-two string quintets and more than sixty string quartets. While Beethoven's quartets were understood and lauded by a few, Krommer's were played literally wherever four people got together to scrape the catgut, and, in those days, that meant everywhere. Quartet-playing, in the period of transition from clavecin to hammer-klavier, from Silbermann to Erard, had become an epidemic. It was the house music of rich and poor, of cultured and simple folk. Musicians played Mozart, Haydn, and Boccherini. Amateurs had Rosetti, Fesca, the two Rombergs, Gyrowetz — the last of whom wrote thirty symphonies and seventy works of chamber music, lived from 1763 to 1850, and dismissed Beethoven, Weber, and Schubert as "chaotic." They had furthermore Pleyel, Rode, Neubauer, and Onslow — poor Onslow, the prototype of the highly cultivated and refined composer, the pet of society, admired for his "originality," called to succeed Cherubini at the Institut de France, and soon forgotten. Musical history is full of Onslows!

We can hardly conceive how difficult it was for Beethoven to break up this cohort of quartettists, and it is not surprising that these difficulties should have made him feel disappointed and embittered. H. W. Riehl vouches for the truth of the story according to which both Krommer and Beethoven were guests, one evening, at Count Lichnowsky's palace in Vienna. During the opening number of the programme, a quartette by Krommer, Beethoven showed such undisguised contempt for the less gifted but more popular colleague, by talking and sneering, that the host had to take him to task.

Among the many stars of various magnitudes that studded the musical firmament of Vienna at the beginning of the nineteenth century, there was none perhaps who with a gentle little twinkle succeeded in producing as dazzling effects as did Sigismund Neukomm. Josef Haydn had been a father to him and taught him all that could be taught. After journeys in Sweden and Russia, Neukomm arrived in Paris about 1812. Talleyrand, the Machiavellian, who was the only one to see beyond Napoleon, had just lost his private pianist, Johann Ladislaus Dussek. Friends recommended young Neukomm, and he obtained the position. Talleyrand became very fond of him. He took him along to the Congress of Vienna, and there a Requiem for Louis XVI, composed by Neukomm, was sung at St. Stephen's before an audience of kings and princes. Several hundred singers took part in this memorable performance. And to think that for such an occasion no worthier composer could be found! Neukomm travelled much. He went to Brazil, in 1816, with the Prince of Luxembourg, Ambassador of France. In 1826, he saw Italy. Walter Scott met him the year after. He accompanied Talleyrand to London in 1830, and liked England so well that he settled there. He visited Algiers, Constantinople, Greece, and was on the point of embarking for New York when sudden illness overtook him in Manchester. He probably wrote more than one thousand compositions. To this day, the Universal Catalogue of Pazdirek contains three full pages listing works by Neukomm which were evidently published at some time or other. Neukomm wrote songs and choruses to texts in German, French, Latin, Russian, Italian, Bohemian, Portuguese, and English. Have you ever heard anyone sing them? Fétis, who saw him in London and later, in his travels, at Paris and Munich, unwittingly pronounces judgment over this amiable, generous, tactful man by calling him *"un artiste respectable."* In the fight for the fittest the respectable artist has slight chances to survive.

Fétis, the incomparable lexicographer, in his arduous researches must have been appalled by the number of respectable artists he encountered, and by the vast quantity of their music which is hardly remembered by name and of which never a note will sound again. And since he laid down his pen, the amount has grown incessantly. But there are things that Fétis heard which we shall never hear, and which we may well envy him. Should you not like to have been at Lord Saulton's, in 1829, the night when Fétis accompanied at the piano Henriette Sontag and Marie Malibran, who sang a duet from Rossini's "Semiramide"? I should. And I should have liked to have seen Henriette's, then Countess Rossi's, return to Covent Garden in Donizetti's "Linda di Chamounix," when the Grand Duchess of Strelitz, Princess of Cambridge, had secretly commanded London society to be in their seats at the opera when the overture began, and to rise to their feet when the star appeared. That night, between the acts, even old Wellington, the Iron Duke, hobbled behind the scenes to kiss the tips of Henriette's fingers.

The romance of great singers is a fascinating tale retold on a thousand nights and one. There are lesser lights with whom I should be fully contented, if only they would shine into the dark and dusty recesses where gems are hidden and are persistently overlooked for the sake of obvious and tawdry Brummagem that basks in the sun of popular approval. Shall I ever hear Schumann's "Im Zwielicht" and "Auf einer alten Burg"? When will singers realize that the loveliest of Fauré's songs are not among the scant half-dozen which form the sum of their exploring? Singers would derive greater help from looking into a geographical atlas than from the study of publishers' announcements.

A recent recital programme contained a song by Augusta Holmès, once a sure winner, now but seldom sung. It recalled to mind the rôle she played in the life of Henri Regnault, the painter with a tenor voice. Regnault had twice unsuccessfully competed for the *Prix de Rome*. His third attempt, in 1866, was threatening to be another failure, when one evening, during the *concours*, he met at Mme. de Sainbris's the young composer whose strange and lovely physiognomy captivated him. He made two sketches of her that night and in twelve days he completed the painting "Thetis handing the arms to her son Achilles," and the goddess bore the traits of Augusta Holmès. He won the coveted prize. The letters which he wrote to his father and friends from the Villa Medici contain several passages on musical matters in Rome. Camille Saint-Saëns, who used to delight the circle at Regnault's studio in Paris by playing for hours from the scores of Wagner, had sent to his friend, in April, 1867, a "Veni Creator," in manuscript, with the request that Regnault submit it to Abbé Liszt. Regnault describes his visit with a painter's sensibility. He relates how he rang the bell and felt his heart thump as if he were at the door of the dentist. The grand old man received him with *une amabilité charmante,* praised the motet, and then played excerpts of his own "Dante" and his "Tasso." Regnault was in the seventh heaven. Who would not have been, in his place? There is an account of an amusing incident in a letter written in January, 1868, when the painter was very much occupied with his first *envoi*, "Automedon and the horses of Achilles," which now hangs in the Boston Museum. Regnault says: "My little director" — the painter Hébert — "asked me last Sunday to render him a service which, I confess, cost me a great deal and did not fit in at all with my present state of mind. He had asked the French Ambassador to dinner, together with sundry duchesses, countesses, and the like. He was to entertain them, in the evening, with a concert of chamber music, performed by the best players of Rome. But the musicians were obliged to attend a rehearsal at the Teatro Apollo that night. M. Hébert, in his distress, and dreading to see his guests sitting round in the salon yawning, begged me to assume the burden of entertaining his company and to replace the instrumentalists. Although I was in no mood to appear in public, I did my best, so as not to spoil the party. *On a été satisfait.*" That is true modesty, befitting a real artist. What did Regnault sing for his illustrious hearers? Surely a song by Augusta, most likely one by his friend Camille, and possibly one by Emile Pessard, whose portrait sketch he made in 1868. Nor was this the only occasion on which he sang publicly. In March of the same year he sang the tenor part in a requiem mass at the church of Saint-Louis des Français, in Rome, for the unveiling of a monument to the memory of his fellow student Deschamps. All the other singers were professionals. *"Les premiers chanteurs et les plus forts instrumentistes de Rome prêtaient leur concours et il s'agissait de ne pas faire rougir l'Académie de son ténor. L'église était remplie, et bon nombre d'étrangers avaient été conviés. Tout a bien marché, dit-on. Nous nous sommes couverts de gloire."* There is just and pardonable pride in that remark. More glory would have been his had not a Prussian bullet, perhaps the last one fired before the walls of Paris in 1871, killed the patriot, silenced that *"voix si douce et si pénétrante,"* as Arthur Duparc called it, and robbed the world of an astonishing painter, whose genius had hardly begun to develop.

Melancholy as these retrospects may be, the thought is even

sadder that it will not be possible for us to hear all that the future holds in store. Mingled with this regret there is also something of disquietude. Thomas Alva Edison has delivered us into the hands of posterity. We shall stand utterly revealed, from "That Chicken Pie" to Caruso's *Che gelida manina*. What will music be like in a hundred years, when the phonographic records of our luminaries, kept sealed in the vaults of the Paris Opera, are solemnly turned on? Ah, if one could hear ahead!

WHY DO WE DANCE?

Le pantalon
De Toinon
N'a pas de fond.
(Text of the celebrated "Pantalon")

IT WOULD seem fatuous, in one so destitute of Terpsichorean accomplishments as I am, to attempt a discourse on the dance. Far be it from me to feign an authoritative air in speaking of the technical side of dancing as an art. Pleasurably moved or keenly stirred by performers on the "light fantastic toe," and heartily appreciative of the eccentric or riotously gorgeous spectacles that modern ballets offer us, I must plead ignorance of the completest sort when it comes to *"entrechats," "pirouettes,"* and *"chassez-déchassez."* I might as well confess that I am no dancer at all, and that I am equally unqualified to pronounce myself on the relative superiority of the "fox-trot" over the "turkey-trot," particularly as I suspect that the remembered store of my zoological and ornithological studies would be of small consequence in settling so delicate a matter. What I am in quest of are the physiological and psychological principles that underlie the quickened and accentuated movements of the human body, commonly associated with dancing.

This may seem, offhand, a forbiddingly dry and unimaginative way of approaching a subject that is sheer animation and fancy. Yet, in the last analysis, the value of all so-called historic or scientific investigation depends not alone on the establishing of more or less authenticated facts; their presentation and interrelation can gain coherence and reality only when they become amalgamated by an added pinch of "such stuff as dreams are made of." Perhaps it may appear, in the end, that I have helped myself rather generously to that precious ingredient. But let it not be forgotten that in curiously probing the past and questioning the future, we resemble the tourist who is climbing a mountain. We ascend the foothills and gaze on the plain; we rise to the highlands, whence we can see the valleys and trace some of the rivers to their sources. From the loftier peaks we can make out the distant sea; but alas! on reaching the summit, eager to set our eyes upon the farther shore, we find nothing but shimmering mists and vapours at our feet. So shall I ask the reader to follow me, in discussing the dance, from the level of substantiated fact, over the crags of scientific hypothesis, to an altitude of vague and cloudy, though none the less absorbing, speculation.

Let us, then, look first for the physiological basis of dancing.

The quickened and accentuated movements, to which I have referred, spring from the normal walk or the natural gestures of a human being. However, unlike the ordinary walk or actions, they are not prompted by a utilitarian motive, that seeks the accomplishment of some ulterior purpose, such as the walking toward a definite goal or the handling of a specific implement. In order to constitute a dance these movements must be an end in themselves, and must, above all, be governed by ordered progress, or rhythm. By rhythm we understand a periodicity of movement, noticeable to our senses as recurrence of visible events or patterns, or as repetition of audible or sensible accents and beats. Such beats are also called "pulses," a word derived from the Latin noun *pulsus,* to which the ancient Romans attached such diverse meanings as to use it in connection with blood-circulation and breathing; with the motion of feet and oars; with incentive to will and imagination; and finally with such widely but regularly spaced occurrences as the solstice.

In order to realize how all-pervading this periodicity of movement is, we need only remember the measured circuit of the stars, the round of the seasons, the alternation of day and night, of tidal ebb and flow. It is the kernel of all such phenomena as sound, as electric currents of varying frequency; we follow this pulsating or vibratory motion, as it becomes more and more rapid, through the different stages in which it appears to us as heat of increasing intensity, then as light and colour, continuing to about 750,000 billions of rhythmic oscillations per second, which are needed to produce that sombre effluence known as the ultra-violet ray of the solar spectrum. Science has gone beyond this point, although much that lies behind it remains still unexplored. What we know to be a certainty is that, in whatever direction we may look — toward the infinitely large or infinitesimally small movement in this world — everywhere we detect some form of ordered progress, or rhythm.

Is it, then, to be wondered at that man is built on a similar plan? His heart-beat, his breathing, his walk, under healthy conditions, are rhythmic. The mainspring of the human organism, like that of a watch, must keep strict time! We have not, as yet, gained a clear insight into the subtle connections between the law of rhythm and those of gravitation and maintained energy. But it is more than likely that the reasons which make rhythm essential to man hold good for the whole universe, and that nothing can better explain the omnipresence of rhythm than its economic or, if I may term it so, its conservant and labour-saving properties. These beneficent attributes of rhythm are, consciously or subconsciously, guiding every step we take, every move we make.

It was a momentous day in the evolution of man when he discovered that by regular — that is, rhythmic — motion he obtained an automatic movement of whatever limb he used in his work, eliminating thereby the necessity of mental exertion in the control of muscular effort (a thing doubly hard for primitive man). He learned to save his strength, and found that rhythm made work easier. The manual labour of man, as an individual and especially in a group, is unthinkable without adherence to rhythmic precision. Thus the Malays row to the sound of tam-tams; the Arabs pound their coffee to the hum of a rhythmic drone; in China even the whipping of culprits was regulated by the beat of an accommodating drum. In the museum of the Louvre there is a little terra-cotta of very old Greek origin which shows four women

DANCE IN A CEMETERY—(*XVIth Century*)

kneading dough to the accompaniment of a flute-player. And to this day, domestic, agricultural, or industrial labour obeys this rhythmic law.

The concentration of group effort can be achieved only by sounds which succeed each other at regular intervals and emphasize a rhythm that is felt individually, by each worker, and is responded to simultaneously, by all of them. Witness the sailors' chanties, the marching-songs of soldiers. These practices date back, undoubtedly, to a dim and distant past, when they were even more needful than they are in our motor-driven age. We find a curious instance in Athenæus, according to whom the trumpeter Herodorus of Megara, at the siege of Argos, had the power of animating the troops so much, by sounding two trumpets at a time, as to enable the soldiers to move a ballistic machine close to the rampart, which they had in vain attempted to do for several days before, on account of its enormous weight. Now, the playing of one man on two trumpets, contrary to Athenæus's inference, had no part in the success of this exploit. It was the trumpeter's signal, or rather his repeated signals, that enabled the men to work *in concert* at their military engines, for want of which signals their previous efforts had been scattered and ineffective.

And here I should like the reader to ponder what I believe a possible answer to the puzzling question of what the trumpets blew that had such disastrous effect on the walls of Jericho. In an age that knew not the use of steam or electricity, and in which the simplest mechanical devices were comparatively undeveloped, the only method of moving heavy objects, such as battering rams, was by the combined force of a great number of hands, timing their muscular impulse to given signals. And thus the signal probably came to stand for the action ruled by it. Therefore the trumpets circling seven times round the mural defences of Jericho must have meant that the battering rams had to be applied seven times to various parts of the fortifications before the conquering breach was made. This knowledge and rational view of what has long been allowed to pass as a miracle does not materially add to the sum of human happiness, but there is a certain solace in what is more than a suspicion — namely, that the age of wonders probably never existed, or has not yet begun — which for all practical purposes of the present is the same.

That rhythm should exercise this regulating power over the movements of the human body lies primarily in the fact that the rhythmic sense is innate in man and that any appeal to this sense is not only general, but contagious. Herewith we turn from the physiological to the psychological properties of rhythm. The infectiousness of rhythm may be observed, with mingled feelings, at orchestral concerts when some misguided enthusiast, seated behind us, is tapping with his foot an obvious measure against our chair. Nor are these "assistant conductors" the most musical members of the audience. On the contrary, the rhythmic pleasure derived from hearing music is the lowest form of satisfaction that this art is able to afford. Savage tribes, as a rule, content themselves, for what we might call "musical entertainment," with hammering on all sorts of drums, the beats ranging from a simple and stolid repetition to a remarkably involved and furiously aggressive metre.

Thus we see that rhythmic motions of the body have their physiological foundation in being natural and helpful to man. This contributes again to the fact that they are also pleasurable. But pleasure is not the sole nor the first psychological motive for dancing. This pleasure, consciously sought and found, is of a higher order only when the rhythmic motions of the body become eurhythmic — that is, when they follow some æsthetic ideal and assume the character and responsibilities of an art. Primarily, these dance motions are, as I have said, merely emphasized gestures. And, as such, they are nothing but the bodily reflex of heightened emotions, or affects. As our emotions are directly influencing our heart-action, by quickening or accentuating our pulse, so do they react upon the quickened or accentuated movements of the body. In these bodily gestures which are inseparable from certain affects, I would place the origin of all dances. Awe, fear, anger, joy, lust, are accompanied by movements of the body indicative of the particular affect that causes them. Each affect, according to its nature, inevitably throws the body into an attitude of attack or defence, into a motion of shrinking from, or grasping for, an object or person. Granted that dancing is nothing but a deviation from our walk under normal conditions, and takes on more or less the form of skipping and jumping, let us remember that the horse, when frightened, no longer walks, but jumps; that the dog, in anger or joy, skips about and rises on its hind legs; that in mating-time the restlessness of certain animals leads them to perform what for want of a better term we can only call a dance. It is to heightened affects, then, that we must trace the psychological roots of dancing. And the next conclusion, supported by the theories of modern psychology, is that — *vice versa* — agitated movements of the body will induce a corresponding state of agitated emotion.

Now, the elementary emotions, such as awe, fear, anger, joy, love, must be occasioned in man by his relation to a source or cause outside of himself. I should class these affects or emotions, according to three chief sources, as resulting from the relation of:

1. man to the supernatural, or God;
2. man to man;
3. man to woman.

This leads to a classification of dancing into its three great groups; namely:

1. religious dances — to worship or placate a deity, or to incite an ecstasy of spirit in the dancers;
2. war dances — to intimidate an enemy, or to incite a heightened aggressiveness in the dancers;
3. profane dances — to further the relations between the sexes, or to incite a greater passion in the dancers.

Everything that has been called "dance" in the history of mankind may be referred to one of these three groups. And in each instance the psychological motive becomes self-apparent by the very character of the dance.

There remain, however, two interesting questions not answered by this classification. One is, why the first and third of these groups show recurrent tendencies toward degenerating; the second, why these tendencies should coincide with periods during which the live forces of humanity are subjected to extraordinary drain. In touching upon these problems, one is tempted to ask whether the dance in its acutest form and ultimate purpose is not really a reflex or stimulus of the strongest and most fundamental desire in man: his hunger for individual projection of life, the instinct of race-preservation in the masses.

Is it a secret aim of Nature, in times when our life-blood is ebbing too fast, to repair the waste by arousing this hunger, this instinct, more strongly, more brutally, and, one might say, more shamelessly? It is certain that whenever the need of new vitality seems greatest, the passions are permitted to hold full sway in a dance that disregards all our acquired notions of propriety, that grows into a manic obsession. Let us inquire into the history of the three groups of dances, with particular regard to these tendencies.

Sacred pageants seem to be as old as the first devotional rites of man, dedicated to that mysterious being which ordered life and death, ruled the thunder, sent rain or drought, and bound the heavens to the earth with a luminous rainbow. Whatever visible image men gave to this mighty power, they were awed by it into a kneeling posture of humility, their bodies writhed in fear, or, moving round in stately procession, they offered thanks and praise to their master. Before the black bull Apis, symbol of creative productivity and fertility, the priests of Egypt, in their strange attire, performed a cadenced round, as the stars encircle the sun, giver of life, ripener of all fruit. Down to the earliest religious demonstrations we can retrace this interplay of sex instinct and mystic aspirations, seeking expression in rhythmic movements of the body and gradually degenerating into a lascivious dance. And why? Religion is prompted by dread of unfathomable death; it always unites with a spiritual promise of happiness or solace the command to fight the forces of destruction by perpetuating life. "Be fruitful and multiply" is the supreme bidding of Nature. And, whenever necessary, all religions

seem to have adopted ways of heightening that incentive to prolong life after death, not in painting supernal realms where the
soul is supposed to dwell, but in a demand for the material, and
to Nature more important, survival in the progeny of the flesh.

Take the Hebrews leaving Egypt. Led by the wisdom and
counsel of Moses, they succeeded in fording the Red Sea; and the
waves that closed in behind them not only shut them off from
their pursuers, but seem to have cut them off from the rest of the
world, for all eternity. When this handful of men and women,
exhausted from the hardships of their exodus, were giving thanks
to the Lord who saved them from slavery, Miriam, the sister of
Moses, and all the women joined in a dance that must have
fired the blood of those men, must have made them forget the
dangers that lay behind them, the uncertainty they were facing,
and must have whetted their appetite for life, the everlasting
hunger of the race to eternize itself in its children, a hunger that
nobody needed more than that isolated lot of Jews. And this is
not the only instance of dancing related in the Old Testament,
though it is the first and by far the most significant.

Although we have many pictorial records of dances as practised in the early days of Grecian civilization, on mural friezes,
in Tanagra statuettes, and especially on vases, we have no clear
idea concerning the famous mysteries of Eleusis. It was a religious ceremonial in honour of Ceres — goddess of fertility —
lasted for nine days, included various processions and dances, and
culminated in an awe-inspiring rite, which undoubtedly aimed to
arouse the two dominant desires of man, for the immortality of
soul and of body. The festivities and dances held in honour of
Bacchus unquestionably turned into orgies. The Feast of Apollo,
the Feast of Oxen, the Feast of the Earth, the Triumph of Pallas
over Neptune, and countless others were celebrated with dancing.
Every family event, every public function of a religious nature,
was an occasion for exhibitions of the dance. There were dances
which, according to Plato, had that character of gentleness, gravity, and nobility suitable to the expression of the sentiments with
which a mortal should be permeated when he invokes the gods.

There was one dance, the Endymatia, which called for brilliant trappings, was performed in public and in private, and — we are told — "sometimes lost its sacred character." The Hormos, dedicated to Diana, was danced by youths of both sexes, unclothed, but their movements, as became the cult of the chaste huntress, gave no offence to modesty, their attitudes were purely intended to show to their fairest advantage the beautiful lines of perfect human bodies, warmed by the radiant skies of Hellas. These dances were instituted by Lycurgus, the great Spartan legislator. Plutarch tells us that when Lycurgus was reproached for the nudity of the women, he answered: "I wish them to perform the same exercises as men, that they may equal men in strength, health, virtue, and generosity of soul, and that they may learn to despise the opinion of the vulgar." A rather arrogant way of putting it. Nor can one quite repress a feeling that behind the wish of Lycurgus there was the will of Nature.

Since time immemorial funerals were made occasions for dances. In Greece the body was carried to the pyre, preceded by a dancing priest, accompanied by dancing relatives and friends, mourned by hired wailing women who simulated grief and tears. Not only in antiquity, throughout the Middle Ages we encounter funeral dances, meet with turning pairs in cemeteries, find the mourners carousing at the wake. And here again it seems that the presence of death releases in man subconsciously the impulse for preservation and continuation, which is the very foil of death. A civil engineer belonging to the Suez Canal Commission, who visited the Nile countries in 1855, described a funeral at Derr, the capital of Nubia:

The son of the Cadi had just died. We arrived three hours after his death, at the moment he was about to be buried. The population had assembled, the men on one side, smoking their tshibouks, the women further on, emitting moans; all were crouching on the ground, dressed in their best. They began by washing the corpse; then it was placed in a shroud and covered with a burial cloth, which is of a reddish colour. During this time, the tarabouk resounded, accompanying dances which were executed by the women.

Here, too, by the open grave, that curious appeal to the senses of life!

The Romans had their sacred dances, as had the Greeks. Even to the meagre beginnings of their great epoch we can trace religious ceremonies in which dancing had its part. King Numa Pompilius founded the order of Salian priests, whose duty it was to honour the gods with dances. But in Rome, more quickly than in Greece, these performances lost their pure and modest character, and dancing in general tended to gratify an increasing demand for pleasure and obscenity. The history of Rome offers abundant proof that dancing degenerates whenever the vital forces of a race need replenishing. For corroborative evidence we need not look only to the days of decline. As early as the year 364 after its foundation, when the city was ravaged by pestilence, this reaction set in with a desperate abandonment to dancing, approved and recommended by divine oracles. Ancient Rome was not devoid of prudes who condemned dancing as frivolous and wished it confined to professional performers. That was in the days of supremacy and health. When the cancer of Oriental mollification and megalomaniac expansion began to destroy the nerves of the Empire, weakened by the drain of incessant war, the dance took its place at the head of all diversions. Ammianus Marcellinus relates of the imperial days that once, when a famine was raging, all foreign philosophers, orators, and teachers were ordered to leave the city, while three thousand foreign dancing girls [1] were permitted to remain. But not even they could stay

---

[1] The dancing girls from Gades (Cadiz) were especially famous, and, according to Martial's testimony, their peculiar prowess was such that it is easily perceived why no Roman "Midnight Frolic" was complete without them:

> Nec de Gadibus improbis puellæ
> Vibrabunt sine fine prurientes
> Lascivos docili tremore lumbos.
>
> Lib. V, epigr. lxxix.

the fall of Roman dominion on earth, nor of the Roman gods above.

The Moslem and Hindu religions are unthinkable without their preponderance of dancing. And these dances, especially, are apt to take on a libidinous character. For are we not here in the countries of perpetual floods and famine, in the very lair of the Plague? The sacred dancers of India, the Ramdjeniy, sway in undulating rhythm over the floor of polished marble; their arms seem to stretch toward the far-off, invisible god in a gesture of desire. The air is rich with the scent of crushed blossoms; the weird sound of incantations, accompanied by strange instruments, re-echoes from the dimly lighted temple walls on which the gods are represented in appalling hideousness or monstrosity. Rousselet, in his book "L'Inde des Rajahs," speaks of the festival of "Holi," in honour of the goddess of spring, as "feasts of frenzied debauch, knowing no shame, and raised to the dignity of a cult. The dancing girls have for these holidays particular dances, in which all decency is disregarded."

Mohammedanism has its dancing Dervishes. The founder of the sect is said to have turned round his axis for forty days without stopping, to the sound of a flute, to be rewarded at the end of the fortieth day, when he dropped unconscious to the ground, by what we are told was divine ecstasy. What an inhuman price to pay for even so rare a pleasure!

In Algeria we find a religious sect the horrible rites of which call to mind the orgiastic furor of the Bacchantes, those dancing priestesses who in Greece and Rome brought licentiousness to a degree that taxes even modern imagination. In an atmosphere saturated with incense, to a music that becomes more and more strident and vertiginous, these Algerians gyrate until they fall senseless to the floor, when they add to the barbarism of their performance by self-torture and self-mutilation.

This strange combination of the religious and sex-complex is here taking on a form of perversity known in psychiatry as "masochism." And masochism is at the bottom of that peculiar religious mania of the "flagellants" who at various times, during

Dieß liebli@man foll Frölich bey Saures Vögelten ma@en
Emfaldi gut wei@e thl. dem@ fi@ fein@ La@en.

Bereillen Preulligtat, und mit ben fich Gebehren.
Betreiden fei beym Tanck, wer gläu@rölicm wolmt werden.

Be Reichheläut in Tank Tenk Tenk brau@ mu@e S@willen.
Sie find der bälte Mu@ derien me Grülliet Reiller.

CARICATURE OF PEASANTS SEIZED WITH
DANCING MANIA—(*XVIIth Century*)

the Middle Ages, moved in ghastly processions through the countries of Europe. First organized in 1056, vainly prohibited by the authorities, these large congregations of men, girded with ropes, marched through the streets of one city after another, to the rhythmic cadence of lugubrious chants, and with ecstatic gestures scourged their naked breasts and shoulders, until the blood was dripping in the mire of the road. Italy, Austria, Hungary, and Poland resounded with their agonized psalmody. They existed in southern France, under the name of *"blancs battus,"* down to the reign of Henry III. That jaded and weary monarch first encountered these processions when on a visit to Avignon. He was so fascinated by what the old chronicler terms *"ces comédies indécentes"* that he decided to prolong his stay in the city. Finally he became himself a convert to these sanguinary excesses, introduced them in Paris, where the gentlemen and ladies of the court, with the Duchess of Montpensier at their head, paraded through the town in scant attire and wielding murderous scourges in their hands, but doing themselves little harm, beyond an unnecessary exposure to the dangers of catching cold.

It is a far cry from those ambulatory orgies of religious maniacs to the gay farandoles of the Provençals, yet the echo is clear and unmistakable. They are nocturnal dance-processions, made more mysterious by the flaming torches that leave a trail of heavy smoke to mingle with the dust, stirred up by stamping feet; and smoke and dust — before they slowly settle in the distance — have covered with their double veil the chain of agitated couples, whose whispered pledges and confessions are drowned by the strident *galoubet* and the relentless *tambourin.*

Long before the Middle Ages the dance had found a place in Christian worship. Tertullian, who embraced Christianity about the year 190, is our main authority for the fact that the first Christians, persecuted and always in the shadow of martyrdom, danced in singing their sacred hymns and canticles. This practice was never quite abolished until it had degenerated and had lost its religious character, so that the bishops had to prohibit it.

Father Ménéstrier, who in 1682 published a most interesting book on the dances of antiquity and of his day, wrote:

I myself have seen the canons take the choir boys by the hand in some churches on Easter day, and dance in the church, singing hymns of thanksgiving, to say nothing of the scandalous customs, introduced by the simplicity of past centuries, but so corrupted by libertinism that not only have severe laws been necessary for their suppression, but much care and zeal on the part of our prelates to banish these dangerous abuses from their dioceses.

In the Cathedral of Seville, to this day, the choir boys perform their historic dance, dressed in quaint costumes of the time when their privilege was sanctioned by a Bull of Pope Eugenius IV, in 1439.[1]

Within the last century the "Holy Rollers" in America, and the "Jumpers" in Australia, have made some sort of rhythmic bodily exercise the chief part of their religious worship (owing perhaps again to conditions similar to those which the Jews had to face after crossing the Red Sea). Nevertheless, there is no dancing in our present churches. Nor does Nature require it of the church. For that edifice has lost the significance it possessed up to the late Middle Ages, when it stood for the great civic centre of the community. Michelet calls the mediæval church *"ce domaine du peuple."* It is no longer so. From the church the dance in its "acutest" form has long since migrated to what later

---

[1] The Baron Pöllnitz, who visited Spain during the reign of Philip V and was in Madrid about 1725, wrote in his memoirs: "There were Processions during the Easter Week, when the Holy Sacrament was carry'd to the Sick: The Streets and Balconies were on this Occasion hung with Tapestry: The Sacrament, which was carry'd under a Canopy, was preceded by a great Number of Priests and Friars, who had all Wax-Tapers in their Hands: There was also a numerous Symphony, and a great many Dancers, in Masks of several Sorts, leaping and playing Gambols with Castanets snapping in their Hands: And in this manner they danc'd before the Holy Sacrament, and continued it even in the Church, till such time as the Benediction was pronounced."

became the true domain of the people — namely, the theatre and the public dance-hall.

But before we turn to these places, let us briefly review the second and least interesting type of dances, those of a warlike character. These exhibitions, which I have ascribed to a desire to intimidate an enemy or incite *"une belle fureur"* in the dancers, were very popular in ancient times and are still so among uncivilized aborigines of the black and the red races. Greek youths, before going into battle, or to commemorate a day of victory, put on their armour and performed a dance which developed into a simulated combat. We find the same thing later on in Rome. Something of this spirit survived in the tournaments and pageantry of knighthood, and, reduced to more prosaic but perhaps as efficacious a practice, we see it in the exercises and drills to which our present generation of strenuous and neurotic business men submit at the gymnasium. It is the prototype of all athletic sport. But what might still be called a "war-dance" was known as recently as in the days of Napoleon I, whose "Grognards" are pictured in a coloured lithograph of the period as hopping round much after the fashion of the Sioux or Chippewas, with an attentive audience of other warriors yelling encouragement to the least graceful of Terpsichorean artists. You may ask why our boys and the "tommies" and *poilus* did not seem to need that sort of exhilaration before attacking the enemy. As a matter of fact, they needed and received similar exhilaration, but more in the form of relaxation than as an incentive to greater ardour. And that is probably due to the fact that the character of warfare has so much changed. Armies no longer meet on the battlefield by special arrangement and personal invitation of the generals. The note of chivalrous competition has vanished. It is a matter of cunning, of brutality, or surprise and fiendish engines. Yet the horrors of carnage made, on the eve of battle, the call of passion and the dance for pleasure's sake only the more irresistible.

There remains the third and last group of dances, those frankly intended for entertainment only, of purely profane character, a social diversion, and as such reflecting sharply the societies of different epochs and climates. The degree of licentiousness exhibited in profane dances, throughout the ages, varies according to the economic situation and the political fortunes of the times. The more desperate the aspect of either, the lower the level of decorum. By way of proving this thesis, it may be the straighter course to single out the periods of greater hardship and mortality, and to show how they affected dancing.

I have mentioned the visitation of Rome by the pest, in 364, and its consequences. There exist striking analogies between these consequences and the conditions that attended the first appearance of Asiatic cholera in the countries of Europe, in 1349. "The Black Death" — as the malady was then called — had begun to sweep westward out of China; wider and ever wider became its devastation; no precautions, no remedies seemed to stay its murderous progress. News travelled slowly in those days, and the tales of horror had hardly time to precede the fearful visitant himself. Hygiene was unknown. Superstition reigned everywhere. As village after village, town after town, fell a prey to this pestilence, the people of Europe were seized with terror and religious hysteria. The water of the well, the fruit on the tree, the air itself seemed poisoned. The rich and the poor alike succumbed hopelessly and helplessly to this "Avenging Angel." By the time the epidemic had reached Germany, the populace was dying by the millions. The dead could not be buried fast enough. The horrors beggared description. The "Last Judgment" seemed at hand, and the wrath of God ready to exterminate the human race. In the passiveness of their despair, people gave up all efforts to resist this plague, and thereby naturally augmented the danger. At the point of deepest, direst misery, what is it that suddenly kindles the expiring flame of life, whips the flagging forces of humanity into a ghastly but magnificent assertion of their will to live? It is the dance, the fury of dancing! Unbelievable scenes occurred, as recounted by an eyewitness in the famous "Limburg Chronicle." This is, in part, the story:

Anno 1374, in the middle of summer, there was a strange thing

to be seen on Earth, particularly in Teuton Lands, along the
Rhine and the Moselle, namely that people began to dance and
to rave, turning in pairs in one place for half a day, and danced
until they fell to the ground. Thereby they expected to be cured,
and went from one town to another, and they collected money.
And matters became so bad that in Cologne more than 500 people were found dancing. And it was declared a heresy, as it was
done for money, and as many men and women were led by it
into immoral intercourse. For in Cologne alone more than a hundred women and girls were found with men not their husbands.
All of these women were with child as a result of these dances.

And here again, as so often in history, we see the Church
foolishly and vainly trying to step into the path of Nature, by
combating the very means that Life is forced to adopt in an
heroic effort to stem the overwhelming tide of Death. But the
religious authorities are not alone in their blindness to the causes
and effects of those extraordinary conditions. The historians, too,
feel compelled blushingly to register their disapproval. A remark
of F. de Mesnil in his "Histoire de la danse à travers les ages,"
apropos of the French guild of *"ménéstriers,"* those wandering
musicians and dissolute dancers, is typical of this common error:
*"Ces fêtes continuèrent malgré les guerres, les pestes et autres
calamités."* Note the *"malgré,"* which should properly be replaced
by an *"à cause de"*; for the more wars, the more pestilence and
calamities on earth — in other words, the larger the death rate —
the gayer, the more universal and licentious must be the dance!
Nor is it only in the public square, in the village tavern, that in
such circumstances all bounds of modesty are broken. Death, the
equalizer — portrayed by Holbein and other mediæval artists in
a dance with "rich man, poor man, beggar man, thief; doctor,
lawyer, merchant, chief" — Death enters the moated castle as
unceremoniously as the wind-torn hovel. And the reaction remains the same; for, as Michelet tells us, the nobility engaged in
a series of hilarious and unbridled entertainments, ending in *"un
dernier bal enfin, mais celui-ci masqué, pour dispenser de rougir."*

When the dance became one of the community's secular concerns, each national temperament found expression in a typical folk-dance, as distinctive as national speech and costume. But whether it be the Spanish or Italian *"gagliarda,"* called by Prætorius (in 1668) an "invention of Hell," or the Tyrolian *"Schuh-plattler"* in which it is the dancer's aim to swing his partner high into the air so that her petticoat blows up a snowy bell; whether the fiery "mazurka" of Poland, or the Hungarian gypsies' "czardas" with its ominous, slow beginning and its cyclonic finale; the old English "trenchmore" and "cushion-dance," that ingenious excuse for promiscuous osculation,[1] or the Bohemian "umrlec" (death dance) in which a man or woman "plays dead" and lies on the floor, with eyes closed, to receive a "parting kiss" from each member of the company, which blithely turns round the "corpse" — everywhere, in the south, east, north and west of Europe, folk-dances are nothing else than a form of public courting or amorous frolicking; and the more daring the wooer, the better pleased the damsel. What these popular romps were like during the religious wars of the sixteenth and seventeenth centuries, when Death was reaping a bumper crop, can hardly be put in seemly wording. We must read Florian von Fürstenberg's denunciation in his "Tanzteufel (Dance Devil)," of 1567, or Cyriacus Spangenberg's "Ehespiegel (Marriage Mirror)," of 1570, in order to grasp the wicked, untrimmed truth. While the mercenaries of the Catholic and Protestant rulers were decimating each other, not for a paltry "thirty years' war," but for

---

[1] John Selden, in his "Table Talk" (published in 1689), wrote: "The court of England is much alter'd. At a solemn dancing, first you had the grave measures, then the Corantoes and the Galliards, and this kept up with ceremony; and at length to Trenchmore and the Cushion-dance: Then all the company dances, lord and groom, lady and kitchen-maid, no distinction. So in our court in Queen Elizabeth's time, gravity and state were kept up. In King James's time things were pretty well. But in King Charles's time there has been nothing but Trenchmore and the Cushion-dance, omnium gatherum, tolly polly, hoite come toite." The curves on the political barometer paralleled by those of the dance! And in the reign of Charles II the needle fell to the lowest storm-point in the scale.

WALTZERS AT THE TIVOLI, PARIS, 1802 — (*drawn by Sir John Dean Paul*)

"The dance which we saw is a most curious one . . . it is called *valse*; about 200 couples took part in it to the accompaniment of very slow music . . unfortunately my drawing can give but a feeble idea of it; the postures of the women were agreeable and alluring to say the least; as to the men, the less said about them, the better; they were so dirty and vulgar as to be disgusting."

more than fifteen decades, there was hardly a town in Germany in
the annals of which we do not find, for this period, some well-
meaning ordinance directed against the provocative prurience of
the dance. Certain regions were known for their particular celebrations, in which dancing predominated. All these occasions seem to
fall in, more or less, with the phases of nature, which bear the
strongest influence upon the effect that seeks an outlet through, or
is stimulated by, such rhythmic leaps and bounds. Almost every
race indulged in solstice-dances, at the time when the rhythm of
the universe seems to change, as flux and reflux alternate, when a
certain mysterious agitation is animating nature, and the seasons make another step in their eternal round. Mézeray, in his
contemporary "Histoire de la France," relates that in the reign
of Charles V, on St. John's day: "people divested themselves of
all their garments, placed flower-wreaths on their heads, and,
holding each other by the hand, they danced in long processions
through the streets and churches, sang and whirled round until
they dropped, out of breath." It is always the same picture, in
different colours, throughout the ages. These practices were
stopped, by act of Parliament, in 1667.

We are left in no doubt about social dances in Italy during
the sixteenth century, owing to several exhaustive treatises of the
period. There is, in particular, Fabrizio Caroso's dance-book,
"Ballarino," published in 1581, and dedicated to the beautiful
and notorious Bianca Capello. There are Cesare Negri's "Nuove
inventioni di balli," printed at Milan in 1604, and disclosing the
fact that, more poetic than our age with its "bunny hug,"
"shimmy," and allied atrocities, dances then had such pretty and
significant names as *caccia d'amore, cortesia amorosa, amor felice,
nobilità d'amore, torneo amoroso* — "amorous tournaments" they
verily were, one and all, fought not with "rockets," but with
armes à outrance.

The ballet as a sumptuous spectacle, in the modern sense, was
an invention of the *quattrocento,* and came spontaneously into
existence. At least, its connection with an art not unknown among
Greeks and Romans seems to lie solely in the arbitrary choice of

a mythological subject. In every other respect it was an absolutely novel thrill to which the world was being treated. Nor can we find any preliminary steps of development for it, unless we consider as such the singular entertainment devised by Bergonzo di Botta at the nuptials of Duke Galeazzo Sforza of Milan with Isabella of Aragon, in 1489. Its first appearance set a standard which was seldom equalled in what, ever after, remained the costliest, the most dazzling and often criminally lavish display of riches and splendour.

It was in 1581, at the palace of the Louvre in Paris, that Henry III, King of France, late of Poland,[1] commanded the musicians and entertainers of his court to devise fitting festivities wherewith to celebrate the marriage of his "favourite minion," Monsieur le Duc de Joyeuse, with Mlle. de Vaudémont, sister to the Queen, Louise of Lorraine. Seventeen separate functions took place, each host vying with the other in the folly of luxuries; but the most stupendous remained the ballet arranged by the Piedmontese fiddle-virtuoso, Baltazarini de Beaujoyeulx, with music by Lambert de Beaulieu and Jacques Salmon. At this wedding feast of royalty the princes and princesses of the houses of Valois and Anjou participated in a choreographic representation of an old Olympian myth, as gods and goddesses, with their attending nymphs and satyrs. Baltazarini says in the preface of the printed work that he had "blended together poetry, music, and dancing in a manner which, if ever done before, must have been in such remote antiquity that no trace of it remains." And

[1] Henry could not have forgotten how, upon reaching Venice in his flight from Poland, 1574, the *Serenissima Republica* had honoured him with a series of brilliant festivities, among which there was an allegorical and mythological "impromptu," a mixture of dancing, poetry, and music, largely interspersed with choral singing of compositions furnished specially for the occasion by the Venetian madrigalists, just then most plentiful, prolific, and progressive. In the long list of "tips" handed out when the royal guest departed, the musicians were remembered with 300 *scudi*, as much as Luigi Foscari was paid for the use of his palace. The dancers are not mentioned; perhaps they received garter buckles with the princely monogram in precious stones. But, more than likely, the ballet formed a rather insignificant part of the show.

the author emphasizes the novelty of his invention by saying: "I have given the first place to *dancing* . . ." and he might have added, to the rhythmic evolutions of the human body, clad in a profusion of brocades or simply adorned with nature's charms. For while some of the costumes cost as much as eighty thousand francs apiece, those participants whose rôles provided a justification shone by the mere exquisite whiteness of their skin. And thus was born the ballet. Like the opera, which originated in Florence about nineteen years later, it remained for a long time the privileged entertainment of the noble and rich, and more particularly of the regal courts. Louis XIV danced in twenty-seven ballets when he was young, and received the cognomen *"Le Roi Soleil"* from the part he took in one of them. Although lively steps occurred in these ballets or were danced at balls, it is principally the stately measure that prevails in both. Louis was particularly fond of the courante. It must not be forgotten that the costume of the ladies and the swords worn by the cavaliers precluded any helter-skelter mingling of pairs in an animated round. These conditions remained the same until the outbreak of the French Revolution, with the courante making room for the minuet under Louis XV, and the gavot becoming the "fashionable" dance under Louis XVI. Note that every one of these figure-dances, though capable of all the graces and gallantry imaginable, eighteenth-century qualities never excelled, remained nevertheless a rather stiff and dignified affair, in which a certain "distance" was always kept between the partners, a distance that a smile and a look might easily cross, but that was never abandoned for the sake of closer propinquity. Nor did the gallant century in France have to resort to such expedients. Although society, at last, was dancing on top of a volcano, the reigns of the fourteenth and the fifteenth Louis had been glorious and fairly prosperous. What wars had been waged did not demand too heavy a toll of lives. It was a period of stability; and from the dream that nothing could disturb this equilibrium the country was awakened only when it found that in this blissful state of somnolent contentment the reins of government in Paris had slipped out of a soft and perfumed hand, to be snapped up by the coarse and brutal fist of the rabble. The balance turned turtle, the change was almost instantaneous.

In Vienna, the capital of the Roman Emperor of Teuton nationality, the change was more gradual. Not that his throne was threatened like that of his brother-in-law and his sister. But the wars in which Austria had been entangled, especially under Maria Theresa, wars with Russia and Turkey, wars with Bavaria, with France and England, and especially the long and obstinate struggle with Frederick the Great of Prussia, had severely taxed the forces of the Empire and drained its sap. It was in Austria, and more particularly in Vienna, that at this point the waltz made its victorious entry into the world. The rigour of antiquated etiquette was broken, and with the more intimate embrace of the dancers, linked more closely by the sway of a bewitching rhythm, the waltz cast its imperious spell over a disintegrating society. Michael Kelly, the Irish tenor, who sang in Vienna from 1782 to 1786, relates in his entertaining reminiscences:

The people of Vienna were in my time dancing mad; as the Carnival approached, gaiety began to display itself on all sides, and when it really came, nothing could exceed its brilliancy . . . the propensity of the Vienna ladies for dancing and going to carnival masquerades was so determined, that nothing was permitted to interfere with their enjoyment of their favourite amusement.

And Kelly goes on to state the incredible length to which they went in this pursuit. — England, too, had succumbed to the dance craze, after a fashion. Dr. Burney tells us in his "History of Music" of conditions in London, which throw an interesting light on the favour in which the ballet was held at the end of the eighteenth century. Burney writes:

In the year 1781 Pacchierotti [the Caruso of his day] had been heard so frequently, that his singing was no impediment to conversation, or even animated narrative and debate, but while the elder Vestris [the Nijinsky of his day] was on the stage, if during a *pas seul* any of his admirers forgot themselves so much as to applaud him with their hands, there was an instant check put to his rapture by a choral "hu-sh-sh!" [And in 1788 Burney writes:] Within the last ten years, Dancing seems to have encroached upon Music, and instead of being a dependent or auxiliary, is aiming not only at independency, but tyranny.

Remember that the learned and peeved doctor speaks only of the ballet, as danced on the stage. The calm, collected Briton, like the prudish Roman at the summit of his power, standing secure and aloof from the turmoil with which the rest of Europe was contending, could possibly tolerate, perhaps encourage and even rave over the graceful pirouettes of Vestris, *"le dieu de la danse,"* but for the looseness of custom at continental balls, and particularly in public dancing-halls, he had only a disdainful shrug of the shoulders.[1] In 1802, when the peace of Amiens left Europe with a foretaste of General Bonaparte's strategic and diplomatic talents, many Englishmen visited Paris through curiosity, and in search of cheap relics of the *"ancien régime."* One of the most distinguished was the London banker and littérateur Sir John Dean Paul, who with his wife and three friends spent two weeks in the French capital, during the month of August, 1802; and the sights that attracted our travellers most, to judge by Sir John's diary, were those to be seen at the various dancing-

[1] Yet London, in earlier and less glorious days, had known its "Mulberry Gardens" and "World's End," notorious places of intrigue and broad hilarity. Sir John Hawkins wrote that "there was an edifice built of timber and divided into sundry rooms with a platform and balustrade at top, which floated on the Thames above London Bridge, and was called the Folly. At first it was resorted to for refreshment by persons of fashion; and Queen Mary with some of her courtiers had once the curiosity to visit it. But it sank into a receptacle for companies of loose and disorderly poeple, for the purposes of drinking and promiscuous dancing."—Vauxhall originated in the reign of Charles II. Its history, like that of Ranelagh, is redeemed by services to music proper which counterbalance the piquant story of its improprieties.

places, such as Tivoli, Frascati, and the Pavillon d'Hannovre. Sir John was also something of an artist and he has drawn for our benefit various couples dancing the waltz at the Tivoli. His picture is probably several shades more modest than what he saw and what he describes as a dance that could never cross the Channel, wherefrom we may infer that the honourable city banker's financial perspicacity must have surpassed his prophetic gifts as far as concerned the contagiousness of the waltz.

But let us return to Paris in the hour of the crisis, and let us see when and why the waltz found there such fanatic devotees. The extravagance, the sublime indifference of court and aristocracy; a national debt that had reached fabulous figures; new dogmas proclaiming "the rights of man" and assaulting the timeworn tenets of social justice; and finally the shot fired by those Massachusetts farmers at Lexington, re-echoing round the world with the sweet promise of independence — all things combined, resulted in an overthrow of mildewed conceptions, creeds, and customs. After the storming of the Bastille, on July 14th, 1789, events moved quickly. In a steady, breathless *crescendo,* they lead to the climax, the murder of Louis XVI, and the subsequent Reign of Terror. With Robespierre and his accomplices wielding absolute power, the knife of the guillotine had barely a chance to cool off from the blood of the numberless victims that the blind fury of the populace demanded. But the greater the slaughter, the wilder and more licentious the amusements of the people. And with the cast-off manners of aristocratic gallantry and chivalry, the *"Fêtes Galantes"* that Watteau's and Fragonard's brush had immortalized became a thing of the past. The new spirit, which required so copious a baptism with the liquor of life, had to find ways and means of replenishing the wasted stock. It was at this juncture that the waltz appeared in Paris. The days of the Terror knew for the business of the night 23 theatres open in Paris, filled with laughing spectators, and 1800 public dance-halls, overflowing with crowds that sought a brief respite in the whirl of the dance, the insinuative lilt of the music, the lights from a hundred lustres, the perfumes of thousands of women dressed for the feast. Nature left nothing undone to make the lure resistless. Gone, by a stroke of magic, were hoopskirts, furbelows, powdered wigs, and laced corsages. Instead the women modelled their attire after that of Aspasia, with bare arms and breast, sandalled feet, and hair bound in plaits round their heads. Fashionable hairdressers arranged the curls of their customers with casts of classic busts before them. Undergarments were banished and replaced by a knitted silk vest which clung to the figure. In this attire the "belles" of the revolutionary epoch paraded the boulevards and went to the dance. But not only in the public places set apart for such amusements, or in private assemblies, did the populace turn in a surging eddy to the tune of the waltz. Mercier, in describing the conditions he saw, writes:

Dancing is universal; they dance at the Carmélites, between the massacres; they dance at the Jesuits' Seminary; at the Convent of the Carmélites du Marais; at the Seminary of Saint-Sulpice; at the Filles de Sainte-Marie; they dance in three ruined churches of my section, and upon the stones of all the tombs which have not been destroyed.

But the most amazing part of Mercier's recital is his account of the *"Bal des Victimes,"* to which were admitted only the relatives of men and women murdered on the guillotine:

Will posterity believe that people whose relations had died on the scaffold inaugurated, not days of solemn general grief, when, assembled in mourning garb, they might bear witness to their sorrow at the cruel losses so recently sustained, but days of dancing, drinking, and feasting. For admission to one of these banquets and dances it is necessary to show a certificate of the loss of a father, mother, husband, wife, brother, or sister under the knife of the guillotine. The death of collaterals does not confer the right of attending the fête.

And thus Nature, in her cryptic ways of wisdom, destroys,

and immediately proceeds to repair, even in the guise of hysteria and perversion. Lives were needed in France more than ever. What the blood-thirst of the terrorists had left undone, the campaigns of Napoleon accomplished. The dance went on, always giddier, always more licentious. The waltz, once known in France as *"la volte,"* an inoffensive pastime of peasants, then forgotten and reimported from Vienna, was finally legitimized by its introduction on the stage of the Opéra, in 1800, in a ballet by Gardel, famous choreographer in his day, with music by Méhul, and very neatly named "La Dansomanie." [1] What this mania for dancing finally came to can be judged best by the rigour and ingenuity which were required in order to fight it. The Church sent out missions to preach against these abuses. Thirty missionaries who visited the province of Bourgogne during the carnival of 1819, having forbidden all dances and profane entertainments, had a chorus of young maidens sing a long chant to the tune of a then famous aria; two stanzas will suffice to give a taste of this austere sermon in rhymes:

> *Funeste danse,*
> *Triste tombeau de la pudeur,*
> *Funeste écueil de l'innocence,*
> *Le Démon seul est ton auteur,*
> *Funeste danse.*
>
> *Qu'une danseuse*
> *Vous soit un sujet de frayeur;*
> *Craignez son air, sa voix flatteuse.*
> *Qui surprend mieux les yeux, le cœur,*
> *Qu'une danseuse!*

These observations suggest inevitably a parallel between the

[1] This ballet remained in the repertoire of the Opéra for a number of years. It was given as late as on Monday, October 17, 1825, when it formed the "after-piece" to the première of "Don Sanche," one-act opera of the fourteen-year-old François Liszt (not named on the *affiches*).

dancing-craze of 1819 and that of 1919. The capitals of Europe, the whole of the United States, after having endured the greatest hardships and anxieties within the memory of man, were dancing, were furiously and indecently dancing. The middle of the nine-teenth century enjoyed innocuous lancers, quadrilles, polkas, and expurgated waltzes. In France, where the birth rate was beginning to decline, we meet before the outbreak of the Franco-Prussian War with the "cancan," the only dance of the period that was pointedly obscene. The interest in social dancing had become perfunctory; the ballet had turned a barren harlequinade with an abundance of pink tights, white tulle skirts, and fairy tricks destined to gladden the nursery.

Since the Great War we are being treated to an "intermezzo" with a world that is merrily dancing its heels and heads off, danc-ing, perhaps, toward the brink of ruin. So danced Babylon, Nineveh, Byzantium, and Rome — names that stand for vanished civilizations. Must we seek the race that is to rule to-morrow in that one which is still without public dance-halls, *"Palais de Danse,"* for its fretting children, whom Nature is struggling to preserve against all odds?

It is a most absorbing, a most appalling perspective which opens to the gaze that follows the dance, throughout the centuries, from a distant antiquity down to our days. Emerson wrote in his journal of 1822: "Owing to the identity of human character in all ages, there is as much instruction in the tale of Troy as in the annals of the French Revolution." Were Emerson living to-day, the French Revolution might have served him for com-parison with existing disturbances. And so we see, reaching back-ward and projecting forward, a vague outline of recurring events, a cloudy likeness in all pictures. There is forever a similarity of causes and effects, a periodicity of movement, which, spread over thousands and perhaps millions of years, is nothing but the manifestation of that rhythmic law which the incomprehensible stars obey, as does that equally incomprehensible thing, the heart of man, leaping immemorially, with quickened pulses, to the seductive measures of the dance.

JAZZ

(*Read before the Music Supervisors' National Conference in Nashville, Tennessee, March, 1922*)

JAZZ is upon us, everywhere. To deny the fact is to assume the classic ostrich pose, head buried in the sand, tail-feathers to the sun. To shout alarm hysterically from the house-tops, is to exhibit over-confidence in clamorous indignation as a purifier of morals, if it be not wholly to ignore historic precedent.

Let us remember that the worst of our present dances are not beginning to approach in barefaced wickedness the almost unbelievable performances of our forefathers. And let us admit that the *best* of jazz tunes is something infinitely more original — perhaps even musically better — than the so-called "popular" music that America produced in the "good old days," that golden age which lives only in the mythology of disappointed sinners.

Almost every race and every age have known social conditions which result in an unloosing of instincts that nature wisely has taught us to hold well in check, but which, every now and then, from cryptic reasons, are allowed to break the bounds of civilized restraint.

Such excesses have not infrequently attained to tragic madness. The silly, lewd gyrations for which jazz is held responsible by some are the release of tension in a witless, neurotic stratum of society. But such dances were common long before the word "jazz" was coined. Our recent dance craze has known the tango, the "shimmy," the various zoological trots, to much the same purpose that now cries out for jazz.

Whoever wishes to reform the dance must break the grip that

clutches partner against partner, in shuffling, wriggling ambula-
tion. Abolish the comparative intimacy of that twofold company;
make room for the benign third party that turns company into
crowd; devise a dance in which there is general participation, as
there was in the quadrille, the figure-dances, the milder forms of
country reels, and you not only will improve the tone of public
amusements, but possibly may open a way for dance-music to
resume a swifter, ampler, and more sweeping gait, instead of
the repeated, jogging, stubborn motives which lead to stupid, short,
reiterated movements.

For the present I am not concerned with dance reform, nor
am I interested in jazz as an accompaniment to Terpsichorean
atrocities, but rather in the musical side of jazz — how it originated, what it represents, and what it may lead to.

*   *
*

To a great many minds, the word "jazz" implies frivolous or
obscene deportment. Let me ask what the word "sarabande"
suggests to you? I have no doubt that to most people it will
mean everything that is diametrically opposed to "jazzing." When
you hear mention of a "sarabande," you think of Bach's, of
Handel's slow and stately airs; you think of noble and dignified
strains in partitas, sonatas, and operas of the eighteenth century.
Yet the sarabande when it was first danced in Spain, about
1588, was probably far more shocking to behold than is the most
shocking jazz to-day. The sarabande seems to have been of
Moorish origin. Then, as now, the Oriental, the exotic touch gave
dancing an added fillip. When Lady Mary Montagu, writing from
Adrianople in 1717, described the dance that she saw in the
seraglio of a rich Mussulman, she made allusions which leave
no uncertainty as to the exact nature of these proceedings. Something of that character must have belonged to the earliest sara-
bandes. They were the proud Hidalgo's hula-hula.

A French author, Pierre de Lancre, wrote in 1613: "The

courtesans who mingle with the players have given this dance such a vogue on the stage that there is hardly a young girl in the country who cannot copy them to perfection." How truly the same might be said of our generation! It is the stage that starts a novel mode of dancing, the public which is alert to ape it and outstep it. Father Mariana, in his book "De Spectaculis," published in 1609, devoted a whole chapter to an attack on the sarabande, accusing it of having done more harm than the bubonic plague which devastated Europe in the Middle Ages.

Again, we hear it alleged that the moral corruption worked by jazz is vastly more calamitous than was the material havoc wrought by the World War. And yet, as we know, this once objectionable sarabande finally became a matrix wherein the greatest musical composers cast some of their loftiest and purest inspirations. Dances, popular and no doubt shocking in their day, have furnished the soil for the cyclic growth from which has sprung, by way of the concerto and sonata, the grandest form of absolute music, the orchestral symphony.

What the waltz was when first it set Vienna spinning, when it turned Paris into one big whirlpool, has been variously chronicled by pious and blushing witnesses, none of whom was more perturbed than the impious poet Lord Byron.

> Not soft Herodias, when, with winning tread,
> Her nimble feet danced off another's head;
> Not Cleopatra on her galley's deck
> Displayed so much of leg or more of neck,
> Than thou, ambrosial Waltz.

Yet Weber was to vest such bareness in the spacious mantle of his art, and Chopin crown it with the coronet of quality.

I have taken the licence of rapidly rehearsing these few historical facts to answer those who might question my saneness in bestowing upon the musical side of jazz so much as a particle of studious thought. Without speculating what the future development of jazz may be, what ultimate contribution to musical styles it may make, there is an excuse for believing that long after the dance known as jazz will happily have vanished, investigators in the field of musical history will have occasion to search for the inception of these peculiar tunes, to seek for traces of contemporary opinion on their merit or their faults. I frankly think that it would set us down a rather jaundiced lot if those investigators were to discover no sign of unbiased appraisement, nothing but wholesale ranting against a laxity of morals which was inveterate before the frenzied beaters of pots and kitchen kettles became entitled to full membership in the Musical Union.

Let me emphatically state that I in no way sympathize with these perpetrators of infernal din, who are giving a poor imitation of the admirable savage, with his highly perfected and astonishingly diversified art of sounding pulsatile instruments.

The savage stands far above the clownish tricks of rubbing sandpaper, blowing shrieky sirens, or hitting at random a battery of gongs. The savage is immeasurably more cultured than the person who belabours a piano with his whole body and, thrumming two or three ill-assorted chords, frantically fumbled together in endless and stale repetition, tries to tell you that he is playing jazz. As a matter of fact, he is doing nothing of the kind.

Like any other type of music, jazz can be bad or good. I am not defending bad jazz any more than I would defend a bad ballad or the bad playing of Beethoven. I have no intention of standing up for the insolent plagiarists who misappropriate and disfigure Rimsky-Korsakov, Puccini, and that superlative master Johann Strauss. I am certain that the apostle of vulgarization who should try to rewrite Shelley's poems in slang would be broken on the wheel and quartered. And I should be delighted to help set up the punitive machinery if musical barbarians were to be similarly executed.

So much, then, to clear the stage, and range into a solid background these protests and restrictions, upon which I shall ask you to fix, from time to time, a reassuring glance, while I step to the proscenium and speak my little piece. The burden of it is this: there exists such a thing as *good* jazz music, and *good* jazz is a great deal better, and far more harmless, than is a bad ballad or the bad playing of Beethoven. And, if you are open-eyed in surveying our musical tendencies, you cannot pass blindly over the unspeakable riff-raff of our male and female balladists: the "Smile" songs; "Bubble" songs; "Mother," "Mither," and "Mammy" songs; the sloppy "Sweetheart" drivel; above all, the unpardonable maltreatment of the classics by the multitude of amateurs — offences infinitely worse than good jazz. And to the latter I now come.

*   *

*

Jazz as a state of mind is symptom, not malady. Jazz in the guise of music is both anodyne and stimulant to the afflicted. To the immune it is an irritant. The term "jazz" as applied to music is rather elastic. It embraces not only the noisy-noisome sort, the jumble-jungle kind, but a type that refines upon and meliorates the racy stuff of wilder species with matter of a distinctly and engagingly musical nature. Good jazz is a composite, the happy union of seemingly incompatible elements. Good jazz is the latest phase of American popular music. It is the upshot of a transformation which started some twenty years ago and culminated in something unique, unmatched in any other part of the world. Fifteen years ago we had progressed to the insipid "Waltz me around again, Willie," to the coon-song and rag-time factories in the back parlours of the West Twentieth streets of New York. With the period of "Everybody's doing it, doing it, doing it," about 1912, we reached the short insistent motive which was to usurp the prerogatives of songfulness.

Then, one fine day, in 1915 — or fine night, I should rather say; for, if I remember correctly, it was in the second act of a mildly entertaining operetta — we were treated to "The Magic Melody." A young man, gifted with musical talent and unusual courage, had dared to introduce into his tune a modulation which was nothing extraordinary in itself, but which marked a change, a new régime in American popular music. It was just the thing that the popular composer in the making had been warned against by the wise ones as a thing too "high-brow" for the public to accept. They were foolish prophets. The public not only liked it; they went mad over it. And well they might; for it was a relief, a liberation.

Gradually the courageous young man found imitators more daring than himself. Harmonic richness and variety entered victoriously where stereotyped cadences, barren and threadbare progressions, had reigned *ad nauseam*. Mind you, I am not setting milestones with the tunes I have named; I merely wish to suggest to you different stages of a continuous evolution, by songs which were typical of each.

I have not given the subject sufficient study to say definitely at what point the course of popular American music took a new turn, but, unless I am very much mistaken, "The Magic Melody," by Mr. Jerome Kern, was the opening chorus of an epoch. It is not a composition of genius, but it is very ingenious. While it is almost more tuneless than was "Everybody's doing it," if that be possible, and largely adheres to the short, insistent phrase, it stands on a much higher musical plane. Its principal claim to immortality is that it introduces a modulation which, at the time it was first heard by the masses, seized their ears with the power of magic. And the masses, as usual, showed excellent judgment.

Mr. Kern subsequently proved to be one of the most fertile, tasteful, and characteristic composers of light music. When he tries to be purely melodic, he is apt to fall back upon plain sentimentalism, tinged with spurious folk-song colour. But his little harmonic device had a hue all its own; and popular parlance decided that it was "blue."

A veil of mystery covers the first dark deed that went by the name of "blue." Forever hidden, perhaps, is the identity of the melancholic culprit who perpetrated it, although stout hearts are ready to cite the man, the place, and the tune. They are not apt, however, to tell you of an ancestral and *bona-fide* "blue chord," which Richard Wagner deliberately chose in order to make more graphic the word *blau* when Tristan, in the beginning of *Tristan und Isolde*, refers to the green, but distant, shore as shimmering still in a blue haze. That is the sublime instance.

The ridiculous one is the maudlin *glissando* on ukulele and steel guitar, the tear-duct of popular music. What stainless ears considered a rather weird turn of the melody, a morbid shifting of harmonies, entered the dictionary of professional jargon as "blue note," or "blue chord."

I am under the impression that these terms were contemporary with, if they did not precede and foreshadow, the period of our innumerable musical "blues." What the uninitiated tried to define by that homely appellation was, perhaps, an indistinct association of the minor mode and dyspeptic intonation with poor digestion; in reality, it is the advent in popular music of something which the text-books call ambiguous chords, altered notes, extraneous modulation, and deceptive cadence.

The trick had irresistible charm; everybody tried it. It was in the preludes and interludes of the popular songs that the radicals began to break down the old order — that is, in those measures where the voice did not interfere with their freedom. The hackneyed "Till ready" was mercifully dispatched to limbo, and superseded by some dexterous harmonic tricks that not only stood, but demanded and deserved, rehearing. Instead of the traditional sequence of dominant, diminished-seventh, and dominant-seventh harmonies — which formed the time-worn transition into the refrain and accompanied the chanted announcement: "When he to her did say" — there sprang up a diversity of the freshest, most unexpected modulations, which fell upon the ear like drops of evening rain upon a parched and sun-baked soil. The various shades of blue in which untutored harmonists indulged ranged all the way from faint cerulean to deep indigo. The last could often be more fittingly compared to mud.

Between the earlier "rag" and the "blues," there was this distinction: the rag had been mainly a thing of rhythm, of syncopation; the blues were syncopation relished with spicier harmonies.

In addition to these two elements of music: rhythm and harmony, the people — who in the beginning had known but one
thing: melody, fastened upon a primitive and weak harmonic
structure of "barber-shop" chords — the people, I say, who had
stepwise advanced from melody and rhythm to harmony, lastly
discovered counterpoint. And the result of this last discovery is
jazz. In other words, jazz is rag-time, *plus* "blues," *plus* orchestral polyphony; it is the combination, in the popular music current, of melody, rhythm, harmony, and counterpoint.

*   *

*

Each of these four ingredients bears racial features which are
unequivocally American. Yet this Americanism is not exclusively
a tribal one; it is not content to borrow from the Negro, to filch
from the Indian. What marks of Oriental inflections it shows hail
from the Jordan rather than from the Congo River. While the
primitive syncopation was taken over from the coloured man,
while the Semitic purveyors of Broadway "hits" made us an
invaluable gift of their more luxurious harmonic sense, the contrapuntal complexity of jazz is something native, born out of the
complex, strident present-day American life. Where did you hear,
before jazz was invented, such multifarious stirring, heaving,
wrestling of independent voices as there are in a jazz orchestra?
The saxophone bleats a turgid song; the clarinets turn capers
of their own; the violins come forward with an *obbligato;* a saucy
flute darts up and down the scale, never missing the right note
on the right chord; the trombone lumberingly slides off on a
tangent; the drum and xylophone put rhythmic high-lights into
these kaleidoscopic shiftings; the cornet is suddenly heard above
the turmoil, with good-natured brazenness. Chaos in order —
orchestral technic of master craftsmen — music that is recklessly
fantastic, joyously grotesque — such is good jazz. A superb, incomparable creation, inescapable yet elusive; something it is
almost impossible to put in score upon a page of paper.

For jazz finds its last and supreme glory in the skill for improvisation exhibited by the performers. The deliberately scored jazz tunes are generally clumsy, pedestrian. It is not for the plodding, routine orchestrator to foresee the unexpected, to plan the improbable.

Jazz is abandon, is whimsicality in music. A good jazz band should never, and actually never does, play the same piece twice in the same manner. Each player must be a clever musician, an originator as well as an interpreter, a wheel that turns hither and thither on its own axis without disturbing the clockwork.

Strange to relate, this orchestral improvisation, which may seem virtually impossible or artistically undesirable, is not an invention of our age. To improvise counterpoint was a talent that the musicians in the orchestras of Peri and Monteverdi, three hundred years ago, were expected to possess, and did possess, to such a high degree that the skeleton scores of those operas which have come down to us give but an imperfect idea of how this music sounded when performed.

A semblance of this lost, and rediscovered, art is contained in the music of the Russian and Hungarian gypsies. Just as that music is a riotous improvisation, throbbing with a communicative beat, ever restless in mood, so is jazz. Just as the gypsy players are held together by an identical, inexplicable rhythmic spell, following the leader's fiddle in its harmonic meanderings, each instrument walking in a bypath of its own, so is the ideal jazz band constituted — that is, the jazz band made up of serious jazz artists.

Franz Liszt could give a suggestion of gypsy music on the keyboard. He had a way of playing the piano orchestrally. There are few people who can play jazz on the piano. Jazz, as much as the gypsy dances, depends on the many and contrasting voices of a band, united in a single and spontaneous rhythmic, harmonic, and contrapuntal will.

Jazz, fortunately, can be preserved on phonographic records for our descendants. They will form their own estimate of our enormities. If we had such records of what Scarlatti, Couperin,

and Rameau did with their figured bases, we should need fewer
realizations, restitutions, and renditions by arranger and deranger.

*   *

*

Jazz is a more typical, a more comprehensive expression of the
modern American spirit than all our coon-songs, our pseudo-Indian
wails, the regional songs of a hundred years ago, the tenth-rate
imitations of stale English ballads, the imperfect echoes of French
impressionism. Good jazz is enjoyed by capital musicians, by men
who are neither inordinately immoral nor extravagantly uncul-
tured. It has fascinated European composers like Stravinsky,
Casella, Satie, as Debussy was fascinated before them by rag-
time. "Golliwog's Cakewalk" and "Minstrels" are works of the
purest art, notwithstanding the fact that the essence of their
peculiar charm was filtered from the emanations of the music-hall.

If jazz music has any of the gypsy music's fitness for survival,
it will leave a trace, unsoiled by memories of indecorum and
police raids. Meanwhile the curious and heretical inquirer may
be pardoned for dwelling reflectively upon so odd a case as that
presented by the gradual accession of melody, rhythm, harmony,
and counterpoint to the leading rôle in the popular music of
America, a process covering barely more than five decades. It has
no parallel in musical history, unless we take musical progress as
a whole during the last five centuries. Good jazz, once brought
into the focus of unclouded criticism, reveals, aside from the
grosser features visible to a naked eye in the dark, some finer
lineaments, which make it appear justly entitled to the benefit
of honest doubt, based — if on nothing else — on the examples
of the sarabande and the waltz.

Of course, someone may interpose that we cannot drive jazz,
waltz, and sarabande in one and the same harness; that the musical vehicles of 1922 are as different from those of 1822, or 1722,
as is a snorting eight-cylinder automobile from a featherweight
Tilbury or a pompous state-coach drawn by six.

Quite true. Yet some argumentative and jazz-loving person may come along and retort that, while the means and speed of locomotion have changed, human nature has remained stationary, or, at least, much as it always was and will be. Said person might add to our embarrassment by averring that perhaps the real trouble is a momentary shortage in Handels, Webers, Chopins. And how shall we prove him wrong?

TRITONE

BEETHOVEN'S MYSTERIOUS MALADY

"A CENTENARY is always an ubiquitous temptation to indulge in rhapsody at the expense of veracity." Thus writes Mr. Ernest Newman on the first page of his book "The Unconscious Beethoven." And forthwith he yields to another temptation: he celebrates the event by over-indulging his fantasy in the absence of certainty. But he does it with such apparent belief in his own candour, with so great a show of anxiety about "the truth," that no one will question the motives that prompted the recounting of the whole unvarnished tale, told with Mr. Newman's usual dialectic skill. The only thing that might be questioned is whether the centennial air, heavy with rose and laurel, had after all been noticeably cleared by the addition of the doubtful fragrance from Mr. Newman's bouquet of hints and guesses.

Mr. Newman calls his book "an essay in musical psychology." True to the technique of some of our most eminent psychologists, whether musical or not, Mr. Newman's procedure, in the main, is that of the little boy who delights in playing with mud. Mr. Newman declaims against "the romantic and sentimental rubbish" which has a way of accumulating about the figures of great men "during the course of a century or so." In the name of "historical criticism" all dirt of this sort must be removed, even if nothing else will do but to substitute for it dirt of another and possibly more unpleasant kind. It would be indelicate to suggest that anything Mr. Newman writes could be likened to rubbish. He is too frequently original as a thinker, too uniformly brilliant as a writer.

If Mr. Newman's is an illuminating book, it throws more light on the author than on the author's subject. The book is bare of any facts concerning Beethoven not known before; it merely spins out and twists up certain theories long held as plausible, without adducing a single scrap of new evidence or positive proof wherewith to substantiate or clarify them. Herein the book is disappointing.

Mr. Newman's object is "to dig out the real Beethoven from the romantic plaster-of-Paris in which he has gradually become encased." The excavation carries a long way forward what the author began in his study of Wagner, the man and the artist. In both cases he has shown himself particularly interested in the man; and for reasons. If the man and the artist are far from the same, they are inseparable. However, the man with his failings is always humanly nearer to the rest of us than is the artist in his ivory tower or barbed-wire stockade. The man we can possibly measure by the yardstick of our own troubled existence, whereas the artist remains to most of us an elusive or incomprehensible being we love to theorize about, in a vain endeavour to explain the one through the other.

Beethoven, like Wagner, was content to realize in himself the power of genius without aspiring to the condition of saintliness. Genius is an affliction; or, as Goethe put it, a demon. In Beethoven resided a demonic force and will which disregarded everything except the work of creation. That is the mark of the possessed, of the creative artist. And with it is stamped out immediately and necessarily much that in the ordinary man is the behaviour resulting from accepted notions of righteousness or morality. Genius stands not only above the society of men, but outside of it. Here begins the everlasting conflict.

* *

*

Mr. Newman has found it incumbent upon himself to knock off the legend of Saint Ludwig by throwing at it all the adverse testimony ever given against the man Beethoven. The thrower works hard, the sentimental plaster flies to right and left. But it is wasted energy; for when Mr. Newman is done with his job, we discover nothing that we did not already know. Beethoven was fond of flattery, he lacked consideration, he was obstinate, he had rude manners, he could be contemptuous of his lesser colleagues, he was ungrateful, he suffered from colossal arrogance, he was self-sufficient, his natural suspiciousness and distrust were aggravated by his deafness, he was officiously interfering, he gave the reins to his meddlesome despotism and vile temper, he used scurrilous language, he even descended to questionable business methods. In short, he was an impossible person.

Alas, Mr. Newman undoubtedly knows that geniuses are not easy to live with; they cannot be recommended as household pets; they must be handled with infinite tact and forbearance. Since very few people can clash against super-man wrapped in the hard shell of his egoism and stand the shock without hurt, the "contemporaries" of geniuses are often willing but biased witnesses for the prosecution. The contempt of the great arouses the jealousy of the small. Misunderstandings beget misrepresentation. And so little as a suspicion of unfairness is needed to start the biographical artist-in-plaster, anxious to build up the defence. In our own day we have begun to hear whispered stories — not surprising nor unbelievable — which give accounts of the man Debussy strangely contrasting with the perfection of his music. So soon as the gossip will become louder or get into print, we must be prepared for the counter-move of a Debussy legend. It will no more improve the beauty of his scores than any subsequent plaster-wreckers can abstract from it.

Thayer was by no means the only one who truthfully pointed out Beethoven's weaknesses. All except the most superficial biographers laid on black paint, or at least a dark grey, where the shadows projected. Fifty years ago, when the prophets of Wagner in England were accused of seizing upon Beethoven as "a link in a chain of musical progress supposed to find its culmination in the latest productions of a special school of musicians," H. H. Statham in the *Fortnightly Review* wrote that the best proof of Beethoven's greatness lay in the fact "that even his admirers have not been able to write him down. . . . Hardly anything that has been said of Socrates or of Christ equals the tone of solemnity in which Beethoven's moral greatness, and the future mission of his music in regenerating mankind, are spoken of by some of these zealous apostles. Beethoven was neither a Socrates nor a Christ; nor is music a moral agent, except in the indirect sense in which all high and intellectual pleasures are moral agents." And Statham — an architect — belonged to the plasterers' union.

It was late in the day, therefore, when Mr. Newman girded up his loins and slew the slain. But he went through the motions of a great battle simply because he was afraid that some small portion of the "romantic rubbish" had been permitted to survive, even by the honest and ruthless Thayer. So he decided to do away with it once for all. No better occasion could have been chosen for the alleged cleaning operation than a centenary, which always gathers so much dust.

The one point Thayer deliberately passed over with only parenthetical or veiled allusions is the matter of Beethoven's obvious strayings from the path of purity and the consequences he "is said" to have suffered. Beethoven never married, though most of the time he was "in love." It was not his fault that he remained single; more than once he rashly proposed marriage. He longed for a home and family. His conceptions of wedded life were strict and lofty. But the right woman, fit to bear the crown and the cross of being the wife of Beethoven, did not exist. Merciful luck preserved him from getting tied to the wrong one.

Beethoven's celibacy does not imply chastity. He was no Joseph, nor Sir Galahad. His exuberant vitality, especially in the prime of his life, was blended with a large dose of sensuality. It forms a natural attribute of the creative vigour and the artistic temperament. Duclos, French moralist and friend of Rousseau's, travelling through Italy in 1767, observed that castrates make excellent singers but poor composers; and he shrewdly inferred that *"ce dont on les prive a de grandes influences sur les facultés de l'âme."* Beethoven's soul was as ardent as the sap in his veins, and the ardour overflowed into his music. Yet there are critics who deny this. Paul Bekker declares that Beethoven's art "shows no indication of erotic tendencies, his music is outside the realm of sexual impulses." And Mr. Newman thinks that "Beethoven's music has probably fewer sex-connotations than that of any other composer except Bach's." How the sturdy *Kantor,* father of twenty children, would smile at that! The sex-connotation lies in the creative urge itself. And to be erotic, music need not be tinged with the pale, dejected passion of Chopin, the purple frenzy of Liszt, or the flame and gold of Wagner's paroxysm. Cannot a scherzo, without being giddy or bizarre, spring from the playful daring of amorous pursuit, and an adagio, without being saturated with chromaticism, reflect the warm glow of content in fulfilment? The very absence of a loud or unhealthy erotic shade in the colouring of Beethoven's music must be interpreted as a sign that his "love-life" — such as it was — was essentially normal. When in a letter to Ries he bemoaned the fact that probably he would never possess the "one woman" of his desire, he carefully added: "Yet I am no woman-hater." [1]

And still, Mr. Newman would have us believe that Beethoven suffered from "a perverse sex-obsession," that he was plagued by "a morbid sex-complex." Why? Because his well-grounded disapproval of the wives of his two brothers expressed itself in violent hatred for these decidedly frail ladies, and because he wished to keep his nephew Carl away from dangerous company, just as he had warned his brother Johann, twenty years earlier, to "beware of the whole tribe of bad women." In order to justify his deductions, Mr. Newman assumes that Beethoven's "own life had been radically changed for the worse by a youthful imprudence." This leads us to the question of the venereal disease, or diseases, from which Beethoven "is said" to have suffered. The whole question might well have been left where it stood, in comparative darkness; for no matter how it is answered — if a positive answer should ever be found — it makes little difference now.

[1] Vienna, May 8, 1816: *"Alles schöne an Ihre Frau; leider habe ich keine; ich fand nur Eine, die ich wohl nie besitzen werde; bin aber deswegen kein Weiberfeind."*

What may be of interest is to look for a moment at the critical methods of Mr. Newman, the historian.

* *

*

Of course, Mr. Newman is not the first one openly and fearlessly to discuss these things. He quotes from Grove (1879) and Frimmel (1912), besides freely helping himself from the book of Dr. Schweisheimer (1922) on "Beethoven's maladies, their influence upon his life-work," which is really the source of the only pertinent remarks he contributes on the medical side. If the book by Guglielmo Bilancioni, "La Sordità di Beethoven, considerazioni di un otologo" (1921), was known to Mr. Newman, he did not mention it among his references. Beethoven's maladies have always received a good deal of attention, especially in their relation to his deafness. One of the likely causes that have been advanced for it is syphilis. Frimmel, in his recent "Beethoven Handbuch," under the head of "Krankheiten," does not forget *"die ominöse Lues."*

The suggestion was Grove's that the autopsy revealed in Beethoven's body conditions which were "most probably the result of syphilitic affections at an early period of his life." Although the form of the statement is a relatively guarded one, Grove himself was apparently convinced that it was actually true. In a foot-note to this passage he said: "This diagnosis, which I owe to the kindness of my friend, Dr. Lauder Brunton, is confirmed by the existence of two prescriptions, of which, since the passage in the text was written, I have been told by Mr. Thayer, who heard of them from Dr. Bertolini." That is a somewhat roundabout route. But people have been hanged and reputations blasted on flimsier grounds than this.

The first objection — and one we shall have to return to later — is that the diagnostic findings of Bertolini-Thayer-Grove-Brunton did not specify whether it was a case of acquired or congenital syphilis. There is a great difference between the two, as far as the "moral" implications go. Either might have been possible, with similar effects upon the hearing. But instead of being "most probably," or even conceivably, the cause of deafness, it is in decidedly exceptional cases that a syphilitic affection damages the aural mechanism; and it is highly improbable that the damage should be symmetrical. Beethoven's post-mortem revealed nothing that required the acceptance or supposition of syphilis as a necessary or likely cause of any diseased conditions in the ear or any other part of the body. Doctors have been known to disagree. In medicine, more than in any other science, the scope of verified knowledge is constantly being widened, and much of this knowledge is of surprisingly recent date. The later doctor, then, is apt to know more than did the earlier one. In Grove's chain of hearsay diagnosticians only the first and the last links were medical men. That does not make them the stronger links now. Time has corroded their prestige.

Dr. Lauder Brunton was an eminent physician in his day. But that day is no more. His deductions from Beethoven's post-mortem were made in the light of what knowledge he possessed. His opinion may properly have had weight with Grove; now it must be taken with all reserve. In Brunton's time the study of venereal diseases had not advanced to the point it has reached to-day. They were still held responsible for various conditions now recognized as resulting from other causes. Therefore, Brunton cannot be accepted as an infallible authority on venereal diseases; nor can Bertolini. In Beethoven's lifetime the medical world was woefully hazy on such things. As a matter of fact, the definite distinction between gonorrhœa and syphilis dates only from the tests made by Philippe Ricord in 1838, eleven years after Beethoven's death. Prior to that time syphilis, chancroid, and gonorrhœa were confused as manifestations of one systemic disorder and were treated in more or less the same manner, especially as regards the administering of mercury. In Beethoven's time mercury was still a sort of panacea and general tonic or alterative. Because it was found efficacious in some maladies, for which it happened to be a specific, it was used in others for which it was not. Kipling was right when he wrote:

Wonderful little, when all is said,
Wonderful little our fathers knew.
Half their remedies cured you dead —
Most of their teaching was quite untrue —

It would be a peculiarly distressing thought to picture a hypo-chondriac Beethoven taking one useless medicine after the other and going from bad to worse, a victim of those who tried to fasten on him a disease he never had.

Likewise the two prescriptions of which Grove was told by Thayer, "who had heard of them from Dr. Bertolini," give us no promise of a solution until we have actually seen them. The presence of mercury in two prescriptions dating from ca. 1815 would hardly establish in themselves a presumption of syphilis, much less an absolute proof. The only document alleged to be first-hand "evidence" and still in existence is "an as yet unpub-lished note in Beethoven's own hand referring to a cure that leaves no doubt as to the specific nature of his malady." But here again we shall have to verify before we can be certain. The note is said to be in the private possession of a German scientist. Now more than ever the owner of this note is placed under the moral obligation to publish it and submit it to critical scrutiny. The danger of rhapsodizing is apparently as great on the darker side of Beethoven's life as it is on the luminous one. Veracity is not identical with the gathering of every bit of unverified scan-dal; least of all can the method claim to have anything in common with "historical criticism."

*   *
*

There is one piece of direct testimony that stands in par-ticular need of critical inquiry, as it comes nearest to establishing the fact of Beethoven's sexual mishaps. In 1852, Otto Jahn went to Vienna to collect material for the Beethoven biography he intended to write. Bertolini was still alive; Jahn visited him twice and each time took notes. At one of these interviews the physician remarked that *"Beethoven hatte gewöhnlich eine Flamme, die Guicciardi, Frau von Frank, Bettina Brentano; daneben 'miselte' er auch gewöhnlich, wobei er nicht immer gut wegkam."*

The noun *misel* and the verb *miseln* belonged to the German "fashion words" of the late eighteenth century. Probably they were imported into polite speech and writing by no less a person than Goethe, who must have learned them during his student days in Strassburg. *Misel* [1] is the diminutive of the Alsatian *mus* and means "little mouse"; it acquired the significance of "maiden" when lovingly applied to one; thence *miseln* stands for *liebeln*, which in English is flirting or philandering.[2] By forced analogy the Alsatian verb *miseln* may be pressed to do service for the German *mausen*, that incorrigible failing of the little rodent, to furtively steal its food. Thus it may come to signify any lighter form of pilfering; and by bending it over completely, it may be made to lean toward the German *naschen*, the meanings of which range all the way from an innocent nibbling of sweets to "illicitly to enjoy." It was a typical student word, and we can well imagine that the young Goethe in Strassburg, head over heels in love with Friederike Brion, found it attractive and useful. He kept it in his vocabulary. But where he employs it, as in his letters [3] to Frau von Stein, it suggests no more than a harmless flirt.

[1] Fr. L. K. Weigand, Deutsches Wörterbuch, 5th ed., Giessen, 1907: Misel, n. (Pl.—s) Mädchen, ein Lieblingswort des jungen Goethe, eig. elsäss. Dim. von *mus* "maus." ABL. miseln, v., liebeln.

Victor Henry, Le dialecte Alaman de Colmar, Paris 1900: misele = petite souris.

[2] Thieme-Preusser, Neues vollständiges kritisches Wörterbuch der englischen und deutschen Sprache; Gotha, 1859.

[3] Goethe Briefe, ed. by Philip Stein, Berlin, 1902. Letter of June 12, 1777, to Charlotte von Stein: *"Seit Sie weg sind fühl ich erst dass ich etwas besizze, und dass mir was obliegt. Meine übrigen kleinen Leidenschaften Zeitvertreibe und Miseleyen, hingen sich nur so an dem Faden der Liebe zu Ihnen an, der mich durch mein iezzig Leben durch ziehen hilft."* The editor added to this passage: *"Miseley soviel wie Liebelei, miseln gleich liebeln. Misel eine aus Demoiselle* [!] *entstandene Bezeichnung für Mädchen."*

We must assume that in Jahn's notes the word is not his, but Bertolini's. If the Viennese of 1852 used the word in the graver sense just indicated, it would imply that the old physician knew of some of Beethoven's escapades between 1810 and 1815 from which the composer did not always (*"nicht immer"*) return unscathed. The suggested repetition of these misfortunes strongly points to the probability that they had nothing to do with syphilis, but were re-infections or recrudescences of a different nature, which the medical men of those days had not yet learned to distinguish. In fact, the whole profession had been thrown into complete confusion by John Hunter, the famous English physician, who during the last years of the eighteenth century maintained and thought he had proved by experiments that syphilis, chancroid, and gonorrhœa were due to the same virus. Although Bertolini lived to see Hunter's error corrected by Ricord, in 1838, it is doubtful whether these later discoveries were in his mind when he discussed Beethoven with Jahn in 1852. Whatever venereal disease Bertolini may have thought he was treating in Beethoven, there is so far no convincing evidence or even good reason to fix upon syphilis as that disease.

Without going deeper into medical details, we have settled this much:

1. Since Beethoven's incipient deafness had declared itself by 1800, it is impossible to conceive that a venereal disease contracted ten or fifteen years later, if indeed such was contracted, had anything to do with his deafness; and of "syphilitic affections at any early period of his life" we have no proof, nor does his medical history lead us to believe that such an affection existed.

2. Any diagnosis of a venereal disease prior to 1838 must be accepted with the greatest reserve, and not even a prescription or a "cure" involving mercury treatment gives trustworthy evidence of syphilis.

If Dr. Bertolini, as Thayer reported, burned in 1831 (when he believed himself at the point of death) all the letters which Beethoven had written to him, "because a few were not of a

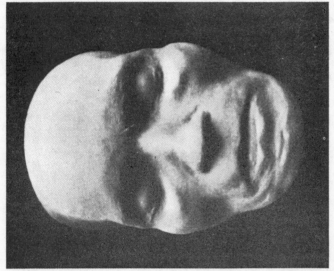

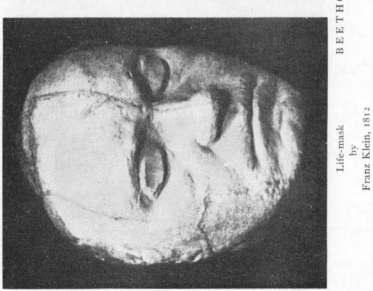

Life-mask
by
Franz Klein, 1812

BEETHOVEN

Death-mask
by
Josef Danhauser, 1827

nature to be risked in careless hands," the precaution speaks well for the doctor's discretion, but offers no positive clue to the nature of these confidences. Should they have been concerned with a malady "that had not merely physical but moral connotation," the deduction — unsupported by other proof — that this malady was syphilis can hardly be called "critical." For the sake of argument it might be objected that, in view of Beethoven's constant intestinal troubles and his blunt modes of expression, the letters, without touching upon amorous misadventures at all, may have been sufficiently "Rabelaisian" to make it seem desirable to Bertolini that they be kept out of "careless hands." Moreover, it would be interesting to know whether in 1831 Bertolini destroyed only Beethoven's letters or those of some other patients as well.

Suppose Bertolini in 1831 — believing his death from cholera near — destroyed the greater part of his medical correspondence. Years later Thayer looks him up and asks to see the letters of the great man to his physician. The physician admits he has them no longer, he burned them. Thayer throws up his hands in horror. What better excuse could the embarrassed physician give than to explain his act of vandalism as an act of pious caution?

In the last analysis, not even Bertolini's *"miseln"* need have the "incriminating" meaning suggested above. Mr. Newman himself tells us that in 1848 (or only four years prior to the Bertolini interview) the editor of Goethe's letters to Frau von Stein gave the meaning of *misel* as *schöne* [a belle or a sweetheart] and *miseln* as *schönthun* [act the gallant or flirt]. Note that the doctor opposed the term to what he said about Giullietta, Christine, and Bettina. These three were "flames" who burned as much in admiration for the composer as he burned in love for them; they were women of a certain prominence, known to have accepted Beethoven's homages more or less enthusiastically; but besides these known attachments Beethoven "habitually" (*gewöhnlich*) flirted with pretty women, unknown and of lesser station, without always capturing his prize. Indeed, there may have been occasions when his attentions were severely rebuffed and the poor love-sick bear must have looked rather sheepish. Ries tells of an instance in Baden when he surprised the composer with an unknown woman who had apparently taken offence at something that Beethoven had said or done; when Beethoven failed in his attempted mending of the wrong move (to slow music played by Ries!), the tilt ended checkmate and the lady left. There is nothing to prevent us from interpreting Bertolini's remark as importing just this, that the flirtatious Beethoven, who had exceptional luck with some women (see Wegeler's reference to conquests an Adonis might have found impossible), was occasionally snubbed; or — to translate Bertolini's words literally — Beethoven did "not always come off well" — that is, victoriously — in his habitual philanderings. The idiom is the same in English as in German.

Nothing obliges us to see an injury to Beethoven's health in what may have been no more than a wound to his vanity. It is less of a strain to put a direct and innocent interpretation upon Bertolini's expression than an equivocal one. Thayer may have thought it a delicate point, for he quoted the first half of Bertolini's remark, the one about Beethoven's "flames," and kept silent about the *"miseln."* That was in a line with Thayer's "exceptionally judicial habit of mind." Since the remark was made to Jahn and not to Thayer, the latter could not judge, any better than we can now, what special meaning the speaker's "inflexion" might have imparted to the phrase. Certainly, in Goethe's letters to Charlotte von Stein the word *"miseln"* and its derivatives were used in the sense that is currently applied to the English "flirt" or the slangy "necking." And the "innocent" explication is offered here simply to show how much there is yet to be ascertained before any other construction can be built on a foundation of facts.

* *
*

The time is past when Beethoven needed "shielding." We make ourselves ridiculous if we attempt to throw the cloak of our conventions round the shoulders of a giant. The thought no longer shocks us that the composer of a "Missa Solemnis" had promiscuous sex relations. We must be reconciled to the whims of nature, which dooms the spirit who conceives the music of a "Credo in unum Deum" to pursue indifferently pretty *Graben-nymphen* or unkempt servant wenches, to become flesh in their embrace.

The probability is greater of our discovering the truth in what the living Beethoven confessed about himself than of finding it in what Mr. Newman imagined about him one hundred years after his death. We have Beethoven's own word for it that he was "no woman-hater"; and at the time he wrote this he had no reason to lie, nor cause for wanting to appear in the borrowed plumes of Don Juan. They were his own. And to judge by what we know of his life, he did not shed his feathers at an early age. It is sophistry to postulate "a youthful imprudence" and a syphilitic affection merely in order to explain Beethoven's anxiety for the moral welfare of his brothers and nephew. The violent hatred for his dissolute sisters-in-law, his solicitude for the weak brothers and weaker nephew, were all perfectly natural. Any healthy person imbued with the least family pride and family love would have done as much. And we know that Beethoven's pride was exceeded only by his capacity for love. Complex and extraordinary as his character was, Beethoven showed no trait of mind, no singularity of behaviour, that has been observed exclusively or predominantly among syphilitics. Mr. Newman's suggestion of a "perverse sex-obsession" and a "morbid sex-complex" based on the presence of syphilis is interesting. But it so happens that Beethoven's "abnormalities" can all be explained quite simply without resorting to an assumption for which we are still lacking the first scrap of indisputable proof.

The first one openly to include syphilis among Beethoven's half-dozen or more maladies was Sir George Grove in the first edition of his famous "Dictionary" (1879).[1] The main prop for

---

[1] It looks as though the glory of having been the first to discover Beethoven's "syphilis" must be conceded to British diagnosticians. But among

the syphilis-theory was Beethoven's deafness. But that prop collapses when we bear upon it with our present-day medical knowledge. Whether Beethoven's deafness was due to an impairment of the conducting mechanism of the ear, secondary to a disease of

them the honour of individual priority is still disputed. Thus — in the *Musical Times* of June 1, 1927 — Mr. William Wallace claims that in 1923 he had the privilege of being the first "to bring forward a piece of evidence which clinches the diagnosis." Mr. Wallace is not only a very able composer and writer, he happens to have had some medical training. His words deserve to be pondered. Mr. Wallace's "evidence" is a photograph of Beethoven's skull, taken at the first exhumation in 1863. This photograph is supposed to show "that the bone in the region of the right ear is enormously thickened"; by this condition, Mr. Wallace believes, "Mr. Newman's minute analysis" is clenchingly upheld. Now, first it should be borne in mind that Beethoven's skull, in 1863, was found to be in a very bad state of preservation. On the whole subject of the skull, see Frimmel's article *Schädel* in his "Handbuch." Through excisions at the autopsy "the bony parts of the head were much altered." Here, then, we are on rather unsafe ground. Moreover, deductions made from the photograph of the reconstructed skull or a plaster-cast are open to question; such photographs would have to be taken under carefully arranged lighting so as to prevent small surface irregularities from appearing as gross asymmetries. Undoubtedly, there existed some pathological change in the petrous portion of the temporal bone. The autopsy already stated that "the whole substance of the *os petrosum* showed a similar degree of vascularity, being traversed by vessels of considerable size, more particularly in the region of the cochlea." The localization in that anatomical region, the thickening of the bone which contains the ear structures, the increase in the number and size of blood-vessels, the degenerative changes in the terminal nerves, all combined strongly suggest a case of otosclerosis (see the summary of recent ætiological observations presented in Ballenger's "Diseases of the Nose, Throat and Ear" [1925], pp. 746-52, in the chapter on otosclerosis). Even Dr. Schweisheimer, who does not accept the latter diagnosis, categorically rejects as baseless the assertion that the thickening of the bone in Beethoven's skull was due to syphilitic action, and goes to great length in proving his point (see Schweisheimer, "Beethoven's Leiden" [1922], pp. 83-6). Mr. Wallace's "evidence," therefore, was thrown out of court one year before he brought it forward. If this sort of scandal-mongering guess-work proves anything, it is the grim determination of some syphilo-maniacs to de-deify Beethoven. But he would remain Beethoven, and be the greater, had he belonged to that distinguished company of *buveurs très-illustres, et vous vérolés très-précieux!*

the middle ear, or to a chronically progressive affection (otosclerosis) of the inner ear, of indeterminate ætiology, in neither case would it be necessary or normal to presuppose a syphilitic origin. The autopsy, contrary to Lauder Brunton's opinion, did not describe any condition which suggested the effects of an acquired or congenital syphilis. Dr. Schweisheimer is categorical on that score. He sees no correlation between the deafness of Beethoven and syphilis. He believes that Beethoven suffered from a disease of the inner ear (labyrinth), not of the nature of otosclerosis, but due to a simple infection. Bilancioni is convinced that it was a case of otosclerosis (*Per me si trattò indubbiamente di una otosclerosi*) and points out that this affection is not limited to the middle ear, as Schweisheimer thinks, but can spread to the inner ear (*È erroneo quanto sostiene il Schweisheimer che nella otosclerosi il processo si limiti all' orecchio medio*). Frimmel adheres to Bilancioni's diagnosis, first made by Dr. Leo Jacobsohn in 1910.

Whatever we know from Beethoven's own descriptions about the progress of his deafness — the pains, the inner noises he heard (tinnitus), and the vanishing perception of higher notes—is in accordance with the clinical picture of an otosclerosis, particularly that form which involves anatomically the osseous labyrinth (hyperostosis of the cochlea). The autopsy revealed that "the Eustachian tube [the canal connecting the middle ear with the naso-pharynx] was much thickened, its mucous lining swollen and somewhat contracted about the osseous portion of the tube; in front of its orifice and toward the tonsils some dimpled scars were observable." This raises the belief that one of the several and severe "colds" from which Beethoven suffered at an early age resulted in a low-grade infection such as might be caused by a streptococcic invasion; in character the process is analogous to that which affects the joints, or the valves of the heart, or the glandular organs, producing always degenerative and fibrotic changes. The primary disease, which eventually induces these later degenerative changes in the ear, may arise from infections situated remotely, or may develop by direct extension through the Eustachian tubes from infections in the naso-pharynx.[1]

On the one side, then, we have a few inferences of the most doubtful validity, whereas on the other we have facts which are admissible as significant evidence, because they represent direct observation in respect to clinical symptoms and anatomical conditions found at autopsy, and also because they harmonize with statistical probabilities based on the collective experience of the medical profession. With our present knowledge, the only conclusion possible is that Beethoven's deafness was not caused by syphilis, either congenital or contracted.

*   *

*

Mr. Newman is not content with putting the human, all-too-human Beethoven under his lens and pronouncing him a syphilitic; in the second half of his book he takes the "unconscious" composer under the microscope and bids us look at Beethoven's musical "finger-print." One cannot hold back the suspicion that a musical Bertillon system would show too close a resemblance among most of the thumbs of one generation to give it great value; at a certain distance, yes — but there again it would be rather the foot-print of a colossus marking a stride in the advance of music. However, let us examine Mr. Newman's discovery.

The musical "finger-print" of Beethoven, according to Mr. Newman, consists in a "figure of three ascending notes in con-

[1] Professor János Bókay, director of the Pediatric Clinic of Budapest University, an ardent musician and president of the Medical Philharmonic Club, commemorated the centenary of Beethoven's death by reading to the medical society a paper on "The Deafness, Last Illness, and Death of Beethoven." Prof. Bókay, after careful review of all the known circumstances, concluded that "the cause of deafness, according to our present conception, was some disease of the labyrinth, and in view of the constricted tube, there is justification in concluding that in the tympanic cavity serious anatomic changes must have been present."

junct motion that generally come in about the same place relatively to the melodic design as a whole, and are unconsciously used to perform the same expressive function."

It was comparatively easy to deal with Mr. Newman the syphilologist. Mr. Newman the finger-print expert is more problematical. First of all, it is difficult to follow Mr. Newman in his ideas about the processes of musical composition. He thinks that "all composers' minds are more or less unconscious mechanisms." Perhaps he means that most artists — whether prose writers, painters, or musicians — automatically develop certain technical idiosyncrasies which are in general easily recognized. They make up what is called a man's style. But once these peculiarities of style are formed — with their selective, and therefore conscious, aids to expression — they require the most vigilant attention, lest they degenerate into mannerisms. Fortunate the artist who successively evolves different styles. Beethoven, Wagner, Verdi were such lucky chameleons. There is an advantage in cultivating versatility. Bach saw it; he tried his hand at the French, Italian, and English manner. Handel was saved when he quit manufacturing operas and went into the oratorio business. Grieg and Debussy belong to the other type. Their "unconscious mechanism" ran in one groove, after one pattern. The wheels slow down when they are clogged with manneristic grit. They need the oil of conscious revolution.

Instead of giving himself over to an "unconscious expression of forces profounder than the merely personal," the artist is the finer, the more sensitive or the more aware he is of the workings of his mind. There are no forces profounder than the ego. And the artist above all others should obey the Delphic injunction to plumb his own depths. It is possible that Nevin's "Rosary" sprang from an unconscious mechanism; it is certain that Fauré's "Prison" sprang from a highly conscious one. Nevin's song is sung by millions, Fauré's hardly ever. Is it because the "Rosary" is the more profound of the two?

We know there is that unaccountable thing called inspiration, which sees to it that the blind hen does not starve and that Beethoven should hit upon the themes of the "Eroica." But whereas the blind hen swallows her corn and cackles, Beethoven has to chew upon his themes and nearly choke. The artist is the tireless artisan, the fashioner, who polishes his verse or his gem until it has that appearance of flawless perfection which hides the pains it cost and makes it seem inevitable. A masterpiece is forged in the white heat of super-consciousness.

Mr. Newman is far too astute not to see the weak points in his theory of the unconscious. Toward the end of his dissertation he admits that "obviously Beethoven was something more than an instrument of the unconscious; he sought consciously for his themes, and did a good deal of conscious manipulation of them and designing of them." Shades of Tartarus! What man sweat drops of bitterer agony than did Beethoven, the conscious manipulator of his themes? And does not Mr. Newman realize that in the "something more" we have the difference between the sightless bird and genius?

When Mr. Newman speaks of the "unconscious repetition of the same formulæ" in the works of certain musicians, we think of the personal idiosyncrasies first, and second of the stylistic devices peculiar to a whole school or generation of composers. In the first instance it is a definite "trick" — such as Franck's cumulative melodic expansion or harmonic restlessness; in the second, it is a general tendency — such as we find in our present atonal and poly-tonal music. If it were not that certain tricks are so easily discerned and can so faithfully be copied, we should not have with us always the unintentional imitator of the masters, or the amusing intentional mimicker, like Mr. Edward Ballantine and his variations on "Mary had a little lamb."

The characteristic note must be original with someone before it can be imitated by others. But Mr. Newman's "three blind (and unconscious) mice" in upward scale formation can hardly be called a personal "formula" that originated with Beethoven. They are a purely structural tool of musical expression, as impersonal and generally employed as the conjunction "and" is in speech. In music it is a connecting bridge, or what some German analysts have called an "anlauf." [1] In speech, the "and" construction may gather the momentum, the live force, of an idiom; it did in ancient Hebrew; and thence it passed into the translations of the Old Testament. In a moderate measure it remains indispensable to all cultural languages, but it is happiest when left unnoticed. In the hands of a verbal artist the humble "and" may, on occasion, be pulled up from its modest station, to perform a rhetorical feat that lifts it high above its usual functions. Overdone, it would be an unbearable mannerism. It is not, it never can be, a personal "formula"; to stamp it as such would be folly.

Yet it is not too much to say that this—comparatively speaking—is precisely what Mr. Newman has done with his "three notes." Only he goes still further. Imagine a literary critic who tells us that he has detected the personal "finger-print" of a writer in the use of the conjunction "and." Not satisfied with counting how often the little word of three letters occurs in his author's text, he bids us behold these letters unconsciously, mysteriously, irrepressibly creeping into such words as hANDle, brANDish, cANDid, mANDarin, sANDals, commAND, AND a hundred others—always "for the same purpose of emotional expression at very much the same point." Peals of laughter would greet the literary critic and his discovery.

Mr. Newman, the musical critic, expects us to keep a serious face while he calmly takes an integral group of four or five notes out of a musical context and plucks from it the three notes he

[1] The immediate parent of Beethoven's "finger-print" was a form of the ascending *port de voix* prevalent in the music of the eighteenth century. But the ancestry goes back to the ascending *ternaria ligatura* of the mensural notation, to the *scandicus* of the Gregorian chant, and backward to the dim beginnings of modulated human utterance, when the short ascending "speech curve" first acquired its emotive stress, its accent of pleading, the suggestion of *Innigkeit* which is the true characteristic of the three, and sometimes more, ascending notes as used by Beethoven in certain places with such felicitous effect. He neither invented the device, nor used it more than others did. Older masters knew its value. See the emotive "anlauf" of three notes to the culminating *herzig* in Mozart's phrase *"Es war ein herzig's Veilchen."* That is a typical example of a common usage.

thinks best suited for the demonstration of his theory. In one
instance (his Example 24) he picks a scale succession of six sixteenth-notes from a group of eight, splits the six in the middle,
and naïvely announces that here we have two "finger-prints" of
three notes each, one right after the other. Think what fun Mr.
Newman could have in hunting for Beethoven's musical finger-
prints in Czerny's "Schule der Geläufigkeit."

Of the same order is Mr. Newman's claim that the numerous
Beethovenian motives, built on the notes of the tonic triad, belong
to one "brotherhood." Obviously they do. But we perceive an
endless horde of rich and poor relations clamouring for admission
to the same fraternity. Mozart and Wanhal, Haydn and Dussek
are equally eligible. The company is not what you might call
"strictly exclusive." Already Messrs. Bourguès and Denéréaz
("La musique et la vie intérieure," 1921) observed that *"Beethoven a l'idée fixe de la Tonique."* But so had his whole
generation.[1]

Mr. Newman is lavish with examples which are supposed to
prove Beethoven's "obsession" of the three-note figure. Unfortunately most of these examples prove either too little or too
much. Take four out of the first five, and you will find that in

---

[1] The "scale of nature" and the natural intervals of the overtones have
long been associated with the musical expression of elemental ideas, sug-
gesting the vastness of nature, the grandeur of creation, sentiments noble,
heroic, or awesome. Beethoven's "Die Himmel rühmen" and Ponchielli's "Cielo
e mar" are cousins german. Of the same tribe are Weber's "Ocean, thou
mighty monster" and Wagner's innumerable "nature" motives, from the
Flying Dutchman's angry sea to the accommodating rainbow of the gods.
Long ago the fanfare became fanfaronade. It was the formula best suited
to the grand, or rather grandiloquent, manner of the eighteenth century.
The motival use of broken chords was as essential to the symphonist as to
the opera-composer. Take the opening movement of the E flat Symphony
(Opus 4, No. 4) of Franz Xaver Richter. The Mannheim influence was not
lost on Mozart. Half of his forty-odd symphonies begin with the tonic
flourish, not counting his chamber music and the rest. The tonic triad, strut-
ting up and down, was a form of musical Johnsonese. Beethoven, like all
of his contemporaries, could still indulge at times in the most approved
eighteenth-century grandiloquence.

each one of them, besides Mr. Newman's ascending three mice, there are tucked away somewhere three descending notes — always an interval of a second followed by an interval of a third. In point of design and "emotional expression" they are quite as characteristic. Nothing prevents us from declaring these three, instead of the others, to be a "finger-print," if frequency of appearance is a sign of the obsession. As regards the latter, may not Mr. Newman, rather than Beethoven, be the real sufferer?

* *

*

If "an essay in musical psychology" is merely another name for fiction, we must hail Mr. Newman's book as an extremely well-written, gripping tale. Put forward as a piece of "historical criticism," it mistakes the meaning of history and the office of the critic. Mr. Newman's avowed purpose in writing his book was to remind us that on the occasion of a centenary "we ought to try to see our subject as he really was." Call him Mr. Newman's subject, and insist that neither a syphilitic patient nor an unconscious musician had anything to do with the late centennial celebrations that overwhelmed us with a flood of Beethoven concerts. If we took a pessimistic view, we might say that the world one hundred years ago killed Beethoven, the man, by not giving him enough; and that in the course of the centennial year it did its best to kill the composer by giving too much of him. Chances are, the composer will survive the ordeal — to the possible disappointment of some people. That the outspoken, peppery fighter should have been dead and buried these hundred years can be a matter only for congratulation. Were he alive, what would he not do to Mr. Newman?

POET AS PROPHET

THERE surely never was a place or a time less fit for the pursuits of the scholiast than our handsome capital at the height of summer. Oppressiveness of the atmosphere engenders lethargy of the mind. Thoughts stick, the brain comes to a standstill.

Not long ago some Labour members in the British Parliament questioned the necessity of providing funds for the temporary removal of His Majesty's ambassadorial establishment from Washington to the coast of New England. Let these honourable and laborious gentlemen draw hither and learn. Even so, an ambassador enjoys certain extraterritorial privileges for his relief and restoration — in cold weather as well as in warm — which do not belong to a law-abiding, dried-up music librarian. All the more reason why the American Government should provide funds for the permanent removal of the whole city of Washington to a less debilitating clime. Or — well, for the alternative we must look to the next Congress and the referendum.

You will say that when it is hot, it is so nearly everywhere. Quite true, and may it console the philosophically minded. But there are differences in degree; the qualifying (or disqualifying) adjective has a comparative as well as a superlative. And the latter indubitably is the distinctive attribute of Washington. Under such circumstances it is impossible to write critical reviews of anything heavier than the lightest fiction. Yes, if I were to discuss with you, let us say, the amiable books of André Birabeau that I just finished — "Le Bébé Barbu," "Le Voyage à l' Ombre," "Le Parfum de la Femme Coupable" — excellent summer reading, I assure you, and not to be disdained in winter.

It needs no further word of explanation why I have lacked the

courage to plunge into profound investigations of Gregorian
rhythms or why I passed by, with a faint shudder, another com-
pact little treatise on the music of the ancient Greeks. I have not
even been able to bring myself to read one or the other of two
new lives of one of my favourite composers, Couperin. (How I
should love, this very minute, to hear Landowska play "Le Bavolet
Flottant" and "Les Barricades Mystérieuses"!) There are a dozen
or more books staring at me reproachfully for my neglect, books
that will be so much more interesting in December, unless by that
time other and still more interesting books have come to hand. It
almost seemed as though I should have to beg off, altogether,
which would have been a terrible calamity. But there hurried to
my rescue a little volume which greatly entertained me and which
I want you to enjoy with me, if you have not already seen it.
Its title is "Antheil and the Treatise on Harmony" (Paris, Three
Mountains Press); its author is Mr. Ezra Pound, the well-known
poet. I admit that the penetrating, the witty and gently ironic
M. Birabeau is perhaps more amusing than is Mr. Pound, who
only now and then is really funny, and more often is a bit bump-
tious. But, all the same, I found his *opusculum* good reading when
the thermometer "at the kiosk" on the shady side of Pennsyl-
vania Avenue was crawling up to 105° and higher.

You have, of course, heard of Mr. George Antheil; and if you
have not, let me tell you in Mr. Pound's own words that Mr.
Antheil is "possibly the first American or American-born musician
to be taken seriously." This is good news, although one could
have wished for more assurance in Mr. Pound's conclusion. That
"possibly" mars the sentence, as it does the verdict. Under-
statement is not Mr. Pound's habitual manner. He can be
devastatingly emphatic.

Mr. Pound's provocative little book comprises four sections.
The first is given over to his "Treatise on Harmony"; the second
one deals more particularly with Mr. Antheil; the third contains
"Notes for performers by William Atheling [*recte* E. P.] with
marginalia emitted by George Antheil"; and "Varia" — half a
dozen pages of left-overs — bring up the rear.

Mr. Antheil, we learn, was born on July 8, 1901, at Trenton,
N. J. "Trenton makes, the World takes!" Could it be that the
Trenton Chamber of Commerce is unaware of what the city's
product is doing to Paris, France, and is about to do — in Mr.
Pound's estimation — to the rest of the world? Mr. Antheil's
parents are Poles; his name is German (it means *share* or *portion*,
and in American, I am told, it should be pronounced so as to
rhyme with *peel* and not with *pile*). Mr. Antheil writes American
music which is neither like Brahms nor like jazz; and sober judges
count it to be better than both. So far, unfortunately, I have not
heard a single note of it myself. Therefore I am still disposed to
accept all that Mr. Pound has written of Mr. Antheil as the one
composer living who is "writing music that couldn't have been
written before."

However, for the sake of fairness and completeness I must
report the opinion of at least one critic, M. Boris de Schloezer,
who differs on that point with Mr. Pound. M. de Schloezer is
generally one of the first to welcome the new or unusual; he cannot be dismissed as a crabbed conservative. Proof of it is that
when he reviewed Mr. Antheil's "Symphony" (conducted by Mr.
Golschman in Paris) for the "Revue musicale," he thought the
composer had "something to say" and "knew his business," although neither the sayings nor the business had anything strik-
ingly novel to commend them. In fact, contrary to Mr. Pound,
M. de Schloezer detected in this score "not only reminiscences,
but entire phrases" of music that had been written before, and
explained it as a "disdain of originality deriving evidently from
Stravinsky, whose shadow hovers over the whole work." The symphony was followed by Mr. Antheil's ballet music for player-
piano and sundry other mechanical contraptions, all manipu-
lated by the composer in person. It is the music of levers, gears,
transmitters, motors, batteries. As such it certainly is the music
of our time, something that could not have been written before.
But is its newness matched by its excellence? M. de Schloezer
thinks not. To him this ballet music "spoiled completely the hopes
that the symphony had raised." He saw in it merely a caricature

of Stravinsky's "Noces." When critics of such eminence disagree, what is one to do? The public in Paris, with the exception of a few Antheilians led by Mr. Pound, lustily hooted and jeered. That used to be a sign of something worthwhile happening, and on the strength of it cautious critics were safe in proclaiming the rise of a great prophet in Israel. Such was still the case with Mr. Arnold Schönberg, whose earlier compositions unloosed public riots, led to fist-fights and law-suits, but whose latest lucubrations are reverently and politely listened to by the *conoscenti* and the *innocenti* alike. Now M. de Schloezer throws doubt into our hearts by saying that *"actuellement, le scandale n'est plus une preuve."* The bottom drops out of musical criticism.

*   *

*

That this "revolutionary" music should be discovered, recognized, admired by a poet while musicians still reject or deride it is in accordance with the best tradition. The ordinary musician's ears are dulled by iteration, clogged with prejudice; his eyes are riveted precisely on all that has "been written before." The poet Baudelaire acclaimed Wagner when the musicians, from Berlioz down, sniffed him with suspicion or growled at him angrily. The thing that could not have been done before, in art, is always suspected or denounced at first. Because it generally means the death of all the weak and ephemeral stuff that immediately precedes it. The craving for novelty is exceeded only by the fear of innovation. Novelty is king for the moment at least, while the next usurper is plotting dethronement or worse. Therefore the innovations in one art often find their first and loudest heralds in the followers of a sister art, since they have less to fear from it and so have a partially open mind. The poet stands to lose little by an upheaval in music, but he can win much if the insurrection follows along the lines of his own previous revolt.

The case of Mr. Pound, ex-vorticist poet, is not, however, a perfect example of what I am trying to describe. Not because he falls short of the standard, but because he far surpasses it. Mr. Pound is a paragon of open-mindedness. Long a writer of polished verse, he has lately joined the ranks of composers. At least he "accommodates notes to words," as he himself puts it, outside of which he claims to be, in music, no more than "an incompetent amateur." Tush, tush! He recently had some of his compositions performed in Paris, settings of poems by François Villon. Poet and musician, he is Mr. Antheil's Baudelaire and Liszt.

But this does not exhaust the versatility of Mr. Pound; he is also a theorist. I should almost call him an academician. For he explains that "academicism is not excess of knowledge; it is the possession of *idées fixes* as to how one shall make use of one's data." Now no one would accuse Mr. Pound of being burdened with an excess of musical knowledge in spite of his apparent acquaintance — nay, his intimate familiarity — with Raphael Socius, Giambattista Doni, Prosdocimus de Beldemandis, Dom Bedos de Celles, Franco of Cologne, Marchettus of Padua, and Dolmetsch of Haslemere. Moreover, if Mr. Pound's data are not dancing a perpetual passacaglia over the *ostinato* of his *idées fixes* (including Mr. Antheil), then our whirling world had better revise its concepts of fixed stars and suns (including Mr. Antheil).

* *
*

The first thing Mr. Pound's little book sets out to show is that, from Aristoxenos to Schönberg, no treatise on harmony has laid proper stress or has so much as touched on "the element of Time." There appears to be necessary "a time-interval" which must elapse between one sound and another "if the two sounds are to produce a pleasing consonance or an interesting relation." Instantly our curiosity is pricked, we sit attentive to learn at last what constitutes a pleasing consonance, what forms an interesting relation. But we are bilked again. Instead, Mr. Pound promulgates his basic axiom (set in all caps.), to wit, that "a sound of any pitch, or any combination of such sounds, may be followed by a sound of any other pitch, or any combination of such sounds, providing the time-interval between them is properly gauged; and this is true for any series of sounds, chords, or arpeggios."

You could not ask for a clearer, terser definition of this hitherto "grossly omitted" element. Nor can you fail to note that, in spite of the new liberties granted, there is still a wholesome restraint suggested in the proviso about those "properly gauged" time-intervals. The restraint goes farther. Even Mr. Pound's system has limits, physical if not æsthetic ones. He points them out presently: "The limits for the practical purposes of music depend solely on our capacity to produce a sound that will last long enough, i.e., remain audible long enough for the succeeding sound or sounds to catch up, traverse, intersect it."

All this is not nearly so revolutionary as the cover *couleur de Moscou* of Mr. Pound's little book would lead one to expect. Here emerge cheerfully our tried old friends the chords and arpeggios, the pleasing consonances and interesting relations; why, even practical purposes are dragged out again to put us at ease and make us feel at home. How much more daring was Dr. Burney, music's first transcontinental reporter and interviewer, who already in 1770 foresaw a legitimate place in music for noise. It took a century and a half to fulfil his prediction. Let me hastily add that whatever Mr. Pound's "new paths" may be, they lie not in the direction of mere noise. In fact, he shrinks with ill-concealed disdain from poor, deluded Marinetti and his "dead cats in a foghorn."

Sensitive poet that he is, Mr. Pound has given much thought to rhythm. He illumines the subject occasionally with a bright flash that soars like a sky-rocket and leaves its image on the retina long after darkness has returned. Take this for instance: "The verbal rhythm is monolinear. It can form contrapunto only against its own echo, or against a developed expectancy." That is splendid—keenly observed, brilliantly expressed, and absolutely true. It applies to prose as well as poetry. And the "developed expectancy" is typical of music. Almost the entire art of musical composition consists in knowing how to develop this expectancy,

when to gratify it, and when to surpass it with something beyond
expectation. What we call "æsthetic pleasure" is largely contained in the relish of a proper balance between the two.

On the whole, however, Mr. Pound's observations on rhythm
are neat and sensible rather than original. He believes in an
absolute rhythm. So did Heraclitus. So do most of us, for that
matter. But what the secret is of a flowing line of verse, or a
felicitous prose cadence, Mr. Pound does not pretend to divulge,
any more than he can probably tell us why in music a heavenly
asthma (take the accompaniment of Bach's "Golgotha") can be
as beautiful as a long melodic phrase coiling up and down on a big
chest full of wind.

*   *

*

When Mr. Pound waxes eloquent on frequencies and combined
frequencies of notes, he recalls the dreariest of text-books, without
always attaining to the soundness that the best of them possess.
And as regards his dictum that "the time-element affects harmony," it belongs to the genus *castanea*, or chestnut. I well remember an experience of my own, twenty years ago — oh, for
those irretrievable time-intervals! — when I showed a piece of
music to a man for whose critical ear I have always had the highest regard. In dissecting a certain progression and trying to
analyse what was wrong with it, he finally pointed to one note
and said: "I hear that note entering one-eighth too soon." That
was all. The progression was corrected, it was good. I had learned
something, and it was nothing but the harmonic significance of
Mr. Pound's "time-element." But, alas, to gauge it there is nothing, nothing but an ear, a sharp, rinsed, unbuttoned ear. Or the
superhuman imaginative concentration, helped by "remembered
analogies," of that deaf crank Beethoven.

Here is a question Mr. Pound must have addressed expressly
to me: "Why, *mon contradicteur* [!], have masters of music speci-
fied that certain compositions be played at a certain speed?" I
bow and reply: to have the directions disregarded by performers

— when these know better. For as there is absolute rhythm, there is specific time. One is born of the other. And there are cases on record when even masters of music have for some reason or other failed to indicate that specific time correctly. But in most instances a musical (and rhythmic) person will sense the time unmistakably, just as a sensitive individual, in walking with someone else, will know whether the pace is too fast or too slow to suit the other walker and the purpose of the walk.

Mr. Pound does not miss the opportunity of reminding us that he had a prominent part in drafting the "Vorticist Manifestoes" and in the activities of the "movement" whose short but promising existence was rudely ended in August, 1914, when our globe was engulfed in a mightier eddy, compared with which the noise that the "Vorticists" made was as the swish of the receding waters in a bathtub. *Bon dieu, qu'il y a longtemps de tout ça!* If I feel like Methuselah, it is not because of my forty-odd years (most of them wasted), but because I can look back upon distant vistas of "movements," one following the other like Egyptian dynasties.

With the war came hysteria. Other pathological states, already latent, were developed by it. They affected the arts. "Dadaism" and "Maschinenkunst" may seem to-day remoter than the reign of Thothmes. But the younger artists would all be machinists, engineers.

The constructing engineer is the great dare-devil of the day. He leads. His science and his craft accomplish wonders. If nature has any laws left inviolate, he will break them and establish laws of his own. In the revolt against "what has been done before" he offers daily new samples of unparalleled achievement. He has evolved, or is evolving, incidentally a new order of beauty, too strange yet to be comprehended in all its potentialities. Time will tell how and to what extent they can serve the needs of sculptor, painter, or musician.

Mechanisms, geometry, and mathematics all have certain well-known relations to art, and probably a few more which are not yet quite understood. But recurrently the idea of this inter-dependence gets hold of people like an obsession. The simple truth is seen in manic distortion. Mr. Pound has hit upon such truth when he defines music as "a composition of frequencies." But like so many other and similar definitions it tells only half the story. Anything that is mathematically ascertainable can also be reduced to formulas, can be communicated and taught. Mr. Pound thinks that if he can only get "the mathematics of these relations so complicated that composers will become discouraged, give up trying to compose by half-remembered rules, and really listen to sound," he will have performed no inconsiderable service to music.

The composer of genius does not work by rules, not even half-remembered ones. He depends largely upon expedients, and these he must find for himself. Half the time he stumbles upon these expedients by chance, or guided by a kindly demon. The expedients crystallize into devices. If the gods are merciful, they let the composer die young before the devices turn into petrified mannerisms. Should the expedients and devices land the composer anywhere, the whole *confrérie* will fall upon them like a pack of hungry wolves, and the theorists, *post factum*, will raise them to the dignity of rules. Then we are treated to a lot of what the Germans call *Epigonenmusik*, which might be translated as "yesterday's hash warmed over."

Parenthetically: there are dishes that taste better the second day than they did the first, provided a little culinary ingenuity enters into their preparation. They are not the *grands plats*. But they represent that delectable class of potted venison, fowl in aspic, or spicy ragouts. Man does not live by roast-beef alone, nor by Bach, Shakespeare, or Michelangelo.

*   *
*

The radical tendencies of Mr. Pound are most sharply defined in the criticisms that he signed "William Atheling" and contributed to the "New Age," from 1917 to 1920. The chief reason for reprinting them in the third part of Mr. Pound's book is the fact that now they come to us enhanced with the pat and tart glosses of the young Trentonian who pays them canine compliments and sprinkles over them the running commentary of his marginalia. The whole encounter is true to the life in its mixture of becoming gravity and charming *sans gêne*.

Art criticism seldom gets beyond a critic's tussle with his own likes and dislikes. Mr. Pound proves a nimble wrestler. Under the weight of heavy argument he pins to the carpet many veteran delusions commonly called "æsthetic creeds." And while he keeps them in a controversial strangle-hold, worthy of Zbisko the Great, umpire Antheil nods approval.

Mr. Pound dislikes the piano — or at least he did so in February, 1918, which was several years before Mr. Antheil discovered new possibilities in the super-dreadnaught (or dreadful) player-piano, which is to the gentle clavichord what the Gattling-gun is to the cross-bow. Mr. Pound's dislike, of 1918, for the piano is even to-day shared by many. But in slapping the instrument and making it responsible for the introduction of the tempered scale, he really hits at the pianists when in his brisk, epigrammatic style he avers that "all keyboard instruments tend to make performers of people not born to be musicians." Evidently Mr. Pound does not own stock in a piano-factory; otherwise he would not imply the ruinous suggestion that the output of the world's piano-manufacturers should be limited to the number of born musicians.

Leaving aside the question of keyboard *versus* fingerboard, does Mr. Pound intend to overlook the enormous debt that Occidental music owes to the tempered scale? Probably he would deny that it is a debt, and stamp it a curse. Mr. Pound believes in "absolute pitch." At least he has some more or less vague ideas as to the salvation of music depending on it. That brings him into sharp opposition to Professor Carl Stumpf and Dr. Erich von Hornbostel. The latter, with the caution characteristic of the scientist, once wrote that "absolute pitch in music is (well-nigh) irrelevant." Be that as it will, without the tempered scale coming when it did, we should not have had Bach's "Forty-eight" and its descendants. The tempered scale gave into the musician's hands the pass-key of enharmonic modulation. It was a marvellous expedient and became a dangerous device. Schubert handled it with the skill of a light-fingered Raffles. Wagner twisted off the bow and left the bit in the lock.

*   *

*

Undoubtedly there is too little regard for beauty of tone, the essentially sensuous and therefore essentially artistic quality of music. Mr. Pound tries to make matters appear worse than they are by contrasting the bad enough present with a past which only in his imagination acquires the virtues that he ascribes to it. He writes: "The attention that was centred in earlier music upon purity of tone, upon sound quality, has been weakened and weakened till I have seen a composer of no small talent utterly impervious to the quality of noise he was making." (To which "G. A." feelingly and illuminatingly adds: "I presume the 'timbre' is meant.")

Here is one of those pleasant and convenient myths that all critics invent at all times. Just what does Mr. Pound mean by the loose term "earlier music" and just how or where was the attention "centred" that produced in a fabled past something which is no longer ours? We have ear-witnesses who tell a different story. If Rousseau, Burney, e tutti quanti are too late for Mr. Pound, we might find him "earlier" ones. Impervious or sound-proof composers — and performers — have probably existed in every age, including the so-called golden one.

It was all right for Mr. Pound to write in 1918: "A concert in a concert-hall is a performance, a presentation, not an appeal to the sympathies of the audience." (He is justly indignant at the "interpreter" who obtrudes himself.) But see how much this simple statement gains in 1925 when appended to it we find a forceful "Yes. G. A." Mr. Antheil is not always so laconic. Nor is he shy in brandishing about with names. For example, Mr. Pound writes: "An era of bad taste probably gathers to itself inferior matter from preceding periods. An indiscriminate rum-

maging in the past does not help to form a tradition." Whereupon
Mr. Antheil jumps for joy and "emits" approvingly: "A splendid
turn for Mr. Casella, Malipiero, Prokofieff, and the Six." Mr.
Pound's assertion that "a sense of rhythm covers many defects"
draws from G. A.: "One might say almost all." Does the glos-
sarist here speak *pro domo?*

When Mr. Pound complains that "there is no place or company where any number of writers and musicians meet to try new
experiments of an 'unpractical nature,'" we must remember that
this was written in 1919. Conditions are changed. Rather an
absolute reversal has set in. Places and companies abound where
a specialty is made of experiments in music of an "unpractical
nature." They have become fashionable, hence lucrative affairs.

*   *

*

So one could go on, here picking a flower, there pricking a
bubble in William Atheling's Notes for Performers. His own performance is not the least entertaining part of Mr. Pound's book.
Moreover, the manner in which it is presented offers food for
thought and invites imitation. Considering the success of the
Pound-Antheil alliance, it would be an excellent scheme for each
musical critic to issue his complete works with marginal notes
"emitted" by some suitable and kindred commentator. Thus I
should like to see the annotated articles of Mr. Newman, M. Marnold, Signor Gatti, Herr Bekker, of our own Gilman, Rosenfeld,
and Hale, gathered and edited as "The World's Library of Musical
Hermeneutics." But the great question is: which critic and
composer should be paired? The problem is too knotty, too involved, to admit of a ready solution, especially in a state of æstival
somnolence, while "the adventurous sun took heaven by storm."

INDECENCY IN MUSIC

PEOPLE whose judgment is generally conceded to be as far from wrong as their virtue is above reproach hold the opinion that music has fallen to a depth of unexampled wickedness. The terms of good or bad, by them applied to a composition, no longer signify success or failure of workmanship and inspiration, but indicate the moral tenor of the music, the edifying or depraving — yes, depraving! — influence it is said to exert upon the hearer. If true, this points to a very alarming state of affairs. Where, under these circumstances, are our Vigilance Committees and Watch and Ward Societies? Apparently, a task awaits these gentlemen, much more severe than any which so far has engaged their ingenuity and perseverance. While they are defending the public against the dangers that lurk in the novels of the late D. H. Lawrence, poisons infinitely more subtle and deadly are being prepared for us by that most "innocent" of Muses, Polyhymnia. Compared with her sinful products, such books as the "Ragionamenti," the "Perfumed Garden," or "Le Moyen de Parvenir" would seem the spotless white of equally ancient nursery tales. What ground is there for these charges?

I am not so sure that music has not to thank the imagination of certain literary persons for some of its lately acquired disrepute. When the Kreutzer Sonata was branded as capable of undermining the foundations of wedlock, there remained hardly a piece of music that was safe from similar denouncement by the *sbirri* of a jealous sister art. Should Paolo and Francesca's accomplice tome stay unrevenged? While the demoralizing exercises in Fagin-Czerny's "School of Velocity" have yet to be turned to account in the story of an agile lady shoplifter, we have been told repeatedly and at great length how the flame of Tristan and

Isolde's music scorched the wings of immaculate maidens and set young men dreaming of "free love" with breakfast on an alcohol burner. The aforementioned Mr. Lawrence went so far as to describe a situation in which two hapless lovers are thrown into the arms of each other through the agency of a musical instrument that a rash punster might be pardoned for calling the tragic flute.

Of course, these accusations were proffered by writers of fiction whose musical understanding was, to say the least, rather vague. To refute them would be almost as easy as to disregard them. But critics who are thoroughly versed in the harmonic and æsthetic laws of music, thoroughly competent to estimate the ethical value of a composition — names shall be given — now tell us that music is headed straight for perdition; unless we stuff our ears with wax or, like Ulysses, lash ourselves to the mast of moral rectitude, we shall succumb to a lure more envenomed than was the Sirens' sweet and pernicious song.

All this is most disquieting, especially because it is so unexpected and finds the majority of us wholly wanting in a knowledge of when to apply the wax. Too long have we trusted blindly to what we thought was the innate purity of music. A writer in John Murray's "Quarterly Review," nearly a hundred years ago, expressed the belief that "there is no Hogarth in music. Punch can give her no place on his staff. She cannot reason, and she cannot defile. She is the most innocent companion of the Loves and Graces; for real romance is always innocent. Music is not pure to the pure only, she is pure to all. We can only make her a means of harm when we add speech to sound. It is only by a marriage with words that she can become a minister to evil. An instrument which is music, and music alone, enjoys the glorious disability of expressing a single vicious idea, or of inspiring a single corrupt thought. It is an anomaly in human history how any form of religion can condemn an organ; for it could not say an impious thing if it would."

The quotation is long, and had to be so, for a reason. Medwin, I believe, reports Lord Byron as saying that it is a common trick of reviewers, when they want to depreciate a work, to give no quotations from it; which was intended as a direct hit at the same "Quarterly." Therefore, no unfairness toward the culprit. The views of this anonymous writer must be given uncurtailed, so as to show the better how complete is the change of things. What was perfectly consistent with the romantic spirit in the year of grace and barricades, 1848, is now hopelessly out of date. Take, for instance, that remark about the organ. An organ remains an organ, after all, whether it stand in a church or in a moving-picture theatre. Yet in the theatre this selfsame instrument has not only acted the wag, it has been made to utter profanities and sounds of unmistakable vulgarity. It furnishes the daily accompaniment to scenes of horse-play and buffoonery which would have made the artist Hogarth blush, and the satirist yawn. Punch was a Hamlet in comparison with Mr. Charles Chaplin. But these, you will say, are not cases of "absolute music" — to call it "pure music" would be irony. I am coming to that.

Music, wedded to words or actions, has indeed been a "minister to evil" long before the projector dimmed the footlights. Nor does the whole guilt rest on the stage. Loose songs have probably existed ever since loose people sang; and that may lie a good deal farther back than most histories trace the evolution of music. The gallant century, in France, produced a rich and varied crop of gallant airs. What is interesting about the songs of that period, such as "Le Manchon," or "Les Vapeurs conjugales," or "Le Sucre d'orge," is that they were published with the official imprimatur of the court librarian and royal censor, and that the printers of such frail and dainty morsels could seriously recommend them as *"les plus propres à former les jeunes gens et les perfectionner dans la Musique."* True enough, the music of the songs has nothing to do with the words. Most of these old airs are charming, and certainly all are pure, not only to the pure, but to everybody. As regards the words, the *"jeunes gens"* of that day were perhaps a little franker than are the young people of ours, but not a whit worse. Our bookstalls may not openly display anything quite so spicy as "The Charms of Cheerfulness or Merry Songster's Companion," containing gems

like "The Inn Turned Out," but there are in private circulation
not a few songs almost as disreputable, and certainly far more
stupid. The armies in the late war knew them by the hundreds.
However, if we have become more careful in the sort of texts
we publish, we have grown bolder in the tunes to which we sing
them. Those eighteenth-century songs, stripped of their naughty
words, stand up without blemish, perfectly innocent and often
exquisite melodies. Quite differently, some of our present street
and dance tunes have a noticeable tendency to remain coarse and
downright vulgar, even without the slightest hint of an under-
lying text. Should music really have lost that glorious disability
of expressing a vicious thought? Could it have learned, unaided,
to be wicked and indecent?

Before taking up these questions, let us admit that one of the
prime factors in the superb unfolding of music, during the last
century and a half, has been none other than the erotic element.
Adolf Weissmann, music critic, historian of Berlin as a musical
centre, biographer of Bizet and Chopin, wrote a little book
entitled "Der klingende Garten." It is a series of "impressions of
the erotic in music." The chapter headings are: The Elements;
Voices; Mozart; The Viennese; Chopin; Symphonie fantastique;
Traviata and Carmen; Wagner; Puccinism; Salome; Conclusion.
This is not enough to indicate the trend of thought that runs
through these chapters, but it will suggest an outline of its
progress; also, it will hint at the direction in which the author
goes for proof of his thesis that the Dionysian is the strongest
motive in modern music. Echoes of Nietzsche are plainly audible.
The whole inquiry leads inevitably to the stage; that is, to the
stage of the opera house. In short and feverish sentences, hurt-
ing each other in constant impact, we are told of the sway that
Dionysos holds — the despotic sway to which all contrary forces
must finally bow. Neither religion nor metaphysics, neither matter
nor form, can long continue to interfere with it. The sparse choral
buds into richer harmonies; the church cantata must suffer the
obtrusion of languid arias and brilliant coloratura; sonata and
symphony fall back upon the dance; not even the fugue can

escape melodic infection. But all roads tend to one and the same point, the opera. Weissmann blames the suppression of the Dionysian element for the latest "aberrations" of music. The only salvation lies in the opera, the synthesis of all sensuous beauty. In the Conclusion we are given to understand that of all modern opera-composers the most authentically erotic, and therefore the greatest, is Franz Schreker.

That pulls the reader up with a start. Has he been deaf to the voice of a prophet crying in the atonal and polytonal wilderness? Doubt in the authenticity of Mr. Schreker's eroticism is quickly dispelled by casting a glance into "Der ferne Klang," "Der rote Tod," "Irrelohe," and all the other operatic "poems" he has written. Nor is it difficult to see why Weissmann believed that in music eroticism and greatness go hand in hand, that on the stage they walk in closest and happiest union. The "Marriage of Figaro" and "Il dissoluto punito ossia il Don Giovanni" might easily be imagined to disturb a stern moralist, even though punishment, in some form or other, can be held up to the weak brother as a wholesome deterrent. But opera is not concerned with pointing a lesson. If there be tragedy, it is one of passion; love has lost nothing in the defeat. It stands glorified even in death. And Dionysos smiles.

That most operas have not been forbidden by the police is largely because the words to which those passionate melodies are wedded seldom reach the ear and understanding of the listener. Also because most singers are too busy watching the prompter or conductor to do the "action" full justice. When it so happened that Tosca-Garden and Scarpia-Marcoux felt sufficiently independent of the guiding baton to put their minds to the business in hand, His Honour the Mayor of Boston felt constrained to intervene, and threatened to close the opera house if everything was not promptly put back on a purely platonic basis.

Offhand, I can think of only two operas in which the motives of love and sex are not predominant; they are "Hänsel und Gretel" and "Joseph" (Méhul's, of course, not Richard Strauss's Veronesian extravaganza). There may be others which I forget

for the moment; but I think that by far the greater number deal
with more or less exciting situations brought about by amatory
entanglements, licit and otherwise. It is common knowledge that
the last Empress of Germany, who vetoed the performance of
Strauss's "Feuersnot" in any theatre run by her impresario husband, would not go to hear "Die Walküre" because of its incestu-
ous crime and the instrumental postlude of twenty-six measures
after the first act curtain has made its precipitous and timely
descent. And this in spite of the fact that European royalty was
more inbred than the population of an Alpine village or a South
Sea island.

If Wagner was erotic, so was Bach, sturdy father of twenty
children. Both were exuberant, dynamic natures. Eroticism and
religion are closely related; but not interchangeable. Abbé Liszt
never quite succeeded in disentangling the smells of frankincense
and patchouli. Wagner's religion was the weaker and more arti-
ficial, because it needed a searchlight and boys' voices aloft in
the wings. The love-sick Olympian, Beethoven, made his own
god after the image of a Solemn Mass. The Catholic Franck and
the Protestant Bach never got away from the protecting dimness
of the organ loft. But each had his restless hours, and to those
we owe some of the best music they wrote.

Bach's noble sensuousness required no trappings. Nor is it,
in the end, important that Wagner composed for the theatre.
When you listen to his finest, most erotic music in the darkened
concert room, it is more marvellous, more telling than when a pair
of corpulent singers strain for high notes and toss each other on
the stage. What is important is the indubitable fact that the
erotic "Tristan Prelude" and the "Liebestod" can be divorced
from the theatre without loss of musical potency, and with an
increase of pure delight to the listener, while certain music of a
more recent date — music to which is tacked no action or "programme," music which belongs to the type known as "absolute" —
has been branded and denounced as dissolute. Let us hear one of
the loudest libellers.

Dr. Alfred Heuss is a musical writer of sagacity and erudition.

He is a musicologist of wide and enviable reputation. For ten
years he was the editor of the journal published by the International Music Society, which was killed by one of the first cannon
shots, in 1914. Dr. Heuss's historical studies may have awakened
in him a greater love and appreciation for the old than he has
for the new. Yet in 1906 he wrote shrewdly and not unsympa-
thetically of Strauss's "Salome." Peculiarly enough, he thought
at the time that Strauss had not written music which was as per-
versely sensual as Wilde's play, and that Strauss could not have
done so had he tried, because the very essence of music repels
everything unnatural and depraved. That sounds not unlike the
1848 reviewer in Murray's sedate "Quarterly." In 1921 Dr. Heuss
was moved to say plain things about Mr. Schreker's operas,
especially about the erotomanic texts and their defenders in the
press. There were signs of growing irritation in that otherwise
very sensible and lucid article.

But now we are come to the astounding criticism that Dr.
Heuss published in the "Zeitschrift für Musik" (February, 1923).
It should be borne in mind that the work reviewed is one of
purely instrumental chamber music, although scored for a small
orchestra. It has no programmatic title. The last movement is
marked "Finale: 1921." Again I shall have to quote without
stint:

It is accomplished! Modern German music has at last succeeded
in tackling life by its most frivolous, most vulgar side; where
orgies of sexual perverseness are celebrated and the French adage
Après nous le déluge is made a German motto. The man who has
worked this "miracle" is the composer Paul Hindemith, in his
"Kammermusik" for small orchestra (Opus 24, No. 1) performed
[in Leipzig] under the direction of W. Furtwängler. . . . We are
here confronted with a music such as no German composer of
artistic bearing ever before has dared to imagine, much less put
on paper; it is music so lascivious, so lecherous, but also imbued
with such unequivocal artistic force of expression that only a very
extraordinary composer could have written it. . . . It is the most

vicious, the most frivolous music possible, also the most realistic; music which in Stravinsky may find its parallel, but hardly its superior. . . . In Hindemith burns the cold fire of selfishness that knows only the ego; he shrinks from nothing; his imagination is keenest and richest when it seeks those fields of modern life most highly esteemed by the dramatists of sex and smut who regret that they may not go farther in their licentiousness than they do. But the composer of purely instrumental music need stop at nothing; and Hindemith is the musician who draws his main strength from this absence of all fetters, from this "intangibility" of instrumental music. . . .

Mercy upon us! What a reversal of opinions! Not so long ago we were assured that only when wedded to words was music considered capable of improprieties. But it seems that music divorced from words has found ways and means of being infinitely more improper. What are we coming to?

After all, it is no concern of ours if Mr. Hindemith, who is indeed an extraordinarily gifted musician, chooses musically to misbehave, or if Dr. Heuss, who is not a hypocrite, sees an offence against public morals in what Mr. Hindemith is pleased to designate, not without apparent reason, as "Chamber Music." It is a symptom of our times, and as such it deserves to be chronicled for a future generation which may understand better than we do what we are aiming at, what we are trying to erect on the latest layer of ruins.

For the moment, it would seem that most people have only one desire — to forget. And there is much of which the recollection might profitably be extinguished. Eros, Bacchus, and Morpheus are the benign dispensers of oblivion. Their ever-willing handmaiden is Music, the "food of love," companion of the cheering (and forbidden) cup, melodious weaver of enchanting dreams. But sleep has been murdered in the cities by motor trucks, steamboat whistles, machine-pianos, ukuleles, phonographs, radios, and houses built so flimsily that you can hear your neighbour breathe. The consoling juice of the grape has been abolished for the sake

of surreptitious poisons. Sex is dragged into the mire, when it is
not scientifically dissected for the benefit of an "enlightened"
public that has lost the sacred awe of nakedness. The factory for
work, the church for worship, are still open. Humanity, at rest
and play, is struggling desperately. Music must come to the
rescue; so must the dance, with consequential unconfinement of
a rather hectic joy.

No one will deny that America is to-day the leading provider
of dance music in the world. Some of this music is unsurpassed
for its originality ..nd healthy verve. Some of it has developed
rhythmic peculiarities that seem to have an almost aphrodisiac
effect on certain people. Dancing has been subjected to much
just censure. But it is not in America that such reproof has been
most merited. Nor is it the American example that has corrupted
the dance, that has prostituted music.

Let these things be well understood. For here you should be
told that Dr. Heuss has set, over his critique of Mr. Hindemith's
"Kammermusik," a title; translated into English, that title reads:
"The Fox-trot in the Concert Hall." Dr. Heuss must permit me
to point out his error if he believes that he has discovered the
first intrusion of this dance into the sacred precinct. He is equally
wrong, I fear, if he concludes that the effect of alleged "obscenity,"
especially in the final movement of Mr. Hindemith's work, can
be laid to the introduction — obvious and not especially felicitous
— of rhythmic and melodic patterns which to Europeans in general, and to a German in particular, may represent the distinguish-
ing marks of a dance admittedly American in origin and known
by the name of fox-trot. The spirit of Mr. Hindemith's music is
so essentially different from the typically Afro-Ebreo-American
that either Dr. Heuss has never heard a real fox-trot or he un-
flinchingly denounced a kind of music that may have its faults
as well as its virtues, but is not as a rule the kind of music that
strives to make its "intangibility" a loophole for obscene phan-
tasms. Mr. Hindemith did not borrow from America only; that
is shown by the "furioso" passage in the same final movement.
It is no longer the vaunted *"furor teutonicus,"* but a rage induced

by the bite of another breed of dog. However, this is not intended to be a critical discussion of Mr. Hindemith's "Kammermusik," which may or may not deserve the opprobrium heaped
on it by the indignant Dr. Heuss. All I want is to move that a
protest be spread upon the record of musical history: if European
composers and critics wish to label musical obscenities with the
names of American dances, they are committing a deliberate fraud.

It is none of our business what Europe does with these dances.
If America can make musical capital out of its first true folk-
music, all the better. If Europe sees in it only an escape into musical idiocy and filth, we do not wish to interfere. But we may be
pardoned for protesting against a possible inclination on the part
of learned musicologists to call this latest chapter in the history
of European music: "The American Infection."

Has the speech of music really been extended to comprise the
salacious vocabulary of the libertine? Was it not enough that he
had seized upon all the other arts for his sorry amusement? The
calamity would be augmented with the danger from the violent
reaction that is bound to arise against music declared to be obscene. As if we did not have a sufficient number of reformers
looking after the welfare of our body temporal and our immortal
soul. Like every reaction, this one, also, will go too far. And
because of a few degenerates we shall see the warm, throbbing
pulse of music stopped — not permanently, but just long enough,
perhaps, for us to be folding up our tents before the new day
starts. The one just coming to a close was fertile beyond measure.
It dawned when Tannhäuser, after oppressive dreams, returned
from the domain of Frau Holda, the pockets of his doublet
bulging with little chromatic notes. They fell by the wayside, and
the morning breeze carried them to healthy, avid soil. They grew
luxuriantly, yet naturally withal; the perfume of their flowering
was pure and rich. Then, in the sun of noontide, began the cultivation of exotic hot-house music. From crepuscular shadows
sprang mad-house music. And with the approach of ominous,
sleepless night, we are promised — but why anticipate? Another
dawn is sure to break.

DECEPTIVE CADENCES

DE GUSTIBUS

A SCOTTISH friend of mine tells this story about his cook:
One day, when she had cooked her master an especially
good soup, he inquired appreciatively what ingredients she had
used to make it so tasteful; and she replied laconically: "There
is thote in t'ilt."

Thought, alas, is as helpful in preparing savoury soups as it
is expedient in making a work of fine art. But the thought alone
might not, indeed it could not, have produced in the cook's case
such excellent results had her imaginative resourcefulness not
been subjected to a critical control — that is, had she not possessed
a discriminating and sensitive palate, or the gift of taste.

Now, we shall not quarrel as to the merits of this or that soup.
You may prefer your lentil soup cooked with a partridge, or with
a piece of venison; you may prefer *crème de crevettes roses à
l'Infante* to *bisque of lobster cardinal;* you may like your clam-
chowder *à la Manhattan* rather than *à la Nouvelle Angleterre.*
Perhaps you are willing to pass all of these by for the sake of a
Taoungakong, Canton style; or you may not feel safe in ventur-
ing beyond a plain and unadulterated *Kraftbrühe.* No one dis-
putes your right to your own personal taste in soups. *Cherchez
l'estomac!* But you must agree that any or all of these appetizing
concoctions might readily be spoiled, for all but exceptional
tongues, by an overdose of pepper or a dash of kerosene. Nor
is the broth made better when you let it burn.

And you will ask: What of Vatel's, Vachette's, and Brillat-
Savarin's gastronomy in a discussion devoted to Palestrina,
Orlando & Co.? — We come to it presently. In Mendel's "Musical
Lexicon" may be found a paragraph on *Geschmack* by "W. W."
(Wilhelm Wundt) which contains the following: *"Eine Speise,*

*welche dem Geschmacksinn nichts bietet, wird als fade, reizlose
verworfen; ebenso wird ein künstlerisches Gebilde, welches dem
inneren Schönheitssinne keine Befriedigung gewährt, für wertlos
erachtet."* [1] Multitudinous and multiform have been the attempts
to define "sense of beauty" and "sense of taste." With what
success? Let us hear Jean Marnold: *"La question qui se pose,
impérative et troublante, est de définir le 'Goût,' puis, et presque
aussitôt, sa cause à la fois et son objet, à savoir ce qu'on nomme
le 'Beau.' Il n'est guère de mots plus discutés et plus vagues,
encore que chacun en use couramment, les accouple et parfois
les oppose."* [2] We shall not chase a phantom. Fortunately there
is enough reality upon which to base a few observations that may
not be impertinent.

Wundt's parallel holds good. The cook needed "thote" plus a
palate. The musical composer, and to a not inconsiderable degree
the musical critic, require thought plus an ear or two. You object
to such trite remarks, and wearily exclaim: "Old story!" Pardon
me:

> *'S ist eine alte Geschichte,
> Doch bleibt sie ewig neu —*

and the reason for dragging it once more from its dusty shelf
was that Lawrence Gilman, in the "Musical Quarterly," seriously
propounded the astounding theory that we had no "touchstones,"
or standards, by which to test the metal of music!

Mr. Gilman admits that "The art of music . . . stands apart
from the other arts." And yet he shows annoyed surprise when
a method that Matthew Arnold recommended to detect poetic
excellence does not prove workable as applied to music. Small

---

[1] "A dish that offers nothing to the sense of taste will be returned as flat
and lacking flavour; for the same reason a work of art that offers nothing
to the inner sense of beauty will be considered worthless."

[2] "The question that arises, imperatively and perturbingly, is to define
'Taste,' and then, or almost simultaneously, to define its cause as well as its
object; to wit: what is called 'Beauty.' There are hardly two words more
discussed, yet more vague, in spite of the fact that everyone uses them
constantly, couples, or again contrasts them."

wonder. Music does stand apart; and necessarily the method by which to detect musical excellence is one peculiar to this art. Walter Pater has pointed the way to it. His words on the subject cannot be quoted too often or too extensively:

It is the mistake of much popular criticism to regard poetry, music and painting — all the various products of art — as but translations into different languages of one and the same fixed quantity of imaginative thought, supplemented by certain technical qualities of colour, in painting — of sound, in music — of rhythmical words, in poetry. In this way the sensuous element in art, and with it almost everything in art that is essentially artistic, is made a matter of indifference; and a clear apprehension of the opposite principle — that the sensuous material of each art brings with it a special phase or quality of beauty, untranslatable into the forms of any other, an order of impressions distinct in kind — is the beginning of all true æsthetic criticism. For as art addresses not pure sense, still less the pure intellect, but the "imaginative reason" through the senses, there are differences in kind of æsthetic beauty, corresponding to the differences in kind of the gifts of sense themselves. Each art, therefore, having its own peculiar and incommunicable sensuous charm, has its own special mode of reaching the imagination, its own special responsibilities to its material. One of the functions of æsthetic criticism is to define these limitations; to estimate the degree in which a given work of art fulfils its responsibilities to its special material; . . . to note in music the musical charm — that essential music, which presents no words, no matter of sentiment or thought, separable from the special form in which it is conveyed to us.

If the sensuous element constitutes and comprehends almost everything that is essentially artistic in art, and if each art has certain responsibilities to its special material, or sensuous element, subject to definite limitations, and if the greater or lesser fulfilment of these responsibilities is the measure of artistic excellence, it remains to be seen how this axiom may find application in the art of music.

The sensuous element of music is tone.

A musical composition is the more artistic the more tone-combinations of a sensuously beautiful order it contains.

The limitations to which musical tone is subject are, on one side, its degeneration into brute noise and, on the other side, its treatment and appeal in a purely or primarily intellectual way.

The responsibilities which the artist has toward tone, as a sensuous medium of expressing emotional and imaginative contents, and of communicating to the listener a peculiar charm by his conception of its inherent beauty and organic perfection, are to guard tone from overstepping its boundaries, and to develop its sensuous or most artistic qualities to the highest possible degree—to make it yield its ripest and most luscious fruit.

And by its fruit ye shall know it.

To avoid misunderstanding, I want to give here, parenthetically, brief consideration to one important point, more typical of music than of the other arts. I mean the evolution of the very material, or sensuous element, of music. The rapid transformation of musical styles, or, more precisely, the progressively varying ideas that we have about concording and discording sounds, are not fundamentally due to a change in æsthetic criteria. Their cause is a physiological one, first brought into the light of scientific research by Helmholtz. The organ which transmits sound-waves to our brains, the mechanism of the ear, is evidently undergoing a process of development, as yet not fully understood. But what seems clearly demonstrated, or at least a plausible supposition, is the fact that owing to these changes the sensuous medium readjusts itself, of necessity and automatically, in order to continue its function of conveying to our aural nerves and brain-cells that peculiar "musical charm," the essence of music. For this reason certain tone-combinations lose their sensuous potency when our ears become overfamiliar with them and dulled to their impress. Other tone-combinations take their place. Weber's "gruesome" diminished-seventh chord no longer fills us with terror. The augmented triads of the Valkyries' steeds have been ridden fast and furiously to their doom. The ninth chord dear to Claude Achille Debussy becomes a blunt weapon in hands of lesser skill than his. We have witnessed the popularization of the whole-tone scale. It found its way into comic opera. It will in turn, and in a not far-distant future, become commonplace, an instrument of torture. Music — that is, our realization of tonal possibilities — is in its infancy. Its stammering is divine. What will the full-grown speech be? Will our aural sense develop until at last we hear the voices from beyond and the much vaunted music of the spheres? Until we reach that day, the stimulus that is required to make us feel the sensuous charm of music will gradually and consistently take on different shades and degrees. We all know how surprised we are when we take up an old piece of music which we loved dearly once upon a time, and find that it appeals to us no longer. — The form or character of musical composition, however, has so far not been affected by equally radical changes. On the contrary, old *forms* still preserve their quaint and lovely grace. But it is useless to deny that most of us, to-day, find greater sensuous charm and more enjoyment in a Pavane by Maurice Ravel than in one by John Dowland (1562-1626).

And that is the salient thing — a work of art must give us enjoyment and satisfaction. Theodore Lipps, the eminent psychologist in Munich, formulated the idea in these words: "*Das ästhetische Wertgefühl ist unmittelbares beglücktes Erleben meiner selbst in einem sinnlichen Gegenstand.*" [1] Baudelaire, after hearing Wagner's music for the first time, referred to his experience as to one of the *grandes jouissances* of his life.

By that sensation shall ye know good music!

Going one step beyond the general axioms which we deducted from Pater's doctrine, let us find a more specific test that might disclose the worth or defects of a musical composition, and thereby probe into the validity of Mr. Gilman's claim. We shall be helped in our task by a sentence in one of Richard Middleton's short stories, so remarkably fine that it would alone suffice

[1] "The sense of æsthetic value is a direct and pleasurable realization of the ego in a sensuous object."

to make his name live among men, after his premature and tragic death. He wrote of one performing the grateful labour of talking about himself: "My words were warmed into life by an eloquence that is not ordinarily mine, my adjectives were neither commonplace nor far-fetched, my adverbs fell into their sockets with a sob of joy." What a *trouvaille!* I propose to paraphrase this sentence for our purpose in this way: "My melodies were warmed into life by a spontaneity that is not ordinarily mine, my harmonies were neither commonplace nor far-fetched, my modulations fell into their sockets with a sob of joy." If you can say this much of your composition, and find others feeling likewise, methinks you have come very near writing a masterpiece. Inventive thought, governed by a critical ear, will work the wonder.

And thereby, also, shall ye know good music!

In art, not more than in soups, the question of taste, of personal preference, is bound up in that of idiosyncrasies and education. But we have agreed not to quarrel about the kind of soup we do or do not like. All we demand is that it really please someone, that "thote" and palate be jointly instrumental in its composition, that it should not be left too long upon the fire, and that it honestly represent whatever style of cooking it may pretend to be.

As far as music is concerned, that is the pith of O. G. Sonneck's terse remark: "Let a quadruple fugue be a quadruple fugue; let programme music be programme music. But both must, above all else, be rich in musical invention!" They will be richest when the composer orders the weaving of his contrapuntal web, the distribution of his chords, the combination of his tonal colours and the pulsation of his rhythms so that the total effect obtains the greatest possible amount of sensuous beauty. I, for one, have never been able to feel the slightest emotional enjoyment from listening to a fugue, as little as a conventionalized design or the busy convolutions on a wallpaper have ever thrilled me. I remember suffering under fugues, and having had to live with wallpapers, that were equally exasperating. Nor is there any

difference between retracing, with our ear, the stencilled walks
of *dux* and *comes,* and following, with hypnotized and helpless
eye, the intertwining branches of an endless rose-chain on a
stupid wall. About programme music there are also differences
of opinion. Busoni, in speaking of the few and trivial effects of
tone that are unequivocally descriptive, said that we debase
tone to noise when we begin to imitate sounds of nature — the
rolling of thunder, the roar of forests, etc. — and that therein lies
the complete stock in trade of programme music. Goethe wrote in
a letter to Zelter: *"Töne durch Töne zu malen, zu donnern, zu
schmettern, zu plätschern und zu patschen ist detestabel."* [1] We
are significantly reminded of Pater's "limitations." The truth is
that when we attempt to imitate the bleating of sheep with the
aid of musical instruments, we may or may not succeed in pulling
off a clever trick. But that is all.

Chopin's piano music shows him to have possessed an "inner
hearing" more delicate than that of Beethoven; Wagner developed a finer ear than Berlioz had; Scriabin had a more sensitive
aural perception than was given to Max Reger. In other words,
taste and technical proficiency are not inevitably linked together,
nor need creative effort of great magnitude always exert the
sensuous charm that a smaller talent may command. Some people
find more pleasure in reading Albert Samain's poems than those
of Victor Hugo. There are composers who possess an amazing
inventiveness, supreme technical skill, composers who are not
necessarily always dull, and yet they never succeed in freeing
their work entirely from platitudes. Take Richard Strauss, for
instance; he does not seem able to outgrow the sentimental
"Liedertafel" themes in thirds and sixths. Look at the one in
"Electra" that is supposed to characterize the House of the
Atrides. Is it not more suggestive of a *Geheimer Oberrechnungs-
auskalkulator's* family than of the royal blood of ancient Greece?

You may not be able to define "taste" in the abstract, as
Jean Marnold fears, but you certainly can tell where it acted as

---

[1] "To paint tones with tones, to thunder, to bray, to splash, and to dash is
detestable."

godfather to a child of human fancy. You can tell where an ear, more finely strung than another, attended the welding of lovely sounds into a work of art. You can certainly tell whether or not a piece of music lives up to the demands that Pater makes upon it. And most assuredly you can tell whether a musical composition has given you something like Baudelaire's *grande jouissance* — that is, if you are fit to be heard in this matter.

Here it behooves us to delve into the question of "taste" in musical criticism. Mr. Gilman says: "I mean by taste . . . instinctive perception of æsthetic excellence." Now, there is Henri Bergson, who writes: *"Ce qu'il y a d'essentiel dans l'instinct ne saurait s'exprimer en termes intellectuels, ni par conséquent s'analyser."* [1] Hence would we seem destined to be disappointed, should we try to define Mr. Gilman's "instinctive perception." Fortunately, and notwithstanding his scruples, the great French thinker himself ventures to give a definition, and boldly sets it down in four words: *"L'instinct est sympathie."* Nothing could be shorter, more precise, and at the same time more helpful in our investigation. According to Bergson's idea, "instinctive perception" would require a certain "sympathy" with the object that is to be perceived. Instinctive perception of æsthetic excellence, then, would seem to require of the observer sympathy with the work of art under consideration. Sympathy with any given phase of art is largely a matter of temperament or native inclination. Its scope is widened by a broader vision of life itself. A moderate eclecticism may prove the wisest stand to take, "on this short day of frost and sun." The monomaniac, the man whose battle name is that of some composer with the syllable "-ite" affixed, is always with us. No matter how worthy the object of his "sympathy" itself, he is too apt to be a bore.

Now, the great confusion that confronts us in artistic evaluation, the contradictory judgments on a work of art — which Mr. Gilman mistakes for proof conclusive that there are no musical standards — are due to the fact that "thote," ear, and sympathy

[1] "The essential qualities of instinct can hardly be expressed in intelligent terms, nor consequently be subjected to analysis."

are seldom found all three in blissful union. Most people making
such criticism are not possessed of the requisite attributes that
make their perception both instinctive and authentic. Nevertheless, they think to have a right to express their opinion, which,
to return to our mutton-broth, is not content to proclaim a soup
too salty or ill prepared, but decrees that you should like heavy
potages, in preference to clear *consommés*. And they demand
considerate attention for their word as gospel truth, because
they believe themselves endowed with "taste." The *amateur* and
would-be *connaisseur* was never branded more stingingly than by
that master musician of the brush, that marvellous etcher of the
pen, James McNeill Whistler, when he wrote:

"Taste" has long been confounded with capacity, and accepted
as sufficient qualification for the utterance of judgment in music,
poetry and painting. Art is joyously received as a matter of
opinion, and that it should be based upon laws as rigid and defined
as those of the known sciences, is a supposition no longer to be
tolerated by modern cultivation. For whereas no polished member
of society is at all affected at admitting himself neither engineer,
mathematician, nor astronomer, and therefore remains willingly
discreet and taciturn upon these subjects, still would he be highly
offended were he supposed to have no voice in what is clearly to
him a matter of "taste"; and so he becomes of necessity the backer
of the critic — the cause and result of his own ignorance and
vanity!

If this applies to "patrons of the arts," to "polished members of
society," it does, sadly enough, apply with equal force to many a
so-called "professional critic." The lot of the music-reviewer is a
hard one. He has earned heaven when he dies, but should be
allowed to dwell in that part of the celestial realm where golden
harps and the angelic choir are out of earshot. He has to write,
often hurriedly, a penetrating estimate of an uninspired work
and soporific performance. Let us not be unkind to the poor
sinner. *Absolvo te a peccatis tuis.* But this leniency is out of place

with the prophets and high priests that offer sacrifice to their various little tin-gods-on-wheels and are not always careful where they pick their sacrificial victim. Too many critics are bent on making literature. They excel in lengthy diatribes, fill column after column with a sickening verbosity, without ever saying anything worth while or to the point. Their task is to impress the ignorant public. They accomplish it by being either frankly and frivolously entertaining, or sententiously obscure and impenetrable. The confusion that reigns in the minds of the uninitiated is rivalled by that displayed in the oracles of the wise ones. Nor is it to be wondered at. We need not be disturbed with Mr. Gilman, when he ponders over the wide difference of opinions on Wagner's "Parsifal" as expressed by Messrs. Runciman and Newman. The one sees in it nothing but "decrepit stuff," and the other calls it "wonderful and impressive." It all depends from what angle you look upon a thing. If you remember the music of "Die Meistersinger," "Siegfried," and "Tristan" while listening to "Parsifal," you may well be tempted to question whether the same vitality and exuberance of beauty that mark the first three are as strongly potent in the last. If you are honest with yourself your answer can only be in the negative. Therefore, "decrepit stuff" may be a strong, but need not be a wrong qualification. On the other hand, if you are more easily impressed by the mystical, religious, and metaphysical of the "Parsifal" poem and score, as such, and apart from what the same composer had previously produced, you may well, and justly, find it "wonderful and impressive." Take the two books of "Préludes" for the piano by Debussy; they contain things of a ravishingly sensuous charm — and, compared with these, there are others that are laboured, dry, and on the verge of being classed among "decrepit stuff." Mrs. Malaprop was right: "Comparisons are odorous." Nor is it always the professional critic who finds the right scent. He is apt to be guided by text-book rules. Now, ugly consecutive fifths and octaves in a four-part exercise of a pupil in harmony are likely to sound badly to-day, and to continue doing so for all eternity. This does not prevent the *tasteful* use of such progressions, nor has it deterred Bach, Chopin, Grieg — not to speak of the younger schools — from using them with fine effect. But the conservative ear is blocked by prejudice. The opposite of the tardigrade is the blindly progressive critic, who indiscriminately hails and praises everything new and revolutionary, for fear that it might ultimately prove a genuine advance in the art, and that his name should be missing in the roll-call of the vanguard. He aids and abets in making of the concert hall a sideshow for freaks and mountebanks.

A writer in the London "Times," not long ago, observed that "Taste may be bigoted, or indiscriminate, or catholic. Bigotry names the stage at which live ideas become dead labels. Music is full of such moments. . . . Lack of discrimination is a lack of humour. . . . True taste in music is neither parochial nor cosmopolitan, but catholic." And this catholicity will become a matter of course, a natural and comforting state of mind, if we let our taste in music be guided by "thote" and ear, both properly equipped and trained. Humbly and dispassionately, but always on our guard, we should cultivate sympathetic receptiveness, submitting our impressions to the test of Pater's "touchstones." The result may be that our temple will hold fewer idols, but those deities that remain enthroned will become holier to us and more benign. Their message will mean more to us, and our faith in it will make us happier and better.

In short, there *are* touchstones by which to prove the carat-weight of music. To deny it is to fling open the portals to underbred composers and overbearing critics. They are in plenty, as it is, striving to enter by the half-open door.

MUSIC, MELODIOUS AND ODIOUS

I would rather be a man of disinterested taste and liberal feeling, to see and acknowledge truth and beauty wherever I found it, than a man of greater and more original genius, to hate, envy and deny all excellence but my own — but that poor scanty pittance of it (compared with the whole) which I had myself produced!

HAZLITT — *"On Criticism."*

IN some deep furrow of my brain — where unavowed suspicions slumber open-eyed, until the ripening rays of disillusionment awake them into blind convictions — I harbour the belief that to a multitude of people music has always meant, and will continually mean, but one thing out of two: something melodious or something odious. Here is the tonic of your critical scale, and here its higher octave. That listless ears must forever confound them is but the natural result of similarity. Nor am I thinking only of her who defined music as "the breath of God made audible," or of him who pronounced it "the costliest of rackets." As a matter of fact, it would require little dialectic to prove that the most odious and the most melodious music are the same. This much admitted, we might as well confess ourselves deaf and remain dumb to boot. But that would be cowardice, or a temper so closely resembling it as to rob discretion of its share in valour. It would stunt the noble courage that makes us enter the tilt-yard of criticism, where we face, not possible defeat in even combat, but the inevitable discomfiture of becoming offensive to our acquaintances and absurd to posterity. We are ever assaulting impregnable windmills, or fighting invulnerable phantoms, for the simple reason that the pedal point in all critical debate on music is that droning diapason: melodious — odious; and never can a reasonable majority of ears be expected to agree: which is the higher, which the lower sound?

Of course, we know this octave spans an infinitude of other ratios; at least, the assumption that it does is the cherished plumb and compass for all intrepid mariners who venture upon the laneless waters of musical arbitrament. But it is nothing unusual to see the sun rising where we expected it to set, because the two polar points of our musical axis, those of melodiousness and odiousness, are so very nearly indistinguishable that each individual sails by a private azimuth of taste. Hence the occasional collisions between opinionated pilots and the general failure to get anywhere. The musical landlubber, being equally at sea, is by his very uncertainty made all the more determined to proclaim his stand on *terra firma*, while he is merely crowing lustily into the world his elevation on a slippery and unfirm mixen. The net result of this condition is the variously edifying legacy of musical dicta to which each successive generation falls heir and adds its portion for the enlightening and the amusement of all the following.

Would it were always as enlightening as it is amusing. Unfortunately, contemporary musical criticism is not kept or read long enough after it was written to prove as instructive as it might be. Only the salient blunders are preserved by tradition for the titter of those who are just as prone to guess the wrong way as were their ancestors. One of the distressing effects directly attributable to this calamity is the fact that so many wary critics, preferring to play safe, stoop to be downright "funny." They hope thus to evade the squibs by quipping. And that is greatly to be regretted. For not the most entertaining article, the cleverest reviling, or the most brilliant persiflage will be as illuminative as is the honest mind of the contemporary reviewer who detected in Beethoven's Ninth Symphony "the obstreperous roarings of modern frenzy," and who suspected the composer of writing "to suit the present [1824] mania!" At a time when Weber's was still "wild and visionary music" and it could be said that "all the songs in 'Der Freischütz,' with the exception of three, are *un*vocal," poor Marschner was accused of yielding "to the prevailing passion of the day — noise!" By people of acumen the melodic invention of "that merry manufacturer" Rossini was called extremely limited; only a few phrases were granted him to be his own, and those he was "repeating on all occasions, whether they relate to the low intrigues of a barber in Spain or to the mighty acts of a prophet in Egypt." Along came Paolo Scudo, who predicted the early and certain fall of "Lohengrin" and "Tannhäuser" because of Liszt's enthusiasm for this music — *"ce qui est de très mauvais augure pour l'avenir de Wagner"* — and proclaimed Rossini's "Moïse" a work of true genius, asserting that neither Mozart, Gluck, nor Weber, *"n'égale la fécondité et la variété d'accents qui distinguent le compositeur italien"*! Who shall blame a music critic after that — and the sampling might be indefinitely prolonged — if he choose to be designedly humorous rather than involuntarily so?

Now, the whole trouble lies in the fact that between melodious and odious there seems to be no secure foothold. The truth and the paradox of music is that both extremes constantly meet, that they are ever undergoing an imperceptible fusion and transformation. The two terms do not express a difference in kind, but in degree; and the degree depends on the listener, not on the music. Keener than the joy of hearing music is that of remembering it. Man dearly loves a tune that he can whistle. But let him go on whistling the finest tune for any length of time and he will drop it like hot coal. The ear must become accustomed to, and conscious of, a sound before it can derive from it full æsthetic pleasure; and with the moment that a sound, or succession of sounds, has been established and accepted, the ear grown used and over-conscious immediately begins to tire of it.

Jules Combarieu has defined music as "the art of thinking in tones." He must have been not a little impressed with his own definition, since he placed it as a motto at the head of his book on the laws and evolution of music. While it does not embrace all the elements, all the aspects, of music any more than do other attempts at concentrating the essence of so volatile a substance, it may serve, if we take into account not only that thought can traverse the whole long range from baseness, through common-

placeness, to sublimity, but also that not all of our thoughts
must necessarily rise to the surface of consciousness. Our subconscious mind has had to take the blame for a lot of things
that we are either too ignorant to comprehend or too ashamed
to acknowledge. The pleasure of listening to music is largely a
matter of subconscious spheres, in thought or in emotion. Only
when the reasons for this pleasure are wholly understood, when
music becomes sufficiently articulate to penetrate our consciousness, does the thought "register," as . it were, and we have
the proud gratification of "following the composer." To lag
behind is no worse than to be ahead of him, which is a not
infrequent sensation derived from hearing the work of certain
men. For if all the arts in common aspire toward the principle
of music, all music aspires toward the state of obviousness. We
may as well go farther and say that music which does not at some
time or other reach this state has never been a natural expression
of a clear and consequential thought. But what is obvious "before
the time" has no claim at all to answer our desire for the
mystifying, the exalting tendencies of art, which quench a finer
thirst, which fill a higher want, and make of art the noblest form
of human satisfaction.

Only what has been so conceived that, once become obvious,
it resolves greater mystery and unveils deeper truth may hope to
live and to avoid the danger incurred by all things that are too
obvious — namely, of growing odious. The finest music is perhaps
that which persistently evades all efforts of the patient investiga-
tor to pluck the petals and pistils apart *in majorem Dei gloriam*,
and yet is manifestly a symbol of cosmic serenity and human
perturbation. Take the ludicrous attempt to explain Chopin's
"Mazurka," opus 17, No. 4, as portraying the altercation between
a Jewish innkeeper and a drunken peasant, earning for it "in
Poland" — so 'tis writ — the name of *"Zydki"* (little Jew)!
Imagine, a silly pothouse brawl, that vaguest and most concrete
bit of Chopin, containing in a few measures the nostalgia of a
whole civilization, the subtlest glimpse of personal revealment,
exhaling the sweetness of cancer, smilingly kissing the hand of

Death, frightful and beautiful like all things tragic and compassionate! God gave the flower perfume, man gave it a Latin name. No, when music is pressed between the leaves of a herbarium, it becomes more ghastly than when organs grind it out in the street, when fiddles scrape it as a seasoning into our food, or when trombone and rattle accompany with it the rites of modern orgiasts.

The most forward, because the most obvious, thing in music is a melodic phrase. Hence it is constantly on the point of becoming odious to someone for whom it has nothing more to resolve, nothing new to unveil. And thus a piece of music will make the wider, the more instant appeal the more obvious it is; and for the same reason it will fall sooner into dislike and oblivion. The so-called "popular" music abounds in pertinent examples. Where are the shows of yester-year? The greater the pity that such gem-like bibelots as the "Japanese Sandman" must meet the abrupt doom of hackneyed clinquant. But all music, in general, obeys this law. All music that lingers without the threshold, all that has too far overstepped the line of consciousness, is apt to be equally odious to different individuals.

At all times a musical idiom is forming in which some of us read a new melodic message, while to the rest it remains unintelligible; on the other hand, we are inclined to regard as stale an increasingly large number of tunes which by many are still held, or just perceived, to contain the magic of melody. "Both are right in what they admire, both are wrong in condemning the others for what they admire." We might announce the perplexing axiom that melody, "the life of music," is its death-germ. Undoubtedly it is the "melodious" type of music that becomes soonest odious, especially if it tries to be too much of a good thing. Which means that melodies should be picked before they are ripe. The Paris version of the "Bacchanale" still throbs with the communicative pulse of passion and flames with scintillating colours, while the "Evening Star" has paled before the splendour of a richer night and the promise of a fiercer dawn. The sands of time are running nowhere faster than in the realm of tone.

Some of the best music is apt to "wear out," and, in the act of wearing, it does not gain enhanced attraction as does an old, familiar suit of clothes. What saves and preserves a great many compositions is the fact that we hear them so seldom.

For my part, I do not require the emboldening authority of Arthur Schopenhauer to own my unswerving attachment to a good tune. But when Mr. Rachmaninoff presents it to the readers of the "Etude" as his opinion that the efforts of the poor, benighted Futurists must fail because of "their hatred for anything faintly resembling melody," I instantly climb upon my little dunghill and crow out, with all the vigour and lung power I command, that a few of Mr. Rachmaninoff's prettiest melodies have to my mind already passed into the stage of odiousness, while a good deal of music that is alleged to be tuneless holds me with potent charms. When all is said and done, the essential thing in criticism is the particular perch from which we view art and from which we do our critical crowing. Let the view be a fairly open one, and let our cock-a-doodle-do be possessed of an ingratiating ring, what more can you demand? We shall not quarrel as to what is melodious and what odious so long as we realize that both terms may be, and are being, applied to the identical music, and that all we require of the critic is to make it attractive and profitable for us to mount with him his beacon, to listen for a "key" note in his call. He must be "the critic as artist." In that capacity, we may well believe that he is a necessity to art, that he is more creative than the artist himself, because "there is no fine art without self-consciousness, and self-consciousness and the critical spirit are one." It matters little, therefore, whether we range ourselves on the side of a waning or on that of a crescent phase of art. There are, indeed, different standards of delight, but there is only one pure, strong fire burning with which to search the whole reach of our ken; and we must give a true account of what we see. For, after all, the highest criticism, really, "is the record of one's own soul."

Fate has been often kind to me; its hardest blows have nurtured humbleness and Christian love within my breast. In all

concerns with fellow men (and women) I try to be a stoic.
Toward music I hold incorrigibly skeptic views. The composers
for whose works I care are comparatively few, but they give much
to me. That does not mean that I am snobbishly impatient with
the rest. My familiarity with the great mass as well as the great
masters of music is far from thorough. Thus have I succeeded in
remaining unperturbed by the former, and in retaining my respect
for the latter. Never having learned to excel on any instrument, I
still can go to a piano or violin recital and find zest of novelty
in pieces that other people, exasperated by over-application,
look upon as bugbears. Nor is my enjoyment marred by constrain-
ing sympathy with struggles overcome. I flee academic fervour and
anything soiled with the sweat of drilling. The best of Cicero
and Molière is irretrievably lost to me by school associations.

Encyclopædic knowledge of opus numbers was never given me.
My musical horizon is closely bounded. But in that narrow space
there are no obstacles to keep me from the sparing stars above.
Their light meets me undimmed and warms me with peculiar
pleasures. The thing is not to lose sight of stellar fixedness, while
our neighbour sets off, with much ado, his Bengal fires, as short-
lived as they are malodorous. Like the moving heavens above,
these musical constellations have a very disconcerting way of
changing. They are subject to frequent shifting — round one or
two suns of prime magnitude. New clusters, ever forming, are
floating into the field of vision with startling suddenness, only to
be eclipsed as suddenly by larger planets. There should be in
music, as in astronomy, an open season for shooting stars. Some
of them cannot be shot too soon to suit me.

I make not the slightest pretence of thinking that my case is
unparalleled. My experience, surely, is shared by many people,
unless they be hidebound — in pigskin, levant, or crushed morocco.
To all intents it is the same. For the assembling of impressions
and beliefs in art, the card index and loose-leaf book are unsurpassed. An occasional rearrangement and weeding-out of cards and
leaves is to be recommended. Hence such frank, if otherwise
unimportant, avowals as mine have at least the effect of a whole-

some catharsis on the individual who makes them; sometimes they help others in doing a little house-cleaning among dusty notions of their own. And nothing gathers cobwebs more easily than the inherited ideas which, like the priceless and useless china of grandma, are reverently placed so high on the shelves of our mental cupboard that the daily feather-duster of doubting does not reach them. Descartes should have been canonized patron saint of critics. Instead of dissipating doubt, most critics cast lavishly of it before the public. Only the very old and the very young enjoy the privilege of being recklessly positive or obstinately negative. For that reason their criticisms make the best reading.

There is nothing more boresome, aside from being well-nigh inconceivable, than an unprejudiced art-critic. Take away from any form of expression the personal note, and you have but an empty blast. What is intolerable is the uninformed critic and the dull. There can hardly be any question that we have too much of the wrong kind of criticism, too little of the right. Here is a pertinent remark penned in 1789:

With respect to all the feuds and contentions lately occasioned by music in France, they seem to have annihilated the former disposition of the inhabitants to receive delight from such music as their country afforded. There are at present certainly too many critics, and too few candid hearers in France as well as elsewhere. I have seen French and German *soi-disant connaisseurs* listen to the most exquisite musical performance with the same *sans-froid* [sic!] as an anatomist attends a dissection. It is all analysis, calculation, and parallel; they are to be wise, not pleased.

And the special bone of contention to which these able surgeons apply their saws is that ossified dilemma: melodious — odious.

The critic as performer of autopsies does not exactly measure up to Wilde's demands. And yet he should use probe and scalpel, but on himself. That is the "record of one's own soul." Is not in literature, in art, the autobiographical the most arresting? And next to ourselves what is there to interest us more than our fellow sufferer? Rousseau's "Confessions" will outlive "Le Contrat social" for reasons other than those that put the book on the Index. The pages of musical self-revelation in "Tristan" and "Die Meistersinger" have other qualities to boast of than the exhibitionist tendencies of a "Sinfonia domestica." Music is becoming less and less autobiographical, nor is it getting better for that reason. By the side of the great confessors in music, Bach and Beethoven, stand Franck with his fervent *de profundis* and Tchaikovsky with his maudlin *miserere*. We have drifted into an era where music, braggartly self-accusing, more often shouts *peccavi*. But, on the whole, ours is reflective music, casting reflections of moods and pictures on the mind. And in this often dazzling play of mirrors the radiation of music has been intensified, while its outline and substance have become diffused. Suggestion has taken the place of statement, and thereby music has learned to say a great many more things than it had ever said before. But again we hear cries of "odious" from those who will not recognize a spade unless you call it by its proper name. Meanwhile the diggers go on with their excavation, which becomes the grave of the old and the foundation for the new. Perhaps we are writing music to-day that is too solidly reposing on dead matter. There is nothing deadlier in music than devices. Christopher Simpson, came he to earth again, might find that his opinion of 1667, "concerning our common scale of musick," needed revision. If ten parts in the ultra-modern Schönberg's compositions are sheer prophetic genius, forty are helplessness and fifty are *vieux jeu* — that is, obvious before the time!

And yet real art should never age. It links remote epochs of history into one spring of high endeavour and makes of alien races kindreds in the search for beauty. Let the artist cater to fashion, and his work will die with the birth of another whim. This is the fate of all things which are only timely, that they recede with time. To create is to build new tombs, to sing is to increase the sum of silence. But to create and sing is, nevertheless, the most precious business we can have here below. It is its own reward, and we must do it in the face of certainty that we can only dream those greater treasures, the intangible, elusive masterpieces of the soul: in painting, a shadowy and fragrant landscape, hushed in the strange light of an unfamiliar hour; in sculpture, a vibrantly respondent hand, held but in passing and forever felt; in literature, a page of opulent imagination, robed in the sober elegance of clean and clinging prose, describing nothing of importance save to the heart that languishes; in music, the echo of a cherished voice, the soft, contented laughter of a mistress known and lost in days when sin was too much innocence. Here is true art; more, here is lasting art. For through it all there moves a thread — all art, all life, aspiring toward the principles of music — a thread of living and expressive melody that will not soon grow obvious or odious.

The skeptic turned sentimentalist — fie! What an unseemly attitude to strike, what a challenge to the giggling crowd!

HARKING BACK AND LOOKING FORWARD

THE history of art cannot be separated from the history of man. The conditions of human life may undergo perpetual change, be caught in the flux of incessant development; but the peculiarities of human nature and the motives of human actions have remained very much the same ever since they have come under closer study. The forms and expressions of art are innumerable and infinitely diverse; but the impulse that drives man to seek in art a higher sort of satisfaction continues to obey a more or less restricted set of abiding principles; chief among them is the principle of satiety and variety.

The power of human nature to relish enjoyment is no more limitless than is its power to suffer hardship. The very essence of pleasurable satisfaction is that it stills a craving only so long as surfeit is not reached. Even pleasure has to be varied, so as to keep from turning stale and dull. Were it not that night and day, winter and summer, for ever alternate, man would tire of sunlight and spring. The less natural the appetite, the more frequent must be the change in its appeasing. Art is the opposite of nature, and the hunger for it is the most unnatural of man's appetites. Therefore, the mode of satisfying it must change the oftener, the more highly developed — the more anti-natural — an art becomes.

Wherever art has been greatly perfected and yet for long periods has remained comparatively free from the tyranny of fashion — as painting in Japan or music in India — wisdom has found a preventive of surfeit. The Japanese hang the walls of their rooms with only a few of their exquisite colour-prints and drawings, but store away in their houses enough of them to replace these pictures with others before the eye has become too familiar with them. The Hindus are so sensitive to the minutest differences in their music that they have special strains adapted to every age and season, to every hour and mood; and thus, even within the smallest circle, they provide for the necessary relief of change. If such sensitiveness of eye and ear can be regarded as a measure of æsthetic refinement, the Oriental races must be considered more artistic than are the Occidental.

No organ seems to tire more easily than does the ear. The notes of the cuckoo in the woods may charm us for a moment; but prolonged, they grow monotonous and cease to be felt as something pleasant. Too long repeated, they finally, and mercifully, are blotted out from our consciousness. Any regularly recurring beat or noise, such as that produced by the works of a clock or the wheels of a railway car, eventually may pass unnoticed. Musical tones neither offer nor permit such escape; least of all when they are skilfully combined. Art, though it be concealed, attracts attention; it appeals to our quickened consciousness; especially tonal art, or music, cries out for notice. Music is the most directly stimulating of the arts; but it has come to be also the most intrusive and the most fatiguing.

The experimental study of fatigue in the auditory mechanism is of fairly recent date. It cannot be said to have advanced far enough to render possible the induction of æsthetic canons from observed physiological occurrences. What we need most of all is an explanation for the probable connection between the latest changes in music and the increase in noise. The progress of music is based on and conditioned by the necessity of constantly overcoming fatigue. And the fatigue of the ear has been hastened or aggravated by the alarming increase in noise to which modern life is subjecting us. Probably our whole nervous system is affected by it, and not to its profit. Where two hundred years ago melodious street-calls announced the approach of itinerant venders and the song of an ungreased axle-tree merely emphasized the ordinary stillness, we now have the involved and strident counterpoint of traffic over an *ostinato* of policemen's whistles and automobile horns. The timid tinkle of the spinet has been replaced by the aggressive tones of the "loud speaker." Loudness and coarseness go hand in hand. Pandemonium in the street, and the home a jazz dive or a roaring Chautauqua — truly, the art of music is hard put to devise new stimuli wherewith to counteract the growing aural disturbance. The wonderful and consoling fact is that music, apparently, is equal to any occasion.

Longer than any of the other arts, music was content with a secondary place as handmaiden to religion and magic or as accompaniment to dance and pageantry. Therefore the past of music is shorter than that of any other art. Music is all future; it is not merely undergoing change; so far it has always advanced. Ever since in the fourteenth and fifteenth centuries it resumed the status of an independent art, capable of stirring the emotions and kindling the imagination, it has baffled all attempts at catching it in a net of definitive rules or theories, it has leapt through the most amazing evolutions, always darting off in a new direction when the old one seemed to lead no farther, always eluding satiety by turning out a fresh variety.

*   *
*

In 1854 Eduard Hanslick (1825–1904), critic and æsthetician, published his famous little book "The Beautiful in Music." In it he admitted that "there is no art the forms of which wear out so soon and so extensively as music." But here the term "form" stands not so much for "shape" or "arrangement of parts" as it does for the formulas, procedures, and devices of musical composition. This is evident from the sentence that immediately follows the one just quoted, in which Hanslick says that "modulations, cadences, progressions of intervals and harmonies, become so obsolete in fifty or even thirty years, that the composer of genius can no longer use them, but is compelled continually to invent new purely musical features." Few critics and æstheticians remember this. Nor did even the one who made these sound reflections.

At the time when Hanslick wrote his book, fifty years had

passed since Beethoven had composed the "Eroica," and little
less than thirty years since Schubert had finished his string-
quartette in D minor (with the variations on "Death and the
Maiden"). Both works are still capable of impressing a good
many listeners with the workmanship, sensuous beauty, and nobility of thought that have gone into their making. But not the
most conservative eclectic or versatile musician would or could
be content, one hundred years after the death of Beethoven and
Schubert, to express himself musically in the manner of either of
these composers.

The "forms" of the symphony and string-quartette, as Beethoven and Schubert left them, had yet a long life of usefulness
before them. However, in 1854 — five years after the death of
Chopin — music had inherited from the frail, consumptive Pole
not only a wealth of new modulatory formulas and harmonic
devices (Moscheles had dismissed them as "inartistic"!), but
nocturnes, ballads, impromptus, and fantasies (Moscheles, too,
wrote impromptus, fantasies, and a ballad, but nobody plays
them now, whereas Chopin's still live): a whole world of eerie,
sombre, tenuous, iridescent sounds, with "Preludes" and
"Studies" as shorter essays, for experiments in a new medium. In
1854 Liszt completed his finest orchestral work, the "Faust
Symphony." The modern orchestra and programme music, children of Berlioz's brain, had reached maturity.

In 1854 Schumann attempted to commit suicide, then lingered
on for two more years in mental darkness; but not without having
shed over music a new light risen from behind the hills of fairy-
land, not without having imparted to musical speech a new
inflexion, the note of an original though morbid passion.

Lastly, in 1854, on the 28th day of May, Wagner had drawn
the final bar-line in the score of "Das Rheingold." Hanslick had
turned from an admirer of Wagner's into an almost venomous
critic of his later operas. He wrote of "Das Rheingold" that
"anything more absurd than Wagner's text from the first to the
last line is hardly to be met with anywhere." Of the musical
style he claimed that it was "declamation instead of singing,

bare of all charm and melody, while in the orchestra the so-called 'endless melody' wallows in deceptive cadences.''

And in December of the same year, 1854, Wagner wrote in a letter to Liszt: "I have conceived a 'Tristan und Isolde,' the simplest but most full-blooded musical composition." While the full-bloodedness of the music could hardly be disputed, the "simplicity" of it was certainly not at first evident. Quite the contrary, to many it seemed intolerably difficult, complex, almost incomprehensible. It was as if music could not go farther and remain music.

Within half a lifetime we have witnessed the revolutionary Wagner's deification over the violent protest of his reactionary opponents, and we have seen a new progressive element relegate him to the fossils; we have heard young Richard Strauss denounced as Anti-Christ, and to-day there are those who would expose him as an old fogey with a bag of tricks; we freshly remember our delighted surprise at the fantastic flowering of Debussy's "poisonous" garden, bathed in the purple magic of twilight, now marked by some intolérant hotspurs as waste land or innocent cabbage-patch; it seems but yesterday that the novelty of Schönberg's "Five Orchestral Pieces" stung us to anger or amazement, and already we have been subjected by our youngest innovators to far more extraordinary sensations.

*　　*
*

Not only has the change in musical styles been greatly accelerated, but the tonal material itself, out of which music is shaped, has been rapidly transformed, recast, expanded. The progress of music, since the fourteenth century, has been a conquest of discord, the liberation of the human ear. We are daily learning to hear new things and are trying to repeat them. At first we may stammer, but in the end we sing. If we could represent the whole substance of tone, the whole audible range of tonal material, as a solid mass, we should trace the development of music by carving into it the earliest and faintest impressions made on its surface, then the pits, the gullies, shafts, and vaulted galleries which, honey-combing, we have wrought into this substance, until in intricacy it resembles the last bead of a Flemish rosary. Or we should show how, climbing from landing to landing the stairs of overtones, we entered one new chamber of sound after the other and made ourselves at home in each. Our youngest are impatiently skipping ahead, knocking at unopened doors, prompt to break them down if the lock will not yield. And the object they seek is a new thrill by virtue of new discords.

What is discord? An irritation of the aural mechanism that results in a greater tension of our auditory nerves. A sensitive musician does not have to hear a discord, he need only see it on paper or just think it, and he will feel the same peculiar effect in his ear. Why is discord? Because the irritation produced by it emphasizes the sensuous element in tone, or what is most fundamental and communicative in music. Discord, then, is something physiological and psychological. While musical art cannot do without it, æsthetically it has no standing, it is not a settled quantity. The proportion of discords needed to tauten our nerves depends upon the individual and the generation. There are no fixed quantities of concords and discords which will give every one the same satisfaction, nor is the same proportion warranted to please the same person at different ages. That point bears remembering. If music "wears" well for several generations, it does so not because of its "sensuous" qualities, and rather in spite of the "formulas" it may employ; outside of mere historical interest, what gives it possibly a longer life is the timeless spirit in which it was conceived and the supreme skill with which it was executed. But these are merits that take on their true value at a distance only. Of our contemporary music and the "music of the future" we have learned to demand discord not merely for the sake of contrast, as a long list of æstheticians would have it, but for itself, as an indispensable stimulus. Already Dr. Burney, in 1770, wrote that discord "seems to be as much the essence of music, as shade is of painting, not only as it improves and meliorates concord by opposition and comparison but, still further, as it becomes a necessary stimulus to attention, which would languish over a succession of pure concords." These were shrewd remarks and extraordinarily forward-looking for the time when they were written. Burney's opinion "that provided the ear be at length made amends, there are few dissonances too strong for it," rested on his belief that "no musical phrase can *end* upon a discord, the ear must be satisfied at last." And both were based upon the creed which for hundreds of years clung to tonality as the only salvation. Logically, the very nature of a "ruling key" demanded that it open and close the piece. Illogically, theorists assumed that tonality was a permanent institution. Rameau, in his "Traité de l'harmonie" (1722), had given the superstition the rank of an axiom in declaring that "the perfect chord is to be used at the beginning and at the conclusion, and for all middle closes and cadences." Would Dr. Burney have accepted Chopin's "Mazurka," opus 17, No. 4, in A minor, with its vague close on a chord of the sixth? This, perhaps, was the first jolt given to a stiff-backed, inveterate prejudice, long before it came tumbling down, broken back and all. The effect of the sixth chord at the end of Puccini's "Madame Butterfly" (1904) is usually spoiled by the precipitate applause of the gallery. These were mild revolts. At last began a hot battle for the most subtle or violent discords wherewith to end a composition. The Russian Scriabin developed a particular talent for strangely evanescent or "unresolved" endings. But almost all composers of the early twentieth century have practised the new fashion in closes, and it has come to be a sign of singular courage — unless it be the affectation of perversity — to end a piece of music on a perfect triad.

Another instance of Chopin's daring and his disrespect for convention may be found in the chain of parallel fifths at the end of the "Mazurka" in C sharp minor (Opus 30, No. 4). When the "Mazurka" was first published, in 1838, Schumann, in his "Zeitschrift für Musik," greeted these fifths with exclamations of vehement approval, although he predicted that the "German cantors," on seeing them, would wring their hands in despair.

Schumann added "by the way" that "different ages hear differently." And so they do. Parallel fifths or fourths, naked and unashamed, charmed the ears of the ninth and tenth centuries. During the reign of strict harmony they were taboo; when they slipped into the work of a master, they were hushed up by common consent of the "learned," which amounted to a conspiracy. No doubt, there are plenty of places in music where parallel fifths and octaves are bad because they violate some very sensible rules of proper voice leading, and in consequence sound bad. There is an equal abundance of examples to prove what great emotional effects can be produced by fifths, stationary as well as in motion. Long passages in fifths or sevenths or ninths, chords built of fifths or fourths, now belong to every respectable composer's stock in trade.

*   *

*

We have no satisfactory explanation why it should be that every discord ultimately turns concord. What the ear rejects at first as too harsh it learns to appreciate for the welcome stimulus of variety and greater sensuous or emotional appeal, unless it be ossified or blocked by prejudice. The history of musical harmony is a fitful story of aural readjustments and revaluations. The ear, in order to enjoy a novel sound, or series of sounds, must get used to them; and practically from the moment that the ear accepts the new combinations of tones without some more or less conscious resentment, the sensuous charm begins to wane. If the listener continues for some time to take pleasure in such music, the pleasure is of an order quite different from that which he first experienced. It may become a purely intellectual delectation derived from technical or historical knowledge; the mere prodigiousness of execution may stir his sense of hazards and difficulties overcome; it may be rhythmical exhilaration only, or the shallow comforts of sentimentality; finally it may resolve into a bad habit, or the defensive armour of an arrested aural development against the onslaught of new discords.

The attack began long ago, but it did not gain momentum until fairly recently. Monteverdi used the diminished-seventh chord in 1608; Weber in 1820 stamped it with the peculiar "weirdness" that it assumed in "Der Freischütz" and retained for two generations; now its effectiveness is spent. Luca Marenzio introduced augmented fifths about 1593; for two centuries and a half they remained a rare exotic; Wagner in his "Nibelungen" acclimatized the augmented triad; soon it flourished rankly; from it sprang Debussy's fertile whole-tone scale, now claimed as everyone's property and sunk to the level of commonness. Chromaticism appeared in Cyprian de Rore's part-songs as early as 1544; but only under the hands of Chopin, Liszt, Wagner, and Franck did it become the supple melodic and harmonic outlet for intenser feelings and tormenting passions; abuse has blunted its edge and dimmed its colourfulness. But each one of these tonal devices was an "innovation" in its day, designed to communicate to the ear a fresh equivalent of the stimulus necessary to relieve satiety by means of variety.

Were it not that, so far, every musical discord has ultimately turned concord, the skein of music would never require untangling and re-winding. Successively new combinations of sounds, producing the desired tonal "rub," are drawn into the working material of the composer, as antiquated methods that have achieved typical significance are dropped by the wayside. Were it purely a matter of contrast, a difference in kind and not of degree, consonance and dissonance would be universal and stable conceptions, in spite of modifications; for light is light in any strength, and shadow always kin to darkness. Nor is it just that the luminous colour of to-day fades into to-morrow's drab or sombre background. The tapping of tonal sources is something different, untranslatable in terms of any other art. It is not a case of finding new pigment; rather of slowly shedding a horny film, thus gradually enabling us to face more light, all the light. Yet within that widening and heightened radiance the proportions and the basic substance of what we see — or hear — should prove constant; the projection of ourselves into the work of art should be imbued with the spirit of noble adventure, burning with the desire for fresh aspects of beauty. That is the artist's loftier aim.

Yet beauty is no more the sole pursuit of art than it is the dominant note in life. Art may be the opposite of nature, but it draws its inspiration from the life within and without us, it holds up to us a mirror that reflects the whole of our interior and exterior world. There we encounter an abundance of what we call ugly, grotesque, cruel, or perverse. And what ugliness life does not suggest, our imagination will invent. Painting and sculpture knew the distorted, ridiculous, or frightful long before music did. Only in recent times has music produced its Breughels, Callots, Daumiers, even its Félicien Rops and Alfred Kubin. However, the absurd or the ugly in art is redeemed by the artist's very presentment. At its best it must be the exception. It may be the outcome of a passing mood in a normal person, or the prevailing mood in an abnormal mentality. Or again, like the "jazz" of our own day, it may characterize a period of disturbed equilibrium, of fermentation or surcharged excitability. The general hysteria of the moment finds vent in grotesqueness, exaggeration, and caricature. The tonal material, made subservient to these ends, has yielded astonishing offshoots and unsuspected fascinations. Yet here, too, surfeit will be reached sooner or later, and change will be inevitable. Perhaps even, after the welter in mock-passion, a benign fate may lead mankind to rediscover serenity. For the noblest music among admittedly great music is that which fills the hearer with a serene earnestness and calm.

* *
*

Whatever seemingly erratic turns the development of music has taken in the past, it has never strayed far from the centre; we are forever turning round the same axis — ourselves, ascending spirally perhaps, leaving behind us excrescences and perversions, outgrowing innumerable stages of childhood. That is the view in historical retrospect. To the majority of contemporary eyes, a new direction taken by music has always presented alarming vistas. One need but remember Monteverdi's "new discords in five parts"; the "crudities" of Dr. Blow; Lully's *"faux accords"*; the choral harmonizations that got Bach into trouble with the worshipful consistory at Arnstadt and nearly cost him his job; Beethoven's last quartettes, which priggish Louis Spohr thought eccentric, unconnected, and incomprehensible, and in which he could see nothing but the composer's "constant endeavour to be original."

Now, this endeavour is justly shared by every new generation, though it is not given to every artist to be original; nor is originality always a pledge of artistry. In fine, then, the future of art lies in the hands of genius. Among the strongest individualities that have helped to shape the music of the young twentieth century are undoubtedly Debussy, Scriabin, Schönberg, Stravinsky, and Sibelius. Debussy, with his musical roots plunged into the soft soil tilled by Gounod and Massenet, and nourished with the intoxicant of "Tristan," began the deliberate revolt against Wagner, the apostasy from the cult of Bayreuth. Scriabin derived directly from Chopin and his hot-house flowers slightly tainted with the odour of death; he lost himself in the nebulous altitudes of metaphysical speculation or descended below to coquet with a dandified Satan. Schönberg is at bottom an unbleached German romantic who has taken it into his head to remake the universe in a test-tube. Stravinsky is the Proteus of modern music, also its Prometheus, shaping the primitive clay of music into stuff unknown before, and animating it with the fire stolen from a pagan heaven. Sibelius revels in Nordic gloom and pessimism, brightened only by the glamour of a heroic past and the glimpses of an enchanted Northland.

It is curious what rapid strides "originality" has made since the advent of improved keyboard instruments, and what help this *tastatura* has afforded genius. The tempered scale may be a curse, but the keys that strike it have been a blessing undisguised. It would seem that instinct leads the hand, and that the hand awakens the ear. Bach's use of his hands on ebony and ivory was

a departure. So was his music. Mozart the improvisor at the
harpsichord surpassed in daring the composer Mozart. Beethoven, deaf, remembered his fingers; the silent reading and
hearing of notes is accompanied in the mind of many musicians
by the imaginary playing of the music on an instrument. The
three boldest musical pioneers of the nineteenth century —
Chopin, Liszt, and Debussy — wrote their best music for that unspeakable piano. And all that in a day when orchestral colours
were growing ever warmer and more suffused. The keyboard has
been the experimental laboratory of music, and a note missed has
often proved a hit, as a mixture wrongly compounded has been
known to account for chemical discoveries. The experimenters are
not through. Some of them may be too reckless in their mixing. In
consequence, their explosives do not always detonate.

*   *

*

The most radical experiments are those which aim to blast
into smaller fractions our tempered diatonic scales. Perhaps the
time is ripe for a new scale, composed of intervals smaller than
half-tones, and for new instruments wherewith to sound them.
Practical success has attended some of these attempts. Busoni
merely theorized about a scale dividing the whole tone into three
degrees. Willy Moellendorff in Germany, Silvestro Baglioni in
Italy, Edmond Malherbe in France, J. H. Foulds in England,
Alois Hába in Czechoslovakia, have evolved systems based on
fractional tones, have built instruments or have written music
introducing quarters and thirds of a tone. The Mexican Julian
Carrillo has constructed string and wind instruments splitting the
whole tone into as many as sixteen parts and has written music
for them which has been listened to with much interest. Notation
of these intervals still offers difficulties. It will take training of
the eye to read what the ear is not yet clearly familiar with. But
there is no reason why the Occidental ear should not learn again
to distinguish what Oriental races have never unlearned.

With scale degrees smaller than half-tones chromaticism will bend more sinuously. Pure intonation, in the process, may oust the ill-tempered scale. A substitution of new and irregular scales for the diatonic scale in its major and minor modes has dealt a last blow to the tottering throne of tonality. Music is gaining new freedom by its unhampered transit through a multitude of keys, without according to any one of them predominance. Tonality was a gauge for the ear. We are being taught to do without that measure. Modulation may go by the board in the process, or at least modulation as we have heretofore understood it. For its charm lay chiefly in the bold abruptness or discursive elegance with which, after a shorter or longer digression, it returned to the point of departure or led into a fresh tonality with the inevitableness that made the step convincing. We shall be able to dispense with modulation, in that sense, much more readily when we realize that another characteristic of music, the motive or theme as a germinative agent, is being abolished. Modulation into other keys was an assistance and a relief so long as, for structural reasons, the composer had to develop his motive, recapitulate his themes. With the abolishment of vacuous imitation, counterpoint became more pliant and less a matter of stencilled repetition or slavish interdependence.

In strict consequence, these tendencies have produced the two most recent and most important types of music, the atonal and the polytonal. The first is music without marked tonality of any kind, without key signature, without cadences or stereotyped closes; the second is music in more than one tonality sounded simultaneously, but not trying to form "harmony" with one another. "Linear counterpoint," "superimposed keys," "planal harmony," "juxtaposition of unrelated sonorities," are some of the technical terms in which the theorists have taken refuge in order to explain the things that happen in the music of Schönberg, Anton von Webern, Paul Hindemith, Křenek, Arthur Bliss, Milhaud, Honegger, Bartók, Kodály, Casella, Szymanowski, and many other "musicians of the future." The movement is general. Nothing can stop it. Theorists like Josef M. Hauer have as uncon-

cernedly built a "system" of harmony upon the quicksands of
atonality as Gioseffo Zarlino on the supposedly eternal pillars of
the major and minor triads. To make up for the lost keys and
tonalities, we are gaining a firmer grasp on tone-values, meaning
thereby the inherent potency of different tone-combinations, much
after the manner in which the painters refer to the arrangement
and "harmony" of pure colour in a picture as colour-values.
Rhythm is falling into an ampler gait; the bar line is removed and
the rhythmic flow unloosened. Melody is a term for something
relative; it has no absolute significance. The outlines in a fine
pencil or a heavy brush both make "drawing." Counterpoint is
slipping off the manacles of rhythmic as well as harmonic depend-
ence. Greater mobility is replacing architectural stiffness. Music
may thus become even more musical, by breaking its alliance with
painting and poetry; it may evolve not only a larger and newer
vocabulary, but a language more direct and specific.

*   *

*

In short, the progress of music consists in the gradual assimila-
tion by the ear of more and more complex sonorities, which
anticipating genius divines, and the slower masses at first refuse
to accept. This has been, and still is, the continual quarrel between advanced and retarded hearing. But the progress of music is
twofold. The one road is marked by the milestones of plain
chant, modal polyphony, the enharmonic scale of the tempered
system, chromaticism, polyharmony, and so forth. It is the essentially musical path on which for over a thousand years, in the
Occident, there has been no turning back. The second road,
which runs parallel with (but independent of) the first, brings us
successively through the eras of Church and Renaissance, Court
and Baroque, Revolution and Romanticism, Socialism and Impressionism, Bolshevism and Post-Expressionism. It is the road of
cultural development in general, of politico-social rounds, on
which a turning back is not infrequent. On every bend of the

road we meet with a new "style," and practically every style finds one or more characteristic "forms" of its own.

The two roads represent separate avenues. We may jump back and pick up music on several points of the second, without receding a single step on the first. For that reason we are able to compose, for instance, a piece of music in the form of a sarabande or passacaglia while using the musical speech of the chromatic epoch without committing an anachronism, provided the result be artistically satisfying. Yes, such borrowing of older forms and filling them with newer contents has a decidedly piquant effect. Also it is true that the pace of progress along the two roads has not always been the same. In matters of "form" music has not advanced so far or so rapidly as it has in those of tonal "material." Musicians of the twentieth century admit as much when they revert to typically ancient forms, as Casella does in his "Partita"; Ernest Bloch in his "Concerto Grosso"; Leoš Janáček in a Concertino for piano, three strings, and three wind instruments; Heinrich Kaminski in a Concerto Grosso for double orchestra, and in vocal chorals and motets; Kurt Thomas in his "Mass and Passion according to St. Mark"; or Darius Milhaud in his "Serenade for Orchestra." The list could be lengthened indefinitely. The archaic trend, as a change from modernistic satiety, as a recoiling from complexity into simplicity, is easily explained.

The situation at the end of the first quarter of the twentieth century may be compared with that which has arisen a number of times in the course of musical development, when at the point of saturation the cry for simplification was raised, when, "the sluices of innovation once thrown open, such torrents of incongruous opinions deluged the world, that seeming anarchy put everything into confusion." Harmonic boldness was the rejuvenating force in some of the Italian madrigals; Thomas Morley (in 1597) complained that the poets who wrote the "ditties" for these madrigals too often indulged in "obscenities which all honest ears abhor" and that, musically, there was "no vanitie which in it [the madrigal] hath not been followed to the ful"; yet he himself adopted the style of the madrigal, and most successfully.

Expressionism was not unknown to the groping Prince of Venosa, whose modulations our old friend Dr. Burney called "forced, affected and disgusting." Where would he find words to express his sentiments could he hear some of the more recent "modulations"? It was Monteverdi who set the seal of genius on the extensions to the charter of harmony which the madrigalists had written into it. The madrigals had the right proportions for an experimental form. And the words helped the composer not only to "shape" his music, but to make it "say" things or illustrate definite emotions which it had not before attempted.

The smaller form is always the favourite during an interregnum. It lends itself better to tentative methods. There is another reason why our modern madrigalists should want to *faire petit:* as a protest against the endless music-dramas and long-winded symphonies. The miniature has come once more into its own as a crystallization of thought or mood. Anton von Webern's opus 5 consists of five movements for string quartette, the longest of which has fifty-six measures, and the shortest fourteen. Of his "Five Orchestral Pieces," opus 10, the first is twelve measures long — if there still can be a question of length — and the fourth lasts six and one-quarter measures, in which nine instruments share in the playing of exactly forty-six notes, all pianissimo.

In the age of "columnists" the essay has given way to the paragraph, the epic to the epigram. Music, too, has become paragraphic and epigrammatic. It has learned to be ironical and satirical. In an age of machines, also, it is but natural that the strident noises and the implacable rhythms of this new world of technical super-beings should find an echo in music. Arthur Honegger's "Pacific 231" for orchestra, and Milhaud's "Agricultural Machines" for voice and seven instruments are telling examples. Orientalism, which had such far-reaching influence on modern arts and letters, has added exotic inflexions to our tonal speech. The borrowing from primitive races corresponds to a recurrent but unfulfilled longing for a return "to nature." Momentarily the supposed primitiveness or crudity may pass as an excitant for limp and weary nerves. Posterity must decide how far it has a rightful place in art. Folk-tunes more than ever have been drawn upon to enrich art-music with the savour of the soil. They sing the artist's perpetual nostalgia for his home in the hills of peace.

*   *

*

It is well to hold apart in music the dual development of form and content. The whole and intricate trend of civilization governs the first. To compare modern music with the cast of modern life is to find its aim and drift. To delineate its conquests of new "discords" is to point to the latest unshackling of sound. It is the ear — and the aural sense alone, as transmitter of sound — which demands this second development. And of that puzzling need of the ear we know nothing. Science owes us still the very first and fundamental explanation. All that we may vaguely guess is its connection with the principle of satiety and variety. And in this dual development technique is but a concomitant. Technique adjusts itself to the transformations of the material. Craftsmanship tells in the end, for it is one and indivisible with genius, requiring that union of skill and inspiration which shapes the masterpiece.

The masterpiece alone does not age. And beauty is not always the quality that endows it with immortality. Not the thing of beauty, but the thing of perfection is "a joy forever." Beauty is relative, is a matter of changing taste. Perfection is absolute, is a matter of permanent criteria. The enjoyment of perfection differs from the enjoyment of beauty. Beauty appeals to our senses. Because they are apt to become dulled, they crave variety after satiety. Perfection addresses itself to what Walter Pater called the "imaginative reason." This reason must be unalterably fixed, maintained on a level of stable rationality. The greatest work of art is that which is wholly beautiful, perfect, and sane.

Of all the arts, music comes nearest to possessing that inexplicable and unqualifiable power of casting over us a spell. It carries us away, it lifts us out of ourselves and transports us beyond ourselves. Music will hold us still and musing, or stir us into irresistible motion. It can lighten our burdens, or weigh our hearts with the load of bitter-sweet sorrow. This is not because music is finer or stands higher than the other arts. The secret power of music must reside in musical tone itself. It must be that musical tone — or the ether in orderly movement — represents in a simple form the trinity of matter, motion, and law. These terms are symbols. And, symbolically speaking, we can say that tone was in the beginning, and that the end of all things is music. Not music in the narrow sense of classical or modern music, or diatonic or polytonal music. It is rather the melody that sings in the laughter of a child, the harmony that decks the wooded hillside in autumn, the rhythm that governs the planets. And the understanding, the love of this music makes of us not only more appreciative listeners and truer artists, but better performers in that exacting and stupendous symphony led by the Great Conductor, the chief musician of the universe.

INDEX